The MENA Powers and the Nile Basin Initiative

Simon H. Okoth

The MENA Powers and the Nile Basin Initiative

palgrave
macmillan

Simon H. Okoth
Virginia Commonwealth University
Richmond, VA, USA

ISBN 978-3-030-83980-2   ISBN 978-3-030-83981-9 (eBook)
https://doi.org/10.1007/978-3-030-83981-9

© The Editor(s) (if applicable) and The Author(s), under exclusive license to Springer Nature Switzerland AG 2021

This work is subject to copyright. All rights are solely and exclusively licensed by the Publisher, whether the whole or part of the material is concerned, specifically the rights of translation, reprinting, reuse of illustrations, recitation, broadcasting, reproduction on microfilms or in any other physical way, and transmission or information storage and retrieval, electronic adaptation, computer software, or by similar or dissimilar methodology now known or hereafter developed.

The use of general descriptive names, registered names, trademarks, service marks, etc. in this publication does not imply, even in the absence of a specific statement, that such names are exempt from the relevant protective laws and regulations and therefore free for general use.

The publisher, the authors and the editors are safe to assume that the advice and information in this book are believed to be true and accurate at the date of publication. Neither the publisher nor the authors or the editors give a warranty, expressed or implied, with respect to the material contained herein or for any errors or omissions that may have been made. The publisher remains neutral with regard to jurisdictional claims in published maps and institutional affiliations.

Cover illustration: kenkuza/shutterstock.com

This Palgrave Macmillan imprint is published by the registered company Springer Nature Switzerland AG
The registered company address is: Gewerbestrasse 11, 6330 Cham, Switzerland

*To the promise of nonconflictual water users:
Kito Valentino, Ellie Okoth, and Mazen Alexander Okoth.*

Foreword

The challenges to cooperation and the need to prevent conflict on a vital major river basin as the Nile is the central thrust of this important book. The Nile River Basin comprises some eleven African countries, as follows: Burundi, Rwanda, Uganda, Kenya, Tanzania, Democratic Republic of Congo (DRC), South Sudan, Sudan, Ethiopia, Eritrea, and Egypt. Burundi, Rwanda, Uganda, Kenya, Tanzania, and the DRC comprise the riparians on the White Nile. Ethiopia, Sudan, and Egypt comprise those on the Blue Nile. The two Niles converge in Sudan and flow into Egypt; so, Sudan and Egypt are the tail-end riparians. Although both Sudan and Egypt are clearly in Africa, they are frequently also associated with the Middle East and North African countries because of their linguistic and cultural ties with the Arab world.

What has made the Nile River basin potentially contentious is that Egypt, with its growing population and as a tailender, depends entirely on the Nile's water for its survival. In fact, it is hard to imagine a country so vulnerable to one critical resource—as this study reveals that about ninety percent of Egypt's water comes from the Nile. This, of course, reminds us of the Greek historian Herodotus's famous and perceptive observation that Egypt "is the gift of the Nile." Although Herodotus may not have known the source of the Nile and the challenges faced by its inhabitants' upstream, modern Egypt and public sector planners, with its current population of about 100 million and growing, can ill-afford not to know the water source of its survival and the need to forge win-win cooperative arrangements with the upstream riparian states.

As countries that are upstream riparians on the Nile have also faced with growing populations and the need to provide them with food and electricity, Ethiopia, one of the larger ones—also with a growing population of about 112 million, has looked up to the Nile for solutions. Ethiopia embarked on the construction of the ambitious Grand Renaissance Dam, with a storage capacity of 74 billion cubic meters, at a cost of some $4.8 billion to provide 6000 Megawatts to meet its energy needs. The construction of the Grand Renaissance Dam has raised concerns and anxieties about water availability among communities living downstream of the Nile in Egypt and Sudan and fears of it triggering possible violent conflict.

This book draws on international experience to show that there are two international models of conflict over shared waters: first, where there is the model of a strong militarily powerful state upstream (a "hydro-hegemon") that shares a river basin with weaker ones downstream. A good example of this is the case of the Colorado River, where the United States is upstream, and Mexico is downstream. In this, the United States (as the hydro-hegemon) uses the international principle of "Absolute Territorial Integrity" and has the "last word" on the resource and there is no conflict. Secondly, there is the model where the stronger hydro-hegemon is located downstream (and may also have alliances with powerful external states) sharing the same waters with weaker ones that are upstream. A good example of this is the case of Egypt, which is downstream and shares the same waters with the other twelve African riparians that are upstream. In this type of situation, the potential likelihood for a violent conflict is intensified if the upstream riparians deprive the downstream of its expected water flow. Egypt's current claims on Nile water are based on "historic rights" and "prior appropriation."

This book does not take sides on the looming crisis over the sharing of Nile water. Instead, it tries to address the factors underlying the growing tensions between upstream and downstream riparian states over the water and comes up with solutions. The book points to the role colonial history had played in muddling the issue of "water rights" over the Nile. The British colonial authorities forged a series of treaties which restricted rights of use of Nile water. The 1902 treaty restricted Ethiopia from undertaking any waterworks on the Blue Nile; the 1929 one allocated the Nile water to Sudan and Egypt and left out the remaining eight riparians; and the

1959 agreement increased water allocations between Sudan and Egypt, excluding other riparians. As upstream riparian countries became independent and tried to address their own food security and electricity needs, the colonial arrangement appeared no longer satisfactory. The late President Julius Nyerere of Tanzania considering having not been a party to the colonial treaties, rejected them and asserted "territorial rights" to use Lake Victoria's water for irrigation farming in northern Tanzania.

Concerned about tensions over the Nile from getting out of hand, in 1999, with the support of the World Bank, the eleven countries of the Nile River established the Nile Basin Initiative (NBI), with a secretariat in Uganda, as a consultation and coordination platform for the sustainable management and development of the Nile water resources and to promote win-win benefits. The NBI, governed by both an inter-Ministerial council and a technical advisory committee, resulted in the 2010 Cooperative Framework Agreement (CFA), which has since been signed by all the Nile river basin countries except Sudan and Egypt, which objected on the issue of the formulation around "water security" and proposed the rewording "not to significantly alter the current uses and rights of other Nile Basin states." This latter formulation was not accepted by the upstream riparian states.

There is scope to resolve current tensions over sustainable management and equitable sharing of the waters of the Nile. This can happen, when the large countries (Ethiopia and Egypt), which have the biggest dogs in the game, recognize that they must be sensitive to each other's development needs and not undertake measures that inflict harm on each other. This book explores a variety of solution-options and even draws on colorful personal experience when it comes to sibling rivalries over a shared common resource and the need for a trusted parent or "convening platform" as a neutral broker. At present, the CFA provides that neutral broker platform where all stakeholders can have their voices heard and where negotiations can be carried out and an enduring solution jointly crafted that is fair and binding. The book proposes a two-tier policy recommendation to help resolve this complex water rights conflict. It first proposes negotiations to lower the temperature—to reduce tensions, the so-called "cease-fire solution." It secondly proposes negotiations to agree on lasting solutions that prevent relapse. This is an important book that will appeal to both policymakers and academics interested in rational solutions to a difficult natural resource challenge, whose joint management or lack of, has enduring life consequences for all countries concerned.

Potomac, MD, USA   Dr. Tijan M. Sallah

Dr. Tijan M. Sallah is a retired former Sector Manager for Agriculture and Rural Development, covering Eastern and Southern African countries at the World Bank. He also worked as senior economist on agriculture and irrigation water development on the Middle East and North Africa, including Egypt.

Acknowledgments

No book is possible without the input of many people alongside the author. Therefore, thanks to the interview participants in Ethiopia (Addis Ababa) and Egypt (Cairo and Alexandria) where the initial field research was conducted. Thanks also to the water scholars whose published material informed my thinking, and to Dr. Tijan M. Sallah, a retired World Bank economist, who shared his thoughts on the issues of water rights in the Nile Basin and wrote the foreword. And to Paul Lewis of Seattle, who, over a period of more than three years, filled my email inbox with the latest updates on the Renaissance Dam conflict. To my colleagues, Professors William Newman and Richard Huff, both of whom shared their ideas from time to time on the project, I share a deep gratitude for your friendship and collegiality. Also, I would like to appreciate the "nods" that I received from professionals in the field, particularly Professor Aaron T. Wolf of Oregon State University who hosts Transboundary Freshwater Dispute Database and to Dr. Omar of Cairo University for his immeasurable insights into Egypt's water situation. Finally, to Sahara Sriraman of Virginia Commonwealth University for the exemplary initial edits, and to the professional, Ms. Angelica E. Bega who straightened the messy work into a format acceptable to the publisher. Thanks also to the Palgrave Macmillan (Springer Nature) staff, and in particular Ashwini Elango who walked with me all the way into the production process. And as always, to my family—Dr. Elizabeth Okoth, Amy Mazzan, Carl, Jona, Emily, and Jesse ("Tray") for their acuities throughout the six-plus-year exercise. As Aristotle would have said, *Efharisto*! (Thank you!).

Introduction

I was born and raised in a rural village in Western Kenya located about 3000 feet above sea level and surrounded by hills and plateaus. The community experiences two extreme climatic conditions: dry and rainy seasons. During the dry seasons, which occur from June to October and from December to March, villagers rely on one major water source: the Awach River. Although roof water harvesting is presently in vogue and provides relief to many during droughts, the local community cannot cultivate crops for their livelihoods. Sometimes, I wonder why my forefathers settled in that area at all.

But accessing freshwater remains a problem for many communities around the world. In Fall 2011, I lived in Kabul where I taught at the American University of Afghanistan. During that brief stay, I witnessed residents of Kabul living in the adjoining hills of the city scrambling for water from isolated sources downtown. Standing by the Kabul River, which traverses the city, I noticed a few things. First, the stench from the heavily polluted water that could not possibly be consumed by humans. Second, I observed men, women, and children walking up the hill with donkeys loaded with plastic water containers. Matters could not be worse for the Lower Gulf States, especially the United Arab Emirates where I lived and taught at Zayed University between 2012 and 2015. Upon arriving at the city of Abu Dhabi, the first thing I asked is why their forefathers were so determined to settle in such a hostile land. A similar question had crossed my mind minutes before landing at King Khalid International

Airport, Riyadh in Saudi Arabia the previous year in October 2011. The cloud of dust that engulfed the airport and its environs presented a picture of doom, as well as human resiliency.

Thanks to Darwin's notion of natural selection, human ingenuity, and the oil wealth bequeathed to the Gulf States, the desert states can desalinize seawater despite the high cost of the process. To provide a clear picture of what it looks like, consider the following. Typically, in any given year, rain comes on average about one to three times, and sometimes none, to the United Arab Emirates. I remember a time when it started to rain while I was teaching one of the classes. The students hysterically requested that I move the session outside of the classroom, so they could feel the joy of rain. It fell for less than ten minutes before quickly dissipating from the ground due to the high temperatures.

In May 2014, I visited Cairo and Alexandria, Egypt to conduct field research on the subject of this book: the Nile water rights conflicts between Egypt and Ethiopia. Upon crossing the Red Sea on a flight from Dubai to Cairo, I immediately noticed the desolate situation in the country, which is famed for its ancient civilization, including the pyramids of Giza and the Tahrir Square revolution that toppled two presidents—Mubarak and Morsi. As Dr. Omar, the professor of linguistics at Cairo University who accompanied me on a trip from Cairo to Alexandria in the north, explained, Egyptians *cannot* exist without the Nile. He pointed at the green fields irrigated by the Nile waters and emphasized that all the food that Egyptians consume would have to be imported if anyone interfered with the Nile water flow upstream. The trip to that country has largely shaped my understanding of why Egypt would resort to any means to ensure its water security.

As I listened to Dr. Omar, along with other scholars at Cairo University and ordinary citizens on the street, it immediately became evident that they were truly angry over Ethiopia's decision to construct the Grand Renaissance Dam. The Blue Nile tributary on which the dam is built upstream is Egypt's lifeline, as it contributes 86% of the water entering the country. Ninety percent of Egypt's water supply comes from the main Nile River (that unites the Blue Nile and the White Nile tributaries). Ethiopians whom I interviewed the same year (between September and October of 2014) about Egypt's disapproval of the dam were not amused. They expressed the belief that they had the right to use the water that emanates from and flows through their territory. The majority of people on the street whom I interviewed expressed their readiness to go to war with Egypt. They also reminded me that it was only the Ethiopians, in the entire African history, that had successfully fended off the Europeans (read: Italians) from occupying their land.

From those interviews, I was much more convinced than before that it is water and not oil, which will attract ordinary citizens to joining national military efforts to wage war against other nations that deny them the right to this important source of livelihood. In this regard, water wars that will likely occur in this century will be different from those that have occurred over oil and other natural resources. With violent conflicts over oil, it is the state machinery that engages in direct combat, while in water wars citizens will willingly join the state forces to defend what they consider a means of survival. The likelihood of these water wars, in which everyone has a stake, will be due to the surge in human population along with water demand, economic growth, and water stress in certain regions due to the looming changes in global climate. Predictably, those areas experiencing reduced precipitation will most likely join forces to secure access either through violence or by collaboration. The possibility of these occurrences will be greater where political hegemons are located downstream, and the weaker ones are upstream.

However, choosing violent conflict or outright war as an option can be costly in terms of human lives, resources, and economic losses. That is why Egypt chose the path of negotiation over war to minimize damages exacted in such a confrontation. But striking a deal in such a complex conflict can be elusive and daunting. As already stated, water claims under historic rights versus territorial rights are enshrined in the international water laws, making it harder for experts, famed consultants, diplomats, and government officials to strike lasting agreements in water conflicts. Presently, how to reconcile these disparate rights is a challenge to those involved in trying to resolve the Grand Ethiopian Renaissance Dam conflict between the governments of Egypt and Ethiopia. That is why it has taken twenty-plus years (1999–2021) to find a solution acceptable to both parties.

Framing the Issue

Some things are worth fighting for, and water is one of them. Presently, there are two schools of thought on this position. The first school insists that though conflicts, as a form of disagreement, adorn nations that share international water systems, these tensions only act as an incentive for cooperation and not violent conflict. These apologists to a "shared water-cooperation link" rely on historical evidence to prove their case. However, the danger with this hypothesis, which to some merits a theory, is its potential to lull us into complacency that war over shared water systems is highly unlikely. It is possible, and rightly so, that the absence of water wars is explained by where the shared water system is located. For example, in the water-rich nations of Europe, the United States, Canada, and Scandinavia, it is highly unlikely, presently and into the future, that violent conflicts will erupt over this life-giving resource. Another favored justification is the presence of democratic institutions. It is argued, mostly in international relations literature, that democratic nations will hardly go to war with one another because they share common values that recognize property rights, among other things.

I also want to add that the absence of violent conflicts over shared waters is predominantly true where (hydro-) hegemons (i.e., geopolitically powerful states) are located upstream and the weaker ones downstream. Examples of the rivers that feature this characteristic are the Colorado River (the United States in the upstream and Mexico in the downstream), the Mekong (China in the upstream and four other countries—Laos, Cambodia, Vietnam, and Thailand—in the downstream), the Euphrates and Tigris with Turkey in the upstream while Syria and Iraq are in the downstream, and the Ganges with India in the upstream and Bangladesh downstream. In all these cases, the international principle of "Absolute Territorial Integrity" prevails; therefore, the hegemons have the last word. Even with the threats of global warming, it is unlikely that these asymmetric power relations can be tipped in favor of the downstream states. Another argument that supports this school of thought is based on the fact that war is costly to both the aggressor and the attacked. In short, no one wins in war unless it ends in the acquisition of a lucrative territory. But, that too, can be costly in the long run.

The second school of thought contends that violent conflict (or war) over shared water resources is inevitable. Although presently there is limited evidence to support this hypothesis, I subscribe to it for several reasons. One, the "it-has-not-happened, it will-not-happen" hypothesis is a dangerous position to take given the present spike in global population and economic growth in the face of dwindling freshwater resources. The situation is exacerbated by the changing climatic conditions as well as poor water management. Two, when an international river serves one or more nations located in an arid downstream, the potential of receiving less water due to droughts or consumptive uses in the upstream can trigger tensions. Three, the likelihood of a violent conflict is intensified if the downstream riparian is a hegemon (politically, militarily, and economically superior). Moreover, most hegemons tend to have extensive alliances with powerful external states that can boost their economic and military prowess. This can elevate the hegemon's ability to face off with nations upstream. Whether a physical confrontation occurs or not, the downstream hegemon can sustain the tensions for as long a time as possible, and when the point of no-return is reached, violent conflict cannot be avoided. The fourth reason is that it is already a challenge to comfortably feed the 7.4 billion people in the world. This is further complicated by unilateral and nationalistic tendencies that jeopardize or threaten to derail globalization, a system that has made it easier for the community of nations to exchange goods and services.

Admittedly, globalization can only facilitate the flow of ideas, technologies, and myriad goods and services, but not life-giving resources such as water. Of course, it is not presently uncommon to export bottled drinking water to neighboring countries; but to do so in large amounts through aqueducts is not only expensive, but also politically unpopular. Consider the possibility of water transfers from the east coast and midwest of the United States to water-starved regions of the west coast such as Arizona and California. Despite having the technological know-how and economic resources to make these transfers possible, claims on water rights by individual states in the east or mid-west are politically infeasible. In fact, because of these claims, several cases have been litigated, while some still linger. At the international level, similar water rights cases have been brought before the International Court of Justice for mediation.

A caveat: This book does not endorse nor propose war as a method to addressing national water rights but rather, acknowledges that such a possibility is not out of the equation given the additional stressors to human survival in the twenty-first century. The word "war" is also used in the context of new technological apparatus, such as hacking and the deployment of biological warfare as forms of retribution or to punish inequitable water use by riparian states in the upstream. But most importantly, the book presents a combination of remedies to the sporadic water sharing conflicts. This is accomplished by examining the twenty-plus years of conflict over the use of the River Nile by the ten riparian countries. The analysis uses the conflict over the Grand Renaissance Dam between Egypt and Ethiopia as the launching pad to understanding the complex nature of water rights for all the members of the basin. The Nile Basin Initiative is an organization that was formed in 1999 to foster cooperation in the use of the shared waters but also to craft a formula for equitable utilization of the resource.

As the discussion progresses, the power of geography and location as explanatory variables cannot be neglected in understanding the causes of water rights' conflicts and the intervention by regional neighbors. That is why the Middle East and North Africa (MENA Region) form part of the book's title.

Although nation-states are linked by mountain ranges, borders, or even underground aquifers, rivers stand out as the most important and unique natural phenomena that connect national territories. A river that begins thousands of miles away in a distant country brings the same water into successive nation-states downstream until it empties into either an open sea or ocean. By traversing different territories with the same water, the river unites nation-states and people who have never met. Metaphorically, the river enables all these strangers to "drink from the same cup." By its necessity, countries linked by one river (that avails water for life) should at the very least, cooperate more than those linked by trade or even technology. Unfortunately, drinking from the same cup can cause conflicts. Consider my early childhood experience.

In the early 1960s among the Luo community of Kenya, it was customary for young male siblings to eat dinner together with their father. At an age of about 5 years, I remember how three of us siblings shared fermented milk from one cup. After each sip, one would pass it on to the other. However, occasional fights erupted as the older brother was accused of sipping more of a mouthful than the others. Fortunately, those fights and altercations that ensued were quashed by my father's reprimands. Given our level of poverty, my parents could not afford to buy extra cups. Think about this for a moment. What could have been the best method, under the same conditions, for sharing the milk more equitably to stem the quarrels among the three siblings?

The ten African countries that share the Nile waters are no different. Squabbles over how best to share the water that links them together have persisted and confounded even the most learned and experienced experts. As will be encountered in this book, the River Nile illustrates this challenge: how to share the water equitably. But it has also given rise to yet another issue: how to resolve a conflict when a state claims territorial rights to use water as they deem appropriate and without regard to those downstream. Just as my father interceded in our fight over milk, the MENA Regional Powers and the countries within and outside of the Nile Basin intervened in the conflict between Ethiopia and Egypt over shared water use.

Scope of the Study

The MENA Region (the Middle East and North African) is comprised of 19 countries, while the Nile Basin countries consist of ten countries (See Figures 1.1 and 3.1). Although they are geographically and politically distinct national territories, the MENA Region and the Nile Basin countries are linked by three discrete features. First, by the River Nile that is shared by eleven countries (Burundi, Rwanda, Uganda, Kenya, Tanzania, Democratic Republic of Congo (Congo DR), South Sudan, Sudan, Ethiopia, Eritrea, and Egypt). Although it has its origin in East Africa, the River drains into parts of the MENA Region (Sudan and Egypt) before draining into the Mediterranean Sea. The Sea, with contents of the Nile, is shared by Egypt, the Gaza Strip, Israel, Lebanon, Syria, Libya, Algeria, Tunisia, and Morocco. But there is a contradiction. Egypt downstream is water-starved while the upper Nile basin is not. This book is about these linkages as well contradictions that together have caused greater anxiety for communities living downstream of the Nile—Egypt and Sudan.

But this work also attempts to illustrate the degree to which addressing anxieties over water use has, by necessity, sucked in the MENA Regional powers including Saudi Arabia, Israel, Qatar, UAE and, to some extent, Turkey. A "regional power" is defined in this work as an independent nation in the MENA Region that wields military power, possesses a strong economy judged by high per capita income (and most likely a rentier state that depends heavily on oil revenues), and has extensive influence in the regional geopolitics and beyond.

Water Rights Conflict

Recently murmurs of war appear to be defacing River Nile's otherwise gentle flow and years of romanticized value. The disruptions of the water flow caused by human activities upstream are turning those murmurs into real conflicts within the Nile Basin. Moreover, the spillover effects have drawn countries of the Middle East and North Africa region (MENA Region) into the equation, thereby complicating the global dimensions and depth of the feud. Hence, the first major challenge facing these two regions (MENA and Nile Basin) is finding a formula to equitably share this valuable resource among the ten riparian states. The second challenge is how to reconcile two opposed international rules that both govern transboundary water rights. The first international rule is the concept of territorial rights that guarantees riparian nations to use any waters that flow within their territories in a manner that does not harm downstream states. The other is historic rights, which assures downstream states of uninterrupted use of the shared transboundary system.

Ethiopia's decision in 2011 to construct the Grand Ethiopian Renaissance Dam (GERD) is the nerve center of the raging conflict between Egypt and Ethiopia. Egypt opposes the project for two reasons. First, under the international law governing shared water systems, Egypt as the downstream State is protected by the principle of historic rights or "prior appropriation." This means that out of the ten nations that share the Nile, it is Egypt that has historically demonstrated substantive use of the river going back to the period of Egypt's ruler, Mohammed Pasha, who initiated the first-ever known irrigation system, the Shadoof.

After that, Egypt was the first in the Nile basin to build the biggest known waterworks within the basin, first, the Aswan Dam in 1902 and then, the current Aswan Dam between 1964 and 1970. Second, Egypt challenged Ethiopia's planned Grand Renaissance Dam based on its potential to impose significant harm. Under the existing international water law, this implies that an upstream state must exercise due diligence not to impose significant harm on the downstream neighbor either through water diversion or projects that might halt or substantially reduce the amount of harm.

The spike in and the continuation of the conflict between Egypt and Ethiopia's efforts to amicably share the Nile waters has persisted for a decade with no substantive resolution. That situation can be attributed largely to assumptions, historical events, power asymmetry, mistrust, and lack of political will. Ordinarily, assumptions can turn out to be credible if supported with scientific data and information. But they can also seem incredulous or untrustworthy.

For Egypt, the idea of a Dam on Ethiopia's Blue Nile, which supplies 86% of its water needs, was conceived as a death knell that portends economic doom or an existential threat. When the first filling of the dam reservoir was undertaken in July 2020, Egypt could still not provide realistic effects that the dam imposed in the absence of a comprehensive study. Historical events, including colonial treaties that accorded Egypt and Sudan Nile water rights, contributed to the state of inertia on the part of the beneficiaries and the unwillingness to face the realities of sharing water rights with the upstream states. Of course, this is to be expected. When a public good whose right has been granted is redistributed to a particular group or a region within a country, opposition or even conflict is expected.

Power asymmetry is another factor that can be attributed to the continuation of the conflict. Egypt, though downstream, has, compared to the Nile basin states, maintained geopolitical power. This is because of its strategic location that serves as a buffer between the western nations and the Middle East. The ownership of the Suez Canal has added to its strategic regional power position during the colonial period and after. Other issues include mistrust and lack of political will.

The right to use the Nile granted to Egypt and Sudan by colonial treaties has, for 70 or more years, grounded a sense of right of ownership. Therefore, any attempt to take some or all that right is tantamount to taking away the means of survival. This explains the heightening of a duel between Egypt and Ethiopia that has lasted for over 20 years (from 1999 to 2020). One expert, Tijan M. Sallah, a retired World Bank economist, who spent years working on agriculture water projects in Egypt, has challenged the assumption that ideally a dam upstream meant to generate only hydroelectric power can substantially reduce the amount of flow downstream. He notes that, ideally, a power-generating dam is a non-consumptive user of water. It can delay historic access to water to downstream riparian states while the water is being held up for storage in the dam but, all things being equal, that water is a non-consumptive use if it is later released to downstream riparian states, such as Egypt. The stored and delayed release of the water could, of course, also have effects on aquatic life in the waters. A concern may also exist with the possible evaporation losses from the stored water in an open dam and the associated evaporation and seepage losses along the way in the Nile's long journey across countries. Growing consumptive uses along the way in upstream states, including Sudan, could also be germane concerns for Egypt. That is why the best way forward is to have a handle on data about the resource and forge a viable cooperative agreement on the water allocation by country (Tijan M Sallah, Personal Communication; June 17, 2020). Dr. Sallah further admits that another legitimate concern is the role that climate change could have on storage in the dam and on Nile flows downstream, especially during periods of droughts in the Ethiopian highlands, which are the catchment area where the Blue Nile tributary begins.

Expert opinions, combined with Egypt's relative disadvantaged location—as a downstream riparian—and the logistical difficulties of forcing a halt of Ethiopia's dam project, compelled Cairo to acquiesce. Even with the signing of a negotiated agreement, the Declaration of Principles in 2015 with Ethiopia and Sudan, the governments of Cairo and Addis Ababa could not agree on the dam's filling plan and its long-term operations. Egypt, for its part, insisted on filling for a determined period, preferably between 10 and 20 years, while Ethiopia preferred two to three years, although that was revised upwards to five to seven years. The periods of preferred filling have continually changed depending on the source of information. Also linked to the filling period was the issue of the amount of water released during that process and what is to be done to guard against future droughts and dry seasons. Another concern for Egypt was the dam's future operations and how unanticipated conflicts are to be resolved. Undeterred by Egypt's concerns, Ethiopia based its position on territorial rights and proceeded with the project because of the benefits it hoped to derive from power generation. These opposed positions of Egypt and Ethiopia presented to the negotiators proved to be one of the most difficult-to-resolve issues on international water rights. Hence the question: how are these different but legitimate interests to be reconciled?

The second challenge was the conflict's spillover into the MENA Region and beyond as the actors pursued avenues to ending the conflict. The entry, for example, by members of the Arab League, the African Union and the United States brought the turbulence in the Nile to new levels, thereby complicating the possibility of striking a deal in a timely fashion.

As attempts were made in 2020 to break the impasse, it became clear that the body politic of The Arab League pulled its weight behind Egypt, while at the same time, Ethiopia engaged the African Union for support. Curiously, Ethiopia found support from some of the Arab League members, including Qatar, Turkey, and Sudan—though diplomatically such support was publicly denied. These dynamics bring to the fore a popular adage: there are no permanent friends in politics, only permanent interests. The case of Sudan implies that after the declaration by Ethiopia to build the dam, the government of Khartoum, a hydro-ally to Egypt for over 50 years and also a member of the Arab League, decamped to the Ethiopian side to ensure that its interest in cheap electricity supply is met.

Moreover, as will be argued in subsequent chapters, the Sudanese move also signified their protection of another interest, the Halayeb Triangle—a contested territory currently occupied by Egypt.

A third challenge in the conflict and to the negotiators is the implications of climate change on the Nile's future water supply and the dam's position in that equation. Egypt, already water-stressed, will experience even greater challenges to ensure water availability for all its development needs. With no other reliable source, Egypt will continue to depend on the Nile waters into an unforeseeable future even as stressors such as population increase, urbanization, and rapid economic growth become more evident. Therefore, because of these issues, addressing the current feud should be futuristic and conducted with the utmost prudence. Moreover, the efforts to address the challenges to the conflict and navigating possible solutions, have been long, winding, and at times as tumultuous as the river itself. Following is an account of that process, both the challenges and what still lies ahead.

THE WHITE HOUSE TO THE RESCUE

The hosting of three African leaders on November 6, 2020, by United States President Donald Trump and Treasury Secretary Steve Mnuchin was a rare occurrence. Presidents Abdel Fattah El Sisi of Egypt, Abiy Ahmed Ali of Ethiopia, and Abdel Fattah al-Burhan of Sudan tasked the White House to help broker a solution to a lingering conflict over the filling period and operation of a dam being constructed by Ethiopia. Egypt is leery about the potential effects on the Nile water, which contributes 90% of all its domestic needs. Cairo preferred a staggered approach spanning ten or more years, while Addis Ababa insisted on a short timeframe, two to three years, once the project is complete. Despite a claim by Secretary of the Treasury Mnuchin on January 31, 2020, that a deal had been reached, Ethiopia has since denied any such agreement. That refutation by the government in Addis Ababa was corroborated three weeks later by Secretary of State Mike Pompeo, that "a great deal of work [still] remains" (Washington Post, Feb. 26). Keeping the water tap open for Cairo is not only an existential issue but also a human right, according to the United Nations' Sustainable Development Goal #6.

The setting and goal of these high-level talks are clear. Egypt and Ethiopia are in an unprecedented conflict over shared Nile water resources. It has taken eight or more years to negotiate as Ethiopia in the upstream constructs the Renaissance Dam, which Egypt fears will reduce the amount of water that reaches its territory. This is because Ethiopia's Blue Nile tributary constitutes 86% of the amount of water on which Egyptians rely. Similar conflicts over dam construction have occurred with new ones ratcheting up in some countries that share the world's 261 river systems. For example, in 1975, there was a military faceoff between Iraq and Syria over the decision by Damascus to construct the Tahba Dam on the Euphrates River. Another event occurred in 1990 when Turkey in the upstream mobilized forces to fend off any attempt by Iraq to bomb its newly constructed Ataturk Dam. That precautionary measure was necessary following its decision to temporarily cut off the Euphrates River flow to fill the Dam's reservoir. The potential of a future war among the three countries (Turkey, Iraq, and Syria) sharing Tigris and Euphrates is higher given Turkey's plan to build 22 dams and irrigational canals under the GAP regional project. Given Turkey's relative military strength, such a war is unlikely unless Syria and Iraq combine their forces against one common enemy. The chances of scaled water conflicts will be prompted by the variability of precipitation due to climate change.

Another example is the conflict between the Upper and Lower Mekong River basin states. China's construction of the Lancang Dam upstream has caused tensions with lower basin states such as Laos, Cambodia, Thailand, and Vietnam, creating concerns about overflow alterations, water shortage, sedimentation trapping, and other environmental effects. It is clear from these examples that Egypt is not alone in its fear of the potential effects from Ethiopia's dam to the upstream. Such tensions are likely to increase in the Nile Basin as the effects of climate change become more pronounced due to shifting rainfall patterns and lengthening droughts.

Moreover, as the demand for cheap energy increases with surging population and economic growth, the harnessing of River Nile waters will trigger further tensions, thereby further endangering Egypt's water security. The biggest challenge, therefore, is how to prevent, mediate, and resolve conflicts caused by shared water rights. Accordingly, and judging by the gravity of the conflict between Egypt and Ethiopia, and the period it has taken to find a solution over the Dam, this book aims to explore the approaches that could have been applied to arrive at an amicable solution. It is also hoped that these suggested approaches can be applied by other riparian states faced with similar or other water-sharing conflicts. Specifically, it suggests a two-pronged approach—one short term and one long term. The short-term approach emphasizes the need for negotiators to, first, focus on the immediate issues and their solutions. The long-term approach suggests the crafting of solutions that are sustainable over time to avoid relapse. The book is thus different from existing works that rely on the international heuristics of an immediate deal; a one-shot solution—negotiate and sign the agreement. Rather, this work contends that such a one-dimensional approach can only be sustainable in selected contexts but not all.

Format

The format of this book is as follows:

Part I: The Conflict, Murmurs of War, and Response:

- Chapter 1 ("Conflict in the Nile Basin") describes the nature of the conflict and the issues of contention over the Grand Ethiopian Renaissance Dam.
- Chapter 2 ("Murmurs of War") provides the background to the conflict by tracing it to the colonial period and subsequent agreements, including the Nile Basin Initiative.
- Chapter 3 ("The Response") reviews specific attempts by Egypt and Ethiopia to find an acceptable solution. This includes a review of negotiations and mediations by external parties as well as technical studies conducted to clarify the issues. The challenges, during the process and how involvement by the MENA (the Middle East and North Africa) powers have complicated the steps to arriving at a mutually acceptable resolution are examined. The analysis extends to the lukewarm role of the Nile Basin Initiative countries.
- Chapter 4 ("Lessons Learned") highlights the lessons learned thus far throughout the planning and negotiation process.

Part II: Navigating Solutions Through Theoretical Lenses:

- Chapter 5 ("Theoretical Solutions") provides a description of Prospect Theory, Collective Action Theory, Cross-Cultural Communication Theory, Intergroup Contact Theory and the Pareto-Improvement principle. The goal is to explain how each theory provides a lens for deconstructing the relevant issues during the conflict and to craft viable solutions.

Part III: Short-Term Solutions:

- Chapter 6 ("Ideal Third-Party Mediation") addresses the importance of understanding the negotiation context, mediator competencies, and arriving at outcomes that last.
- Chapter 7 ("Bilateral Agreement and Negotiations") justifies the suitability of bilateral agreements in water rights conflicts because of their potential benefits compared to multilateral ones. This chapter also suggests litigation as an alternative to resolving water rights conflicts. International experiences with the arbitration by the court systems are provided, including by the International Court of Justice.

Part IV: Long-Term Solutions:

- In Chapter 8, ("Renegotiate, Partition, Apportion the Waters, and Contextualize Negotiation") I argue that it is in the interest of Egypt to renegotiate and sign the 2010 Cooperative Framework Agreement to secure their future water security. That agreement was a culmination of years of negotiation involving ten Nile Basin countries and signed by all except Egypt and Sudan. The ten countries include Kenya, Uganda, Tanzania, the Democratic Republic of Congo, Rwanda, Burundi, Ethiopia, Sudan, and Egypt. The partitioning of the Nile Basin into the upper Nile Basin (UNB) and lower Nile Basin (LNB) is proposed. Such division will make it easier for each sub-basin to better coordinate, manage, and solve any potential conflicts. The chapter ends with the necessity of apportioning water among all the riparian states. The British colonial government was able to do so, albeit inequitably. This proposal relies on widely accepted modalities, supported by the 1966 Helsinki Rules, for sharing water allocation and sound data, to equitably apportion the Nile waters.

Part V: Policy Recommendations and Conclusions:

- Chapter 9 ("Policy Recommendations and Conclusions") summarizes the main policy recommendations of the book. I argue that for a complex water rights conflict such as the one between Egypt and Ethiopia, it is more effective to develop a two-tier resolution approach as opposed to one. The first level (or short-term solution) focuses on the reduction of tension. Fundamental to developing short-term solutions is the ability to understand the negotiation context. This requires understanding the history of relations between two warring nations, the degree of trust between the peoples of the countries and how that might affect cross-cultural communication and the political negotiation climate. It further suggests that if a bilateral agreement cannot be reached, the issue ought to be taken to the courts—at least in situations where independence of the judiciary is firmly rooted.

- Even though negotiators tend to find short-term solutions more attractive because of the reduced transaction costs, over time such solutions are less sustainable. The changes in society that come with population increase, economic growth, increased water demand, and the potential effects of climate change necessitate the designing of a second-tier approach and long-term solutions. Thus, the negotiators should sit at the negotiation table with a two-staged approach; a short-term strategy to immediately reduce the tensions, the so-called "ceasefire solution." The second stage aims at striking lasting solutions that prevents relapse.

Contents

Part I The Conflict, Murmurs of War, and Response

1	**Conflict in the Nile Basin**	3
	The Problem	3
	The Grand Ethiopian Renaissance Dam (GERD)	3
	Issues of Contention	4
	Declaration to Build the Dam	6
	The Context	7
	Historical Commitment	9
	Historical Impediments	10
	Political Instability in Ethiopia	10
	Political Instability in Egypt	13
	GERD Technical Aspects	14
	Value-Based Conflicts	15
	Substantive Issues of Contention	20
	References	27
2	**Murmurs of War**	31
	Significance of the Nile	31
	Invasions	33
	Romanticized	33
	Governance	34
	Politicization of the Nile	35
	19th Century: First Critical Juncture	35

      20th Century: Second Critical Juncture   37
      Creation of the Nile Basin Initiative   42
        History of NBI Formation   43
        NBI and Water Security Goal   47
      GERD Ignites Conflict   47
      References   48

3   The Response   51
    The NBI and Its Limitations   52
      Efficacy of Water Institutions   52
      Successes and Limitations   53
    CFA and Its Limitations   57
      Treaty Ratification   60
      Permanent Institutions   60
      Water Security   61
      Conflict Resolution Mechanisms   65
      Pluralistic Decision-Making   67
      Regional "Capillarity Effect"   84
    Summary   88
    References   90

4   Lessons Learned   95
    Introduction   95
    Strengths   97
      Institutional   97
      Policy   100
      Diplomatic   103
    Weaknesses   106
      Institutional   106
      Policy   107
    Collective Action Problem: Strength or Weakness?   109
    The Tragedy of the Commons: Strength or Weakness?   111
    References   112

Part II   Navigating Solutions Through Theoretical Lenses

5   Theoretical Solutions   117
    Introduction   117
    Prospect Theory   118

Losses, Gains, and Other Premises	119
Collective Action Theory	122
Cross-Cultural Communication Theory	124
Intergroup Contact Theory (Contact Hypothesis)	125
Pareto-Improvement Principle	126
References	127

Part III Short-Term Solutions

6 Ideal Third-Party Mediation — 131
Introduction — 131
Competencies — 139
  Understanding the Context — 139
  Framing the Problem — 148
  Experience — 149
  Pragmatic Strategies — 150
  Distributive Strategy — 151
  Elicited/Integrative — 151
  Transformational Strategy — 152
  Duress-Free Mediation — 153
Outcomes That Last — 153
Compliance — 154
Client Satisfaction — 154
Summary — 155
References — 155

7 Bilateral Agreements and Litigations — 159
Introduction — 159
Bilateral Treaties — 161
Summary — 167
Litigation — 168
Litigation Limitations — 172
Summary — 173
References — 174

Part IV Long-Term Solutions

8 Renegotiate, Partition, Apportion the Waters, and Contextualize Negotiation — 177
Introduction — 177

Renegotiate the CFA 178
Conditions to Renegotiate 178
   Renegotiation Costs: Constraints and Solutions 183
Lessons for Egypt 184
Partitioning the Nile Basin 188
   Free-Rider 189
   Defection and Group Size 190
The Upper Nile Basin (UNB) 192
The Lower Nile Basin (LNB) 193
Apportioning the Nile Waters 194
   Allocating Water Quotas 198
Contextualized Negotiation Model (CNM) 202
   Uniqueness 204
References 205

Part V   Policy Recommendations and Conclusions

9 Policy Recommendations and Conclusions 211
Policy Recommendations: Implications for Egypt and Ethiopia 212
   Going to War (Deploy "Hard Power") 212
   Mitigating Water Rights Conflicts 216
   Resolving Water Rights Conflicts 220
Policy Recommendations: Implications for the Nile Basin 225
References 229

Conclusions 231

Appendix 1a 239

Appendix 1b 241

References 243

Index 261

About the Author

Dr. Simon H. Okoth is an Assistant Professor of Political Science and Director of Internships at Virginia Commonwealth University. He is a member of the Association for Public Policy Analysis and Management, International Public Policy Association, The Association for Middle Eastern Public Policy and Administration (AMEPPA), and Climate Xchange. He serves as a reviewer for *Sage Open Journal*. His research activities focus on international water rights, particularly of the Nile Basin. Dr. Okoth teaches *Middle East Politics, International Political Economy, Public Administration*, and *Black Political Thought*. He previously taught at the American University in Kabul, Afghanistan, and Zayed University in Abu Dhabi, United Arab Emirates.

Abbreviations

AHD	Aswan High Dam
BCM	Billion Cubic Meters
CFA	Cooperative Framework Agreement
CNM	Contextualized Negotiation Model
DoPs	Declaration of Principles
EDU	Ethiopian Democratic Union
ENSAP	Eastern Nile Subsidiary Action Program
ENTRO	Eastern Nile Technical Regional Office
EPRDF	Ethiopian People's Revolutionary Democratic Front
EPRP	Ethiopian People's Revolutionary Party
GAP	The Southeastern Anatolia Project (Güneydoğu Anadolu Projesi in Turkish)
GDP	Gross Domestic Product
GERD	Grand Ethiopian Renaissance Dam
GWh	Gigawatt Hours
HDI	Human Development Index
IJC	International Joint Commission
IPoE	International Panel of Experts
JWC	The Israeli–Palestinian Joint Water Committee
LNB	Lower Nile Basin
MENA	Middle East and North African
NAFTA	North American Free Trade Agreement
NBI	Nile Basin Initiative
NELSAP	Nile Equatorial Lakes Subsidiary Action Program
NELSAP-CU	Nile Equatorial Lakes Subsidiary Action Program Coordination Unit

NGO	Non-Governmental Organization
Nile-COM	Nile Council of Ministers
Nile-SEC	Nile Secretariat
NRBC	Nile River Basin Commission
OLF	Oromo Liberation Front
SAP	Structural Adjustment Policy
SDG	Sustainable Development Goals
TAC	Technical Advisory Committee
TECCONILE	Technical Cooperation Committee for the Promotion of the Development and Environmental Protection
TNC	Tripartite National Committee
TPLF	Tigray People's Liberation Front
UAE	United Arab Emirates
UNB	Upper Nile Basin
UNEP	United National Environmental Programme
UNWC	United Nations Watercourses Convention
USMCA	United States–Mexico–Canada Agreement

List of Figures

Fig. 2.1	Nile Basin Initiative Organization Structure (*Source* https://images.search.yahoo.com/; with permission)	45
Fig. 3.1	Structure-governance-process model	56
Fig. 6.1	External contextual factors	141

LIST OF TABLES

Table 1.1	Existing and planned dams in selected countries	8
Table 1.2	Grand Ethiopian Renaissance Dam—technical comparison with the Aswan High Dam	15
Table 2.1	Percentage of countries in the total area of the Nile basin	32
Table 2.2	Summary—Colonial Nile Agreements and Treaties, 1902–1959	39
Table 3.1	Evaluative criteria for water institution effectiveness	54
Table 3.2	CFA evolution	58
Table 3.3	Endorsement and ratification	58
Table 3.4	Indicators/evaluative criteria for effectiveness of international water frameworks	59
Table 3.5	Negotiation timeline for dam project—success or failure	70
Table 3.6	Evaluative criteria for effective third-party mediation	73
Table 3.7	International water agreements—number and duration	78
Table 3.8	Outcomes of meetings with Trump administration	81
Table 5.1	Relative power parity among Nile downstream states—2019	121
Table 6.1	Ideal mediator competencies	137
Table 6.2	Pragmatic mediation strategies	150
Table 7.1	International water cases adjudicated by ICJ, 1987–2016	169
Table 8.1	Feasibility criteria	196
Table 9.1	Sample international water agreements	216
Table 9.2	Summary policy recommendations—Egypt and Ethiopia	226
Table 9.3	Summary policy recommendations—The Nile Basin initiative	229

PART I

The Conflict, Murmurs of War, and Response

CHAPTER 1

Conflict in the Nile Basin

THE PROBLEM

Satirist Mark Twain once remarked, "Whiskey is for drinking; water is for fighting." That prophetic statement is truer today than it was during his time (1835–1910) given the spate of shared water conflicts. The conflict in the Nile Basin in which a downstream state, Egypt, and an upstream state, Ethiopia, have been sparring over water rights gives further credence to Mark Twain's oracular statement.

THE GRAND ETHIOPIAN RENAISSANCE DAM (GERD)

Both countries have been at odds with each other during the past nine years (2011–2020) over the potential effects of the Grand Ethiopian Renaissance Dam (GERD) constructed in the upstream, nine miles from the border with the Republic of Sudan. However, after the signing of The Agreement on the Declaration of Principles mediated by Sudan in March 2015, Egypt acquiesced to the construction on the condition that the two nations must consult with each other about the reservoir filling and future operations of the dam. It was also agreed that any future activity on the dam must only take place after the completion of formal studies by a neutral and independent team on the potential effects downstream. But as the talks continued, followed by the mediation by the United States and later by the African Union, Ethiopia seemed determined to proceed

© The Author(s), under exclusive license to Springer Nature
Switzerland AG 2021
S. H. Okoth, *The MENA Powers and the Nile Basin Initiative*,
https://doi.org/10.1007/978-3-030-83981-9_1

unilaterally with the plans to fill and operate the dam on its terms. Egyptians seemed convinced, though they did not have supporting data, that how the dam is filled (short or long term) and how much are related to the potential impact downstream at Egypt's Aswan High Dam.

Issues of Contention

Therefore, at the center of the contention, there were three issues. One is the period it should take to completely fill the 74 billion cubic meter capacity dam. Egypt insisted on 12–21 years while Ethiopia preferred 5–7 years. At the seven-year period, the lake behind the dam could stretch 155 miles (250 km) upstream. With both sides unwilling to change their positions, as recommended by the 2015 Agreement, observers hoped that Ethiopia would wait for the results of studies completed by an independent team. However, the planned studies were never carried out.

The second issue was by how much the dam should be filled under different scenarios (i.e., first filling to test the turbines and subsequent fillings). Ethiopia, eager to get an immediate return on its investment and to fulfill power needs to 60 million-plus citizens, preferred the first filling to be pegged at 35 BCM (billion cubic meters). But Addis Ababa deemed it inappropriate to be tied to a specific water amount that they must be able to release in the unforeseeable future. Egypt, however, insisted on a release of 40 BCM and a guarantee on amounts to be released during the period of future fillings. To satisfy both sides, the United States mediators proposed a release of 37 BCM, a plan that was rejected by Ethiopia.

The third issue was the inability to agree on the future operations of the dam. Egypt was concerned about two things: the amount of water to be released should a multiyear drought occur Ethiopia, for lack of data and unpredictability of the climate and weather patterns, avoided engaging in any meaningful discussion on this scenario. Another issue was the failure to spell out how future conflicts are to be resolved. Generally, a conflict resolution mechanism is a necessary condition for an ideal water-sharing arrangement. Moreover, it is a vital mechanism that holds international water rights treaties together. Despite its importance, the negotiation team that met in Washington between November 2019 and 2020 failed to address how future exchange of data and information is to be conducted. This is explored more in Chapter 3.

The stalemate in finding the resolution to the conflict over these issues was further complicated by the involvement of regional powers in the

Middle East and North Africa (MENA Powers). The polarization engendered by external involvement muddied the process by lengthening the period in which a mutually acceptable solution could be reached. For example, the negotiation talks dragged from April 2011 to Fall 2020, with Sudan, the United States and the African Union taking on the mediation role with little success. Sudan, however, mediated the Agreement on the Declaration of Principles signed in 2015. Although it was a major step, the lack of monitoring or institutionalization of an enforcement mechanism rendered it weak and was subsequently violated by Ethiopia. Moreover, those mediation efforts occurred in an atmosphere of mistrust, hostility, belligerence, and claims of a cybersecurity attack on Ethiopia by Egypt.

Intriguingly, the drama seemed unrelenting when Ethiopia, which had expressed interest in finding a mediated settlement decided to proceed with the filling before a formal agreement could be reached (Tadros 2020). The report on their action hit the international media in the second week of July 2020 when the European Space Agency's Sentinel-1 Satellite showed images of what seemed to be a natural backing-up of water behind the Renaissance Dam (Anna 2020). Despite the denial of the correctness of that report, Selishi Bekele, the water minister, stated that any dam construction and subsequent water filling generally go hand in hand. In other words, the filling of a dam need not wait until its completion. By and large, that statement either confirmed or was interpreted to mean that one or more turbine gates had been closed to allow for the first filling to take place. Other reports further confirmed that the increased water levels were not due to the planned rechanneling of the Nile water into the reservoir but rather by the heavy rainfall that had started in June. Thus, what was observed by the European Space Agency was a "natural pooling" enabled by the seasonal rains (Tadros 2020).

Although the described water-sharing problems focused primarily on reservoir filling and future dam operations, the broader conflict has been bubbling since the colonial period, but more so from when, the construction of the GERD was officially pronounced in 2011 by Prime Minister Meles Zenawi. But as briefly described above, the conflict over the dam has largely been technical as well as political. As water researcher Kevin Wheeler of the Environmental Change Institute at Oxford University has cautioned, the problem between the two countries should not be viewed concerning dwindling water supply but rather political mistrust. For now, there is plenty of water to go around, so Egypt should not be worried unless persistent droughts occur in Ethiopia in the future. Moreover, rain in the upstream, especially in the Equatorial Lakes regions (East Africa) where the Nile originates, has been unusually high August 2019 through much of 2020. Thus, Lake Victoria from which the White Nile meets before joining the Blue Nile to Egypt reported an increase in both volume and level. One report showed the lake hitting a new record level of 13.42 m compared to 13.41 m in 1964 (Olaka 2020). A record of water release at the Nile's headwaters in Jinja, Uganda showed the lake level had risen by 2,200 cubic meters per second compared to 1,000 cubic meters in October 2020 (Mafaranga 2020).

To be able to disentangle the nature of the problem and to find appropriate solutions, it is important to fully understand the history of the dam, the rationale for its construction and its technical aspects. That is the goal of this chapter.

Declaration to Build the Dam

The construction of such a structure was long expected. On April 2, 2011, Ethiopia's Prime Minister Meles Zenawi launched the construction of the Grand Millennium Dam (later renamed—Grand Ethiopian Renaissance Dam, or GERD). That declaration was received with jubilation by Ethiopians because the project promised a new lease on life to many. Politically, it was an important breakthrough because previous attempts to construct a dam on the Blue Nile were prohibited by three colonial treaties of 1902, 1929, and 1959. The Prime Minister, therefore, used the occasion to remind critics that Ethiopia had the right to use rivers within its territory to uplift citizens out of grinding poverty. But he also envisioned benefits to neighboring countries through cheap power trade and regulation of hazardous floods downstream. For Egypt, however, the opposite was perceived to be true.

Though for a long time Egyptians had anticipated such an undertaking by Ethiopia, the announcement was met with anger and resistance. With a dam three times the capacity of Egypt's Aswan High Dam (GERD—6,000 MW vs. Aswan—2,100 MW) while sitting on the Blue Nile which provides 86 percent of the water to Egypt, the project implied a reduction in the amount received by Egypt. That would in turn affect levels of agricultural, industrial, and energy supply. Despite bad timing with political upheavals that ousted President Hosni Mubarak in January 2011, the government's response was swift and belligerent in tone. The newly elected President Mohammed Morsi warned Ethiopia that "we are not calling for war, but we will never permit our water security… to be threatened… If it diminishes by one drop then our blood is the alternative." That stern message signified the gravity of the project to Egyptians. In a separate remark, Morsi stated that "all options are open." That remark was understood in Egypt and Ethiopia to mean that a possible military faceoff was possible. In fact, the assertion mirrored Mubarak's earlier warning in 2010 that floated a possible airstrike on any dam constructed on the Blue Nile. According to information posted on Wikileaks, Egypt is alleged to have established an airbase in southeastern Sudan from which it could launch an airstrike against Ethiopia when necessary. Another claim reported by *Sudan Tribune* (Tekle 2017) was that Egypt had negotiated with Eritrea, Ethiopia's enemy to the north, to establish a military and naval base in Nora, Dahlak Island by the Red Sea. Ethiopia speculated that the base could be potentially used to sabotage the dam. Hence, the declaration to build a dam and the events that ensued marked the beginning of a conflict that has lasted close to a decade. To understand the nature and dimensions of the conflict, the following context is important. It also clarifies why it is a project whose time has come, but at the same time, has an undertaking shrouded by competing values.

THE CONTEXT

In Africa, there is one large dam for every 683 people. The average for the rest of the world is one in every 168,000 (Strobl & Strobl 2011, p. 433). In relative terms, this implies that there is still potential for large dams, especially in Sub-Saharan Africa. But the construction of dams is no easy feat. A combination of factors determines construction feasibility.

The foremost concern is water availability. The Equatorial Lake Region, from which Nile headwater originates, receives more than 1000 mm in average precipitation per year (FAO n.d). Another determinant is the economic perspective. In situations where poverty is dire, resources for the construction of dams may not be available unless obtained from external funding. The third factor is the constraint imposed by donors and international laws regarding the construction of dams on shared water systems. For example, a country that plans to build a dam, especially on the upstream, must first get the concurrence of other riparian states.

Even when such consultations are obtained, countries in the downstream will tend to resist because of the perceived negative effects on their existing uses for it. Downstream also views such reservoirs as a major obstruction to full water flow, and more so during low rainy season or droughts in the upstream. Because this has the potential of igniting conflicts, the World Bank, for example, insists on such consultations and gaining the approval by the riparian states in the downstream.

Despite these conditions for the establishment of dams, the Nile River had previously attracted several dams and barrages. The first, Delta Barrage at el-Kanater, was constructed in 1861, Zifta Barrage in 1901, Asyut Barrage in 1902, Isna (Esna) Barrage in 1909, the Aswan Dam between 1899 and 1908 and the Aswan Dam between 1964 and 1970 (Brittanica 2020). As of today, additional dams are planned, as experts believe that the Nile still has the potential for more. Table 1.1 shows existing and planned dams and barrages for the four countries that have invested more in these works than the rest.

Table 1.1 Existing and planned dams in selected countries

Country	Dams/Barrages	Total
Egypt – Completed – Planned	Aswan, Aswan High Dam, Esna, Assuit, Edfina Naga Hammadi	6
Ethiopia – Completed – Planned	Fincha, 1 & 2 Tis Abbay, Tekeze,Tana-Beles Karadobi, Mandaya, Didessa, Mabil, Amerti-Neshi, Baro 1& Baro 2, Chemoga-Yeda, Genale Dawa 3, Gibe 1,2,3,4,5; Gojeb HEP; Halele Werabesa, Koga, Megech, Ribb, Tendaho, Alwero; GERD (Renaissance);	27
Sudan – Completed – Planned	Sennar, Jebel-Aulia, Roseiris, Khashm Algirba, Merowe Kajbar, Dal, Shereik, Nimule, Upper Atbara Hydro Project,	9
Grand Total		42

Developed from World Bank (2001) and Salman (2016), with permission.

Historical Commitment

The commitment to construct a major dam on the Blue Nile started in the 1960s when Ethiopia engaged the United States Bureau of Reclamation to assess the feasibility (Salman 2016). That initiative came about the same time President Gamal Abdel Nasser of Egypt declared the construction of the Aswan High Dam. The almost concurrent conception of a dam by both countries is interesting on two fronts. First, it seemed as if the two nations were on the course of competition with each other, especially over Nile water use. Second, with its project size and benefits to the Egyptian economy, the Aswan High Dam promised to raise Egypt's national and regional political power—because with more wealth comes more power. Similarly, for Ethiopia, such a project could jumpstart its economic progress and keep Cairo's power in check by bringing about some balance.

What happened to Ethiopia's plan for the dam after the completed studies is not clear. What we know is that the dam was to be built close to the border with Sudan, near the same site of the Renaissance Dam. Ethiopia's plan probably failed to take off because, first, the highly discriminatory colonial treaty would have imposed a prohibited legal battle with Egypt and Sudan. Second, it could have viewed Ethiopia's chances of securing funding as limited after the Egyptian experience with the two superpowers.

As already alluded to, Egypt's attempts to secure funding for the planned Aswan High Dam pitted the United States against Russia. When the United States learned that Nasser's right hand was in Washington while the other was in Moscow seeking weapons, Secretary of State Dulles promptly convinced Congress to rescind the funding of the project. Nonetheless, the Soviet Union saved the situation by fully funding the project and providing technical expertise. The project started in 1964 and was completed at the end of 1970.

There is little doubt that upon completion, the Aswan High Dam elevated Egypt's political standing in the region and in the world. It was then the world's tallest dam that subsequently created the largest manmade lake in the world, Lake Nasser. With the dam in operation, Egypt's economic growth improved substantially between 1974 and 1980. Although economists have attributed that growth primarily to the implementation of Structural Adjustment Policies (SAPs) that espoused economic liberalism (*Infitah*) (Weiss & Wurzel 1998), the improved incomes from tourism and increased agricultural productivity are also credited to the opening of the Aswan Dam. Reliability in water supply helped invigorate the productive sector. It is notable that prior to the dam being built between 1961 and 1973, the Egyptian economy recorded low economic growth. That dismal performance was partly due to the policy of import substitution that closed the economy off from external competition but at the same time directed government resources towards investments in public infrastructure such as health and education (Weiss & Wurzel 1998). Lack of stable water supply also undermined the agricultural, industrial, and energy sectors.

Ethiopia, on the other hand, suffered one of the world's most devastating famines between the 1970s and 1980s. The long spell of drought as well as restrictive tenant farming under the imperial regime of Haile Selassie, and Marxian collectivist policies under Mengistu Haile Mariam, contributed to the famine. With that atrocious occurrence along with unabated poverty levels across the country, the idea of a major dam promised a safety net on which industrialization, irrigation, and improved incomes could depend. Moreover, a dam like or even bigger than Egypt's Aswan High Dam guaranteed electrical supply to rural households and the promise to generate revenue for the government through power trade with the neighboring countries. Consequently, Ethiopian Prime Minister Meles Zenawi announced the construction of the Millennium Dam (renamed the Grand Renaissance Ethiopian Dam, GERD) on April 2, 2011. But why now and not earlier? Historical events impeded any such undertaking while the prevailing political conditions in Egypt opened a window for action. Each of these is briefly discussed.

Historical Impediments

Political Instability in Ethiopia

Ethiopia's attention to constructing a dam on the Blue Nile has been inhibited by instances of internal political challenges. First, the imperial regime of Haile Selassie's annexation and control of Eritrea on November 14, 1962 ended in a protracted war for independence. That political struggle concluded in 1991 when Eritrea captured Asmara and subsequently formed a government later recognized by the United Nations. Before that, in 1974, the political dispensation suddenly changed in Ethiopia when Emperor Haile Selassie, who had ruled the country with an iron fist for nearly 33 years, was toppled from power by the Soviet-backed Marxist regime of Mengistu Haile Marriam.

Second, the ascension of General Mengistu's military junta to the country's top office ushered in a moment of euphoria. Too many Ethiopians, the push for "Ethiopia First," "Land for the Peasants," and "Democracy and Equality to all" by the Military Committee (or the Derg), promised a new lease on life after years of imperial dictatorship. But that excitement was short-lived as Mengistu's heavy-handed approach meted extrajudicial executions alongside abrasive policy directives. The unintended consequences for Eritreans included the birthing of revolutionary factions, including the Tigray People's Liberation Front (TPLF), Ethiopian People's Revolutionary Party (EPRP), Ethiopian Democratic Union (EDU), Oromo Liberation Front (OLF), and Eritrean People's Liberation Front. The advent of those factions created an atmosphere of unrest, mistrust, and opened power struggle. All of them aspired to stir up immediate political change.

The first major attempt for political change occurred in 1977 when Somalia invaded Ethiopia's Ogaden province. That invasion redirected the government's attention to economic transformation programs that were being implemented. Meanwhile, the political factions were gaining momentum. In 1991, Tigray People's Liberation Front and Ethiopian People's Revolutionary Democratic Front (EPRDF) succeeded in removing the military regime from power. A new leader, Meles Zenawi, took charge of a country torn by political troubles, from the Ogaden to the Eritrean struggle for secession. It was under his regime that a referendum to grant Eritrean political autonomy in 1993 was held and approved.

Even under Meles Zenawi (1995–2012), domestic political squabbles remained fluid. For example, the Oromo Liberation Front remained restless in pursuit of political equality. Ethnically, they are the largest group, constituting almost one-third of the total population (34.4 percent), with the Amhara at 27 percent, and the Tigray at 6.1 percent in a country of 108.11 million (CIA 2020). To the eastern border, conflicts between Eritrea and Djibouti over the Ras Doumeira region also erupted. And to the southern border, the civil war in Sudan continued unabated from 1969 until 2011, when the country split, legally creating South Sudan as an independent nation-state. Zenawi, therefore, spent a good part of his political honeymoon years trying to foster national unity and to spur economic growth by restructuring institutions.

Drought and Famine
Another challenge was an affront by nature. Despite seasonal heavy rainfalls, Ethiopia is from, time to time, subjected to droughts. Between 1961 and the 1980s, the country experienced unprecedented droughts. The 1983–1985 drought, for example, caused one of the worst human sufferings, with famine triggering deaths of up to one million people. Although drought is generally viewed as the main cause of that tragedy, the implementation of Marxist policies under General Mengistu is partly to blame. The collectivist approach to agricultural production destroyed human motivation for self-improvement. Moreover, citizens were forced to respond to orders rather than to try to improve their economic situation.

Economic Hardships
By all standards, Ethiopia is among the poorest nations in the world. According to the United Nations Development Programme, compared to the rest of Sub-Saharan Africa, Ethiopia was among the bottom fifteen nations in terms of HDI Scores for 2013 (UNDP 2013). HDI (Human Development Index) is a composite measure of how a country is doing in terms of literacy rates, life expectancy at birth and gross income per capita. Although there had been appreciable improvement along all the three dimensions from 2004 to 2013, the mean scores on HDI remained below 0.5. The highest HDI score that can be attained is 1.0. That puts Ethiopia one of the poorest nations in the world. In fact, in 2014, it ranked 173rd out of 187 countries surveyed (UNDP 2013). Reasons for the poor performance include a combination of political instability, war and civil strife, weak public and private institutions. This also translated into weak financial capabilities of both the government and citizens. As one interview participant commented during a field study conducted by this author between and October 2014, "the real issue is that Ethiopia has not, in the past, been able to build a dam because it lacked the financial capacity to do so."

Colonial Treaties
Although colonial water use treaties are detailed in Chapter 2, it is sufficient to mention that the 1902 (Britain and Ethiopia), 1929 (Britain and Egypt/Sudan), and 1959 (Egypt and Sudan) treaties imposed on restrictions on who had the right to use the waters of the Nile, including its tributaries. The 1902 treaty prohibited Ethiopia from constructing

any waterworks on the Blue Nile territory. The 1929 treaty apportioned the water between Egypt and Sudan and left out other eight riparian nations in that legal regime. The 1959 treaty between Egypt and Sudan upped water allocation for themselves and failed to consider other riparian states. In addition to giving monopoly rights to the two downstream nations, the agreements contained a provision that required consultation by an upstream state for any waterworks planned. For Ethiopia, the construction of a dam was blocked by two treaties: the 1902 and 1929 agreements. Moreover, Egypt, for a long time, maintained political and economic hegemony with the Basin region. Egypt has for a long time, especially after President Gamal Abdel Nasser's presidency, also maintained a close relationship with a major superpower, the United States.

Next is an explanation of the key forces that prompted Ethiopia to embark on its most expensive national project.

Political Instability in Egypt

Although not a calculated occurrence, the 2010–2012 political instability in Egypt occasioned by Arab Spring, serendipitously incentivized Ethiopia to move ahead with its dam project on the Blue Nile. The protests that began in December 2010 in Tunisia, quickly spread across the MENA Region, including in Libya, Egypt, Bahrain, Yemen, and Syria. Citizens in these countries demanded a replacement of autocratic rule with a democratic one, the removal of long-serving dictators and improvement in governance that guarantees employment, income opportunities, and economic progress. Subsequently, on January 25, 2011, the protests took place in Cairo and Alexandria. As the crowd grew bigger in Cairo's Tahrir Square, President Mubarak responded by using state security that resulted in multiple deaths. Successive events led to the dissolution of Parliament and suspension of the Constitution. As the court trials of Mubarak continued in 2012, so did the presidential elections. In June of the same year, the Muslim Brotherhood political party candidate Mohamed Morsi was declared the winner and became the first ever elected president in modern Egypt.

Amid all those chaotic events, 2000 miles away in Addis Ababa, President Meles Zenawi took to the podium to announce the decision to build Africa's biggest dam on the Blue Nile tributary. Observers, as well as those interviewed by this author on the streets of Cairo, seemed to agree that Ethiopia took advantage of the chaos to launch the Millennium Dam construction. Moreover, the newly installed president, Morsi, still had a lot to learn on the job while at the same time trying to bring some stability in government. But after hardly a year in office, internal political squabbles and unease in the international community about the Muslim Brotherhood led to a coup on July 3, 2013 (Michaelson 2019). General Abdel Fattah el-Sisi took over as Egypt's new leader.

Undoubtedly, Ethiopia had experienced so many economic and political hardships that it took a toll on its ability to carry out such an expensive venture. But the national resolve to move ahead was made possible first by internal political stability, then by improved infrastructure and economic conditions. Second, a small window of opportunity opened due to political instability in Egypt making the declaration timely. After all, they had been planning judiciously for the dam and logistics were ready. An interesting puzzle to the timing is not only the instability in Egypt but also the conclusion to the joint Cooperative Framework Agreement (CFA). By the time of the Renaissance Dam's announcement, six of the Nile countries had signed the agreement, though only four had ratified it. Ethiopia had done both and Egypt rejected the document due to disagreement on Article 14, which outlined security.

GERD Technical Aspects

The Renaissance Dam measures 145 m in height and has a storage capacity of 74 billion cubic meters (BCM). At completion, the dam will generate about 6,000 megawatts compared to Aswan's 2,100 megawatts (See Table 1.2). The project cost is estimated at between US $4.8 and $5.0 billion.

To appreciate the dimensions of the Renaissance Dam conflict and why it has taken close to ten years to resolve, some of the conflicting values associated with the construction of dams in general, are examined. More importantly, dams, as political projects, engender conflicts because politics is about values (or interests) over which people commonly differ. This is a reality recognized by the World Commission of Dams and will be discussed shortly.

Table 1.2 Grand Ethiopian Renaissance Dam—technical comparison with the Aswan High Dam

Description	GERD	AHD
Height (meters)	145	183
Storage (BCM)	74	162
Size of Reservoir (km)	1800	6000
Length of Reservoir	245	500
Electricity generated (installed capacity)	600	2100
Evaporation (BCM)	2	10
Number of people forcibly relocated	14,000	120,000

Developed from: Salman A. Salman, 2016, p. 516 with permission.

Value-Based Conflicts

Dam as a Political Project

Although the strategic aims of dams are economic in nature (i.e., irrigation and generation of electricity for households and industries), the process of their conception, planning, and implementation is political. In general, decisions to build dams are made by either top elected leaders or by legislators. They must look for funding—a process that can create friction. However, once a consensus is reached and funding is made available, they must then decide on the location of the project. As history tells us, dams disrupt communal living by forcing relocation. Deciding on the site for resettlement can create conflict over land rights. Moreover, resettlement requires substantial financial support. Additionally, public health and social consequences (e.g., waterborne diseases and education for children) can be a challenge to the national government and thereby become highly politicized. In short, the construction of dams is political and can easily spark off conflicts. The following is a review of some of the conflicting laws and values vis-à-vis the Renaissance Dam.

Rights

According to the World Commission on Dams, decisions to construct large dams require an acknowledgement of the inherent rights of all stakeholders, upstream, and downstream. Additionally, an accurate assessment of potential risks, either by the investor or by the risk bearer, is necessary to reduce any contention that might arise. To establish such stakeholder rights for GERD's construction, the logic of this framework dictates that

Ethiopia recognizes and considers not only its rights to the Blue Nile but also those of Egypt. Although Egypt's rights under the 1959 Nile Waters agreement have been a source of contention by upstream states, the new Cooperative Framework Agreement that opened for signature on May 14, 2010 did not immediately convince Egyptian leaders to reassess their position. Instead, reactions in Cairo were swift and resolute. Hardly six months into the office, President Mohamed Morsi issued a pugnacious statement that was meant to caution the Addis Ababa government from attempting to construct the dam. That statement read in part, that:

"Egypt's water security cannot be violated at all. If Egypt is the Nile's gift, then the Nile is a gift to Egypt. The lives of the Egyptians are connected around it… as one great people. If it diminishes by one drop then our blood is the alternative" (BBC News 2013).

That official reaction is reminiscent of a similar reaction by former president Anwar Sadat, who declared that the Nile was the reason Egypt would go to war again after the one with Israel in 1967 and in 1973. A counterthreat by Ethiopia's Mengistu reminded Egypt that Ethiopia has never succumbed to any foreign domination or defeat. They would, therefore, defend their rights to use resources within internationally recognized borders at any time or in the future. The common thread in these intimidations and counteraccusations is the expression of rights and risks. Substantively, operationalizing legal water rights between two warring factions can be contradictory. For example, Ethiopia in the upstream claims its privilege under the principle of territorial rights while Egypt in the downstream, claims hers under historic rights. By exercising its rights upstream, any major waterworks in Ethiopia could potentially reduce the amount of water that reaches the Aswan High Dam. That, in turn, would lessen the capacity to generate power and distribute water to irrigated fields.

Risks

A tangential concern expressed by Sudan is the safety of the dam. Should it break, it could potentially wreak havoc on Sudan's agricultural land and villages. Like Egypt, Sudan fears the water received through the Blue Nile would be reduced. This turned out not to be true after the results of a study by Sudanese water engineers showed that they stood to benefit and not lose from Ethiopia's dam (Salman 2016). For example, the dam would reduce the number of sediments that previously affected the storage of the Sennar and Roseries dams. Moreover, the country would benefit from cheap power import. It is after the assessment that Sudan decided to shift her over 50 years' alliance with Egypt to Ethiopia. That shift exhibits the economic principle of self-interest, in which individuals act rationally to satisfy their utility. In the case of Ethiopia, the project is a rational undertaking to satisfy its national self-interest.

To mitigate these presumed risks, Egypt called for a detailed study by international water experts. The goal was to halt the construction until after the results on potential effects are established, but Ethiopia neglected that rationale and continued with the project.

Equity
Throughout the history of the Nile, equity of access and use has always taken center stage. When it comes to who has the right to use shared natural resources, governments must institute rules or processes to determine access. Often, conflicts will be minimized by making the right to access more equitable to all stakeholders. In the case of the Nile waters, the British colonial government accorded exclusive rights to Egypt and Sudan, thereby restricting use by eight Upper riparian states. Unfortunately, those rights have not changed even with the new Cooperative Framework Agreement that awaits full ratification.

Efficiency
One of the major contentions surrounding the Renaissance Dam is the degree to which it will use the waters of the Blue Nile efficiently, without waste or loss. Egyptian water specialists, along with an international panel of experts, were tasked to study the potential risks of the dam. First on the list of concerns that they noted is the costs versus the benefits of filling the reservoir. This will be discussed further in the next section as it leads to the sticky issue in which negotiation continues.

Benefits Versus Costs
Whenever a large dam is constructed on a shared international water system, the question that arises is about who benefits and who bears the costs. When Egypt built the Aswan High Dam, the government had to seek financial and technical assistance from the Moscow government. Additional funding came from the fees created by the Suez Canal. In fact, that is the primary reason why President Nasser had to nationalize the canal, a decision that caused the Suez Crisis. Bearers of the negative externalities (or costs) of the dam were the Nubian communities. The

artificial Lake Nasser behind the dam forced Nubians from their homes and communities. The resettlement disrupted families and their close-knit cultures.

Economically, Egypt has survived thanks to the Aswan High Dam and others constructed earlier, such as the Low Aswan Dam in 1902. Studies have shown that steady water supply through large dams is positively related to Egypt's economic growth. This is even truer for dams that generate hydropower (Kahsay et al. 2015). The power that run the industries and the water that feeds the crops for domestic consumption and exportation come primarily from the Aswan High Dam.

For Ethiopia, the Grand Renaissance Dam is a big deal. At a cost of $4.5 billion, it is expensive for a country that has a Human Development Index of 0.485, with a life expectancy at birth of 66.6 years, Gross National Income per capita stands at the United States $2,207, and expected years of schooling stands at 8.8 years (UNDP 2020). Although by 2012 Ethiopia was the fastest-growing economy in the Nile basin—at 8.3 percent compared to Egypt's 4 percent (the lowest)—a great majority of people, especially those in the rural communities, are still relatively poor by global standards. In fact, Ethiopia falls within Paul Collier's "Bottom Billion" category. These are the people at the bottom rung of the developmental ladder worldwide. Therefore, for Ethiopia to utilize its thin resources to build this humongous dam, there must be an overwhelming promise that it will generate economic growth and improve the general welfare.

In terms of who bears the cost of the construction, the Ethiopian government looked inside for resources. Other than the tax revenue, the government sold government bonds to the public through the Ethiopian Power Company. Ethiopians in the diaspora invested $5.8 million in bonds. The initiative was launched in April 2011. When this author conducted a field study in Addis Ababa between September and October 2014, a taxi driver said everyone with any form of income was required to purchase the bond. When asked whether it was through duress, he said every Ethiopian not only had the duty to support the dam for its promise of jobs and improving the economy but a national duty to which they must contribute.

In the summer of 2016, a local newspaper called the *Awramba Times* reported the results of the Grand Renaissance Dam Lottery that generated ten million Ethiopian Birr (U.S. $234,000 at the current exchange rate of $1 = 35.20 Birr). The lottery is another source of funding for the dam, created by the National Council for the Coordination of Public Participation for the Construction of the Grand Renaissance Dam Office. Prime Minister Hailemariam Desalegn reportedly bought a lottery ticket worth 5,000 Ethiopian Birr. His action galvanized national interest in supporting the initiative, hence the widespread purchase of the lottery tickets and bonds by millions of citizens.

Interview participants in Egypt claimed that Ethiopia received financial assistance from Israel, Turkey and Qatar. In fact, according to the participants, all three countries were considered suspicious and therefore treated as "enemies". Whether true or not, that view heightened their suspicion about Ethiopia's dam project. The view requires further qualification, however. Foremost, the relations between Egypt and Israel that have, since the latter's war of Independence, the 1953–1956 Suez Crisis, the 1967 Six Day War, and the October 1973 Yon Kippur War, been strained despite the 1978 Camp David Accords that remain valid. Following that accord, the two countries established full diplomatic relations and have widened their cooperation on regional security. However, public opinion in Egypt, according to May 2015 survey by the "Egyptian Center for Public Opinion Research," shows that 88 on a scale of 100 believe that Israel is the most hostile state ("teachmideast.org"). As can be recalled, Egypt was part of the Ottoman Empire, and the two states established diplomatic relations upon the collapse of the empire. In 2013, tensions emerged when Turkish President Recep Tayyip Erdogan chastised Egypt for the removal of its first elected President, Mohamed Morsi. Erdogan's repudiation was tantamount to endorsement of the Muslim Brotherhood and their supporters, a group that Egyptian leaders since the time of President Abdel Gamal Nasser have been trying to tame of their political influence.

The Muslim Brotherhood is alleged to have organized the assassination of President Anwar Sadat on October 6, 1981. Although that lead to a diplomatic standoff, with Egypt recalling its ambassador to Istanbul and expelling the Turkish ambassador in 2013, the relations have never repaired as Turkey tried to flex its influence in the Eastern Mediterranean and North Africa, and specifically in Libya after the ousting of President Gadhafi. In early 2021 however, both countries embarked on mending their tenuous ties through new regional security cooperation arrangements.

Political ties have been equally fragile between Egypt and Qatar, a member of the (Lower) Gulf Cooperation Council (GCC). Foremost, Egypt accused the Qatari government of hosting the Egyptian Muslim Brotherhood leaders, a group accused by the West of being behind terrorist activities. Thus, in 2017, Egypt, along with Saudi Arabia, Bahrain, and the United Arab Emirates (UAE) severed diplomatic ties with Qatar and imposed restrictions on airspace and sea passage for the Doha government and all its commercial entities. After years of negotiations, in January 2021, the four countries normalized their relations after signing a reconciliation agreement in the city of al-Ula, Saudi Arabia. Therefore, there is little doubt from these historical events that Egyptians, particularly those interviewed corroborated the public opinion report, that Israel, Turkey, and Qatar are considered as foes bent on supporting Ethiopia's dam project. Moreover, their actions were considered a direct sabotage on Egypt's political and economic survival.

As stated by the government and corroborated by field interviews, the controversial dam is to generate economic benefits to citizens and the exchequer. For example, the annual revenue from the project is estimated at $1 billion per year. This amount will come primarily from power trade with neighboring countries; Egypt is expected to purchase 200 megawatts-worth of power and Sudan 1,200 megawatts.

It can be concluded that whenever a national project, such as a large dam, is undertaken, controversies emerge over who shall bear the transaction costs and who shall benefit. Often, the benefits are either direct or indirect. Consequently, such incongruences create disagreements and conflicts.

Substantive Issues of Contention

Issue 1—Ethiopia's Unilateral Decision vs. Legal Covenants
At the core of the contest is the unilateral declaration by Ethiopia to build a dam that Egypt argues breaches two colonial treaties of 1902 and 1929. Article 3 of the 1902 Exchange of Notes between the United Kingdom and Ethiopia signed in Addis Ababa on May 15, 1902, read in part, that:

> His majesty the Emperor Menelik II, King of Ethiopia, engages himself toward the Government of His Britannic Majesty not to construct or allow to be constructed, any work across the Blue Nile, Lake Tsana, or the Sobat which would arrest their waters into the Nile except in agreement with his

Britannic Majesty's Government and the Government of Soudan (Treaty Series, No. 16, 1902).

As contentious as the 1902 provision may sound, the treaty was the first to formally provide for Britain's claim on the Nile Basin. Moreover, it fulfilled Britain's strategic interest at the time by blocking the construction of any dam in Ethiopia that could affect the regular flow of Nile waters to Egypt, unless it was under the control of Britain's imperial government. Remarkably, 27 years later, the 1929 Nile Agreement was signed between the Egyptian government and the British High Commissioner in Egypt, with the latter acting on behalf of Sudan and other East African colonies (Okidi 1994; Tvedt 2004). A major clause to that agreement read, in part:

> Save with the previous agreement of the Egyptian, no irrigation or power works are to be constructed or taken on the River Nile or its branches, or on the lakes from which it flows so far as these are in the Sudan or in countries under British administration, which would, in such a manner as to entail any prejudice to the interests of Egypt, either reduce the quantity of water arriving in Egypt, modify the date of its arrival, or lower its level. (Howell and Allan 1994, p. 84).

Another important element to the 1929 agreement was the allocation of the Nile waters, with downstream states—Egypt and Sudan—getting 48.4 billion cubic meters respectively per year. That allocation was afterward hiked to 55.5 billion cubic meters for Egypt and 18.5 billion cubic meters for Sudan under the 1959 agreement between the two countries. The legal dimension of those water allocations failed to incorporate upstream parties into the agreements.

To address the inequity of those colonial water allocations, the Nile Basin States (Egypt, Sudan, Ethiopia, Kenya, Uganda, Tanzania, Rwanda, Burundi, and the Democratic Republic of Congo, with Eritrea as an observer) constituted the Nile Basin Initiative (NBI) in 1999 to (a) jointly manage Nile water use for the benefit of all the riparian states, (b) to share hydrological data to make informed decisions on water use and most importantly (c) to develop a new legal framework for sharing the Nile waters. Such a framework was meant to replace the colonial treaties that have consistently been rejected by the upstream states.

By May 2010, a new pact, the Nile Cooperative Framework (CFA), was ready and formally endorsed by all member states except Egypt and Sudan. The two states refused to sign the document because of disagreements over the wordings of Article 14 (b) that states, "Not to significantly affect the water security of any other Nile Basin State." Instead, they suggested it be rephrased to read: "not to adversely affect the water security and *current uses and rights* of any other Nile Basin State." The added phrase in italics was immediately rejected by upstream states because it implied the endorsement and continuity of the contested historic rights principle implied in the 1902 and 1929 agreements (Kimenyi & Mbaku 2015). In effect, such wording would enable Cairo and Khartoum to preserve unequal water utilization of the Nile waters. It is therefore apparent that Ethiopia's decision to proceed with the project rested on the following considerations: majority rejection of colonial treaties and endorsement of CFA by two-thirds majority approval that gave the new pact legal force. Ethiopia further found a legal backing in the 1966 Helsinki Rules, Chapter 2, Article IV that states, "Each basin State is entitled, within its territory, to a reasonable and equitable share in the beneficial uses of the waters of an international drainage basin." Thus, it is because of these two legal regimes (local and international) that Ethiopia, after over 60 years in the waiting, opted to unilaterally begin the construction of a dam. Egypt and Sudan, however, disagreed on the basis that the CFA had not been ratified by all the Nile Basin members.

This brings us to a persisting dilemma. Egypt and Sudan insist that the provisions provided by the colonial treaties over Nile water use of which they were signatories are still valid. Therefore, they are not legally bound by the new Nile (CFA) agreement. Ethiopia on the other hand, argues that it never signed the colonial treaties and therefore, is not compelled by any of them. Instead, they chose to adhere to the CFA provisions. These contrasting perspectives raise one important question for further discourse: *Whose position shall prevail?*

Issue 2—Negative Externalities?
An externality is a concept typically used by economists and policy analysts to identify the negative and positive effects of an activity within the marketplace. For example, a nuclear plant located in a district provides energy to communities and to industries that employ hundreds of people. However, any spills of radioactive agents will negatively affect the health of those who live nearby. Those affected are not compensated for their

conditions and must pay their own medical bills. The same dichotomous effects apply to dams such as the Grand Renaissance Dam.

Ethiopia stands to benefit from positive externalities including hiked hydropower generation, increased revenues from power trade, power supply for households and improved industrial output and overall economic growth. With improved growth come increases in employment and incomes. However, dams are also known to cause negative externalities including damage to the ecosystem, proneness to water-borne diseases or even floods that damage crops and property in nearby communities. Dams also cause even greater problems for indigenous populations who are displaced and forced to resettle elsewhere. As experiences in Egypt, Thailand, India, Ghana, Indonesia, China, and Brazil demonstrate, displaced communities suffer from loss of land, employment, production system and disruption of social systems and networks that took generations to establish (Cernea 1997). Despite these negative externalities, Ethiopia's decision to build the dam seemed to have been driven by the cost–benefit rationale in which expected benefits were deemed to outweigh the costs, at least in the long term. But as will be alluded to in Chapters 2 and 3, the decision was politically driven.

What of Sudan and Egypt located on the downstream? What type of externalities did the dam pose, given the hostile reactions to Ethiopia's dam?

Except for a joint technical study conducted between May 2012 and May 2013 by the International Panel of Experts (IPoE), no other such official study has been done to showcase specific harm to the countries downstream as at the time of writing this section (March 2020). However, academic work by Bates et al. (2013), Mulat and Moges (2014), King and Block (2014) and Zang et al. (2014) seem to agree that any effects downstream by GERD will be determined mainly by three factors: the hydrology at the time of reservoir filling, the filling policy agreed upon by the parties and implemented by Ethiopia and the actual condition of the receptive dams downstream in Sudan and Egypt. Studies by Wheeler et al. (2016) found the following substantive effects downstream by GERD (pp. 624–625):

1. Aswan High Dam (AHD), Egypt: Annual water release of 35 BCM or more would reduce water shortages, while the release of 30 BCM would inherently lessen the 55.5 BCM that Egypt uses each year.

2. While the release by 35 BCM would increase Ethiopia's energy supply by 11,441 GWh per year, Egypt's production would fall by as much as 1,493 GWh within the same period. Thus, in the short term, Egypt's use of the Aswan High Dam would plummet by about 5 BCM.

    Additionally, any decline in the water supply to Egypt will depend on water levels at Lake Nasser (behind AHD) at the time GERD is being filled and whether there is enough rain upstream or a drought.
3. For Sudan, the irrigated fields would be negatively affected particularly during periods of GERD filling. To mitigate these effects, the study suggests concurrent filling of Sudan's two dams—Rosaries and Sennar—with that of GERD.

Besides this empirical evidence, much of the conflict between Egypt and Ethiopia has been fueled by the perceptions of respective leaders and citizens as reported by the media. Often people perceive a threat when others express the intention to either take or deny them what they consider rightfully theirs. Although such perceptions are informed by several filters, any response to a potential threat is generally fueled by the degree of knowledge one has about the issue or situation. Those who have adequate knowledge will tread carefully by weighing their response, while those who have little may either neglect to respond or surprisingly outdo those who are knowledgeable by overreacting. The unintended consequence of such outbursts is the escalation of what otherwise would have been a simple disagreement to a full-scale conflict. Another trigger to the perception of a threat or fear is the previous experience with the issue on hand.

Soon after the declaration by Ethiopia to construct the dam, Egyptian leaders, including President Mohamed Morsi, and the public expressed fears about a potential of water reduction for their territory. Such action, they claimed, was meant to end their existence as a people because, without the Nile, there simply is no Egypt. This resulted in a pugnacious response by Cairo because, with its location at the end of the pipe, it is more vulnerable to any decision taken by upstream riparian states. This is significant because 90 percent of the country's water supply comes from outside its borders, and Ethiopia constitutes 86 percent of that amount. Clearly, with or without any substantive empirical evidence, any disruption to the flow either through diversion or storage facilities has the potential of reducing water received by the Aswan High Dam, which holds the lifeline to all Egyptians. Moreover, Egypt's overall water demand is currently stretched given the spike in the population that stood at 101.6 million by March 2020, according to the World meter.

Another rare but important unintended consequence of the dam construction, at least in the case of the Ethiopian dam, is the shift in a regional power play. After assessing its economic interests' vis-à-vis its relationship with Egypt, Sudan shifted its alliance with Egypt to Ethiopia. That move was inherent to safeguard its interest in cheap power trade once the dam became functional. Through that new alliance, I argue, Sudan could find backing in its challenge to Egypt's occupation of the contested Halayeb territory located in the northeast of the country. That shift undeniably angered Egypt and led to consternation over the next step in fighting against the dam. I further contend that due to the loss of an ally signaled to Egypt, it is in their interest to find ways of cooperating with all the Nile Basin countries to secure its water security.

Issue 3—Filling and Operation of the Dam
By signing the Declaration of Principles in 2015 along with Ethiopia and Sudan, Egypt had, for the first time, assented to a dam construction by Ethiopia. One issue, however, remained unresolved: the period for filling the GERD reservoir and its operation. To better understand why the filling is at the center of the present conflict, a description of the context is provided.

Located some 20 km (12.43 miles) to the western border with the Republic of Sudan, the Renaissance Dam, as illustrated in Fig. 2.1, has a capacity of 6,000 Megawatts—making it Africa's biggest at a cost of $4.8 billion (Salman 2016). By comparison, it is three times the capacity of America's Hoover Dam with 2,080 Megawatts (Drake 2016). In terms of size, the dam measures 145 m in height with a storage capacity of 74 billion cubic meters. It has an extension with a saddle dam that measures 5.2 km long and 50 m high (International Panel of Experts Report [IPoE] 2012). The reservoir is 245 km in length above the Blue Nile gorge and is expected to cover 1,874 square kilometers once complete (IPoE 2013, Salman 2016). The rationale for its massive size is, first, to accommodate the rise in water levels during the rainy season between June and September. Second, is to account for future variations in energy demand within Ethiopia and neighboring states.

The biggest concern for Egyptians is the potential effects of water flow diversion during the construction and filling up periods. A substantive study on the filling options and possible effects on Egypt and Sudan conducted by Wheeler et al. (2016, pp. 623–627), sheds some light on these fears. By applying models that compare filling under different scenarios, the study noted the following results concerning the time for filling, effects on consumptive uses and on hydropower generation downstream.

1. **Time required to fill the reservoir**: In year one, 560 m of water would be required to test turbines whereas in year three, a fill-up in the amount of 640 m would be needed during the flood.
2. **Potential effects on consumptive use downstream:** A release of 30 BCM or less by GERD could reduce the 55.5 BCM that Egypt annually relies upon under colonial agreement. That has the potential of affecting consumptive uses including irrigation, domestic, and industrial in both Sudan and Egypt.
3. **Effects on hydropowergeneration**: In the short term (first 10 years), Ethiopia would scale up its energy supply by an average of 11,441-Gigawatt Hour (GWh) per year. Under this scenario, and with no adaptations on the part of Egypt, hydropower generation by the Aswan High Dam would plummet, on the average, by 1,493 GWh—assuming an annual release of 35 BCM. Sudan could also lose its power generation capacity by as much as 28 percent (Wheeler, 2016, p. 630) failing to adjust the Roseries and Sennar dams to synchronize with the filling and releases by GERD.

The study concludes that overall risks to Egypt's water supply and hydropower generation will be determined primarily by four factors: (a) the amount stored in Lake Nasser behind the Aswan High Dam at the first filling by Ethiopia's dam, (b) the precipitation patterns at the time of each filling, (c) the amounts of release each time as agreed upon by the three benefactors and d) the policies in place to guide operations of GERD (Ethiopia), Rosaries and Sennar (Sudan) and the Aswan High Dam (Egypt).

However, the problem that remains is the unwillingness of Ethiopia to stagger the filling of the reservoir. As already stated, Ethiopia prefers immediate filling, if possible, between 2 and 3 years although the latest reports indicate within seven years (Hassanein 2020). Egypt, however, insists on a longer period of between 12 and 21 years. Cairo also suggests that the filling should not be done until formal studies by independent experts complete and present their report on prospective harm to Egypt. Another element to this problem is the disagreement over the need to appoint another professional body to conduct a comprehensive study on potential negative effects on Egypt and Sudan. It is difficult to tell whether this will ever be instituted.

At this point, it is helpful to turn to the background of the conflict. Experience shows that issues between nation-states begin in small disagreements but snowball over time if nothing is done to contain them. Sometimes, such inactions are influenced by dynamics such as regime change, ideological differences, demographics, economic imperatives or even by historical hatreds and mistrust between nations. The conflict between Egypt and Ethiopia that has been discussed in Chapter 1, can be appreciated much more robustly by examining the interplay of factors of the past, beginning with the colonial period to 2011. Those historical events are referred to as "murmurs of war" in the next chapter. It is a description of the underlying events that started in bits but recently compounded, shaping the current rift between Egypt and Ethiopia.

REFERENCES

"Egyptian Warning over Ethiopia Nile Dam." BBC News. Last modified June 10, 2013. http://www.bbc.com/news/world-africa-22850124.

Anna, Cara. 2020. "Satellite Images Show Ethiopia Dam Reservoir Swelling." *The Washington Post*, July 14.

Bates, A., Tuncok, K., Barbour, T., & Klimpt, J. -É. 2013. First joint multipurpose program identification: Strategic perspectives and options assessment on the Blue Nile multipurpose development—Working Paper 2. Addis Ababa.

Brittanica. 2020. *Dams and Reservoirs*. Retrieved from https://www.britannica.com/place/Nile-River/Dams-and-reservoirs.

Cernea, Michael, M. 1997. "Hydropower and Social Impacts: A Sociological Perspective." Social Development Papers. Paper No 16, January 1997. Social Assessment Series, The World Bank.

CIA. 2020. *The CIA Factbook*. www.cia.gov.

Drake, Jennifer. 2016. "Ethiopia's New Dam May Cause Trouble with Downstream Neighbours." *The Wire*, 01/9/2016.

Hassanein, Mohammed, A. 2020. "Egypt seeks African Suppport on Nile Dam Dispute with Ethiopia." *Ashark Al-Awsat*. March 18.

Howell, P. P., and J. A. Allan. 1994. *The Nile: Sharing a Scarce Resource. A Historical and Technical Review of Water Management and of Economic and Legal Issues.* Cambridge: Cambridge University Press.

IPoE. 2012. *Nile: International Panel of Experts Visits the Renaissance Dam.* Horn Affairs. Frontmedia. October 19.

IPoE. 2013. *International panel of experts (IPoE) on Grand Ethiopian Renaissance Dam Project.* Final Report. Addis Ababa. May 31.

Kahsay, Tewodros Negash, Onno Kuik, Roy Brouwer, and Pieter Van Der Zaag. 2015. "Estimation of the Transboundary Economic Impacts of the Grand Ethiopia Renaissance Dam: A Computable General Equilibrium Analysis." *Water Resources and Economics* 10(April):14–30.

Kimenyi, Mwangi S., and J. M. Mbaku. 2015. The limits of the new "Nile Agreement." *Brookings, Africa in Focus.* April 28, 2015.

King, A., and P. Block. 2014. "An Assessment of Reservoir Filling Policies for the Grand Ethiopian Renaissance Dam." *Journal of Water and Climate Change,* 5(2), 233–243.

Mafaranga, Hope. 2020. "Heavy Rains, Human Activity, and Rising Waters at Lake Victoria." EOS Science News by AGU. July 7.

Michaelson, R. 2019. "Mohammed Morsi: Ousted President of Egypt Dies in Court." *The Guardian,* June 3.

Mulat, A., and S. Moges. 2014. "Assessment of the Impact of the Grand Ethiopian Renaissance Dam on the Performance of the High Aswan Dam." *Journal of Water Resource and Protection,* 6, 583–598. https://doi.org/10.4236/jwarp.2014.66057.

Olaka, L. 2020. Lake Victoria Could Burst Its Banks More Often in the Future: What Can Be Done. *The Conversation.* www.phys.org/news/2020-06.

Okidi, O. 1994. History of the Nile and Lake Victoria Basins through Treaties. In P. P. Howell & J. A. Allan (Eds.), *The Nile Sharing a Scarce Resource.* London, UK: School of Oriental and African Studies.

Salman, Salman M. A. 2016. "The Grand Ethiopian Renaissance Dam: The Road to the Declaration of Principles and the Khartoum Document." *Water International* 41(4):512–527.

Strobl, Eric, and Robert O. Strobl. 2011. "The Distributional Impact of Large Dams: Evidence from Cropland Productivity in Africa." *Journal of Development Economics* 96:432–450.

Tadros, Amjad. 2020. "Ethiopia Filling Mega-Dam that Egypt Calls an "Existential" Threat." CBS News, July 17.

Tekle, T. 2017. Egypt to Establish Military Base in Eritrea. *Sudan Tribune,* April 18, 2013.

Tvedt, T. 2004. *The River Nile on the Age of the British: Political Ecology and the Quest for Economic Power.* New York: I.B. Tauris & Co., Ltd.

UNDP. 2013. Human Development Report 2013. Retrieved from https://www.undp.org/publications/human-development-report-2013. April 13, 2021.

UNDP (United Nations Development Programme). 2020. Human Development Index (HDI) Ranking. From the 2020 Human Development Report. Retrieved from: http://hdr.undp.org/en/countries/profiles/ETH.

Weiss, D., and U. Wurzel. 1998. *The Economies and Politics of Transition to an Open Market Economy: Egypt*. Paris, France: OECD.

Wheeler, K. G., M. Basheer, Z. T. Mekonnen, S. O. Eltoum, A. Mersha, G. M. Abdo, E. A. Zagona, J. M. Hall, and Simon J. Dadson. 2016. *Cooperative Filing Approaches for the Grand Ethiopian Renaissance Dam*. Water International. N.P.

World Bank. 2001. *Nile Basin Initiative – Shared Vision Program. Transboundary Environmental Analysis*. World Bank.

Zang, Hongzhou., Mingjiang Li, G. M. Kondolf, Z. K. Rubin, and J. T. Minear. 2014. Mekong Delta: Living with Water but for How Long?. *Delta Urbanism: New Challenges for Planning and Design in Urbanized Deltas*, 40(2), 230–243.

CHAPTER 2

Murmurs of War

Egypt and Ethiopia have been at odds with each other over Nile water use from as early as the 1900s to the present. Despite years of acrimony and efforts to find ways to peacefully share this vital resource, the first two decades of this century have been marked by murmurs of war as the two riparian states spar over the Renaissance Dam's negative effects downstream. Lately, the murmurs have intensified creating a hydro-contest that have drawn global attention and the intensified push to find solutions. But doing so requires an understanding of how it all started. As detailed in this chapter, the history and subsequent events that have shaped the murmurs are long, winding and at times as turbulent as the River Nile itself. Hence what follows is a review of the Nile and its significance, the politicization of the Nile and subsequent colonial treaties, efforts by upstream states to assert their water rights claims by way of an institutional framework (the Nile Basin Initiative) and Ethiopia's unilateral decision to construct the Renaissance Dam, as all of these factors have caused this enduring conflict.

Significance of the Nile

The River Nile originates from the East African plateau. From one of the small tributaries that drains into Lake Victoria, then takes off as the White Nile and streams northwards until it reaches Khartoum, Sudan's capital.

There, the river is joined by Ethiopia's Blue Nile tributary for the second portion of its final journey through Egypt and into the Mediterranean Sea. From its point of origin, generally from Lake Victoria, to where it empties into the Sea, the Nile measures 4,266 miles (6,850 km), making it the world's longest. The entire basin covers between 1.2 and 1.5 million square miles or about ten percent of Africa's total area.

The Nile's mean annual discharge measured at Egypt's Aswan High Dam is 84 billion cubic meters; the rest is lost through evaporation. Given its length and geographic coverage, the Nile is disproportionately shared among the 11 riparian states as shown in Table 2.1. The inset data for Egypt and Ethiopia is highlighted in bold, as the countries are the focus of this study.

Of the 261 international rivers that share national boundaries, the River Nile could be considered the most alluring of them all. Several reasons explain this exaltation. First, besides supporting more than 300 million (or 40 percent of Africa's population), the role that the river played in shaping Egypt's early civilization is unmatched by the basin. Second, the Nile's inner prowess, which influenced Egyptian spiritual and cultural lives serendipitously signaled romantic images to the outside world. The amplification of these signals led to the invasion of Egypt and subsequently of the upper Nile valley by external powers. That interest,

Table 2.1 Percentage of countries in the total area of the Nile basin

Country	Area (km2)	Area within the Nile basin (km2)	% of the Nile basin area in the country	% of country area in the total area of the Nile basin
Burundi	28,062	13,860	49.4	0.4
DR Congo	2,401,941	21,796	0.9	0.7
Egypt	**996,960**	**302,452**	**30.3**	**8.99**
Eritrea	121,722	25,697	21.1	0.8
Ethiopia	**1,144,035**	**365,318**	**31.9**	**11.74**
Kenya	593,116	51,363	8.7	1.6
Rwanda	24,550	20,625	84.0	0.6
South Sudan	635,150	520,626	97.7	19.5
The Sudan	**1,864,049**	**1,396,230**	**74.9**	**44.0**
Tanzania	933,566	118,507	12.7	3.7
Uganda	241,248	240,067	99.5	7.87

Source NBI 2012, State of the Nile River Basin, p. 13

particularly in Egypt, is still plenteous today as foreign archeologists, researchers and tourists wonder about the banks of the River Nile to either explain or understand its past. As Cairo-based journalist Farid Y. Farid has observed, the Nile is equally or even more important to Egyptians than the pyramids. Let us consider why.

Invasions

The irresistible beauty and seductive nature of the Nile led to the invasions by the Romans, Greeks, Persians, Turks, Mamluks, Libyans, the French, and the British. Such curiosity was also exhibited by European expeditions to trace the source of this wondrous river in order to explore its history, experience it up close, and control its powers. Additionally, that enchanting characteristic of the river is largely attributed to its spiritual, cultural, economic, and political significance to Egyptians. For example, Egyptian lives were sustained by agricultural production made possible by the Nile for over 5,000 years (Collins 2002). Scholars have also noted that it was the plentiful harvests in Egypt that influenced the Romans to occupy Egypt in 31 BCE. The later invasion of Egypt in 1798 by the French under General Napoleon Bonaparte ended up in a fiasco. They lost to the Mamluks with some of Napoleon's soldiers being marooned by the Nile floods. Napoleon had hoped to take control of the Nile valley. A quarter-century later, in 1822, the British managed to take control of Egypt through colonization. One reason was to control the Suez Canal in order to ensure ease of passage to India and China for commercial interests, the other was to benefit from Egypt's economic bounty made possible by the Nile. Access to the Nile could also ensure the economic survival of Britain's colonies that had extended to the upper Nile countries of East Africa.

Romanticized

The romanticizing of the Nile took several shapes. First, the arrival of Nile floods was welcomed with thrill and celebration. For example, the annual floods were venerated by Pharaonic dynasties in the form of hieroglyphic inscriptions to Hapi, God of the Nile and by building statues (Collins 2002). Kings likewise performed rituals that were believed could increase water levels. For example, papyrus strips were fortified with magic and then thrown into the River. Homer, the Greek poet, is said to have depicted River Nile in the masculine and Egypt in the feminine. Such depiction was based on a local practice that portrayed the river "as the male god Hapi...giving life to the northern and southern Nile". Additionally, Homer's literary depiction took practical forms, as Egyptians celebrated the arrival of Nile floods with romance and love as the following quote testifies:

> When the first wave of the flood reached Thebes and Memphis, when the canals were opened, the great popular festival turned into a feast of love, for the young men were inflamed by the idea that the Nile, on the opening of the canals, took bodily possession of its beloved the dark earth. Under its influence, nights of love and marriages took place, and the young men sang.

Another manner by which the Nile was romanticized was through spiritual matters. It was believed that the Nile possessed innate spiritual and healing powers. Those who drowned in the Nile, for example, were decorated with special ornaments while a woman experiencing labor pains found relief by dipping her body into the water and eating a pinch of dry mud from its banks. Similarly, the sick and emaciated infants were taken to the banks of the river so the mother could throw cakes and dates into the water each time the child cried. The act was assumed to make the baby add weight as well as strength. The Nile valley was also reserved for temples and their gods and as burial sites for the kings. That is why June the 17th of each year (the Night of the Drop) was feted by Coptic Christians throughout the country. Collins (2002) has noted that it is on that day when *Munadee el-Nil*, or the messenger of the Nile, was sent out to officially announce the rise of water levels that ignited all forms of euphoria.

Governance

During the Pharaonic era, the Nile water levels influenced political stability as well as the quality of governance. For almost 200 years after 1797 BCE, the Pharaoh's central government allegedly collapsed because the low water levels reduced resources required for everyday sustenance and for safeguarding the country from foreign incursions. But when the Nile floods resumed between 1550 and 1070 BCE, a new dynasty emerged and flourished. The fall and rise of foreign rulers of Egypt, including the Romans, the Greeks or even by the Arabs have also partly attributed to the changes in Nile water levels. Moreover, the foreign invasions occasioned by low water levels weakened political regimes.

Another interesting influence of the Nile water levels is how they shaped the styles of political leadership. This occurred whenever water levels fell, which thereby diminished the national resource base. It is noted, for example, that the Pharaoh's authority "dissolved into feudal anarchy, banditry, wanton destruction, and civil war" (Collins p.19). The opposite can also be said to be true; when the water levels rose, the kings exhibited more caring and democratic-tolerating behavior. Since then, the link between the Nile and politics has become more prominent and more baffling.

POLITICIZATION OF THE NILE

Extended interests in the Nile and its subsequent politicization gushed in leaps and bounds during the 19th and the twentieth centuries. That spate reached its crest during the second decade of the twenty-first century. But let us travel back in time and review the critical junctures that how those events shaped the present politics of the Nile. More specifically, the reincarnation of the Nile's original values that presently transcend into the MENA Region.

19th Century: First Critical Juncture

After the defeat of Napoleon's soldiers by the Mamluks in the Egyptian Nile valley, another face-off between the British and the French (the 1898 Fashoda Incident) ensued as each sought to take control of the valley inside Sudanese territory (Spencer-Churchill 1989). Following that incident, British Prime Minister, Lieutenant Winston Spencer-Churchill, was asked by *The North American Review* to explain British interests in the territories drained by the River Nile. His abbreviated response was as follows: It all started with the occupation of Sudan by Her Majesty's government. Not long after that, General Gordon, a British representative in Sudan, was killed by Mahdist rebels. It was, therefore, necessary to avenge his death. By 1896, things worsened when eight French mercenaries occupied Fashoda in the upper Nile. They were in pursuit of what Churchill called "a door on the Nile," through which they could conduct commerce with Africa's indigenous people and those in the Far East. It was a situation of "now or never," and that is why they had to be stopped (1989, p. 738).

Despite his doubt of the benefits that Her Majesty's government could derive from the barren lands of Sudan and Egypt, Churchill observed, "it is scarcely likely that we should be so stupid as to abandon the substance of Bahr-el-Ghazal for the shadow of Fashoda. We do not mind how much French merchandise passes up the Nile, provided that the French will recognize that the river flows between banks on which Union Jack is firmly planted" (p. 742). Those developments validate two issues. First is the degree to which the Nile was politicized for commercial reasons. Second, they symbolized what was already taking shape: international clamor for the control of the Nile and political imperialism over the entire basin.

It is also important to recognize that several colonial activities occurred in the Nile basin, from the Congo basin to Egypt, well before the Fashoda incident. For example, to exclude others from the Nile valley, the British negotiated and signed the 1890 Anglo-German Agreement, which specified recognition of its sphere of influence in the Nile valley. A similar agreement was reached with Italy in 1891. These actions were to prevent other foreign interests from entering the Nile from the east.

Another challenge to the anticipated British hegemony was the interest in the Nile valley by King Leopold II of Belgium. By 1885, Leopold had already claimed the Congo basin—which he later renamed the Congo Free State—as a personal fiefdom. To achieve his grand ambition of extending his fiefdom to the upper Nile, Leopold signed an agreement in 1890 with Sir William Mackinnon, the then chairman of the British East Africa Company. The agreement, however, was never endorsed by Prime Minister Lord Salisbury. Despite the lack of an intact legal pact, Leopold insisted on a lease of part of the upper Nile, extending from his Congo Free State to Fashoda in Sudan. As expected, his ambition brought him face to face with the French who were also plotting to occupy area.

The British were keen on keeping the Belgians, and any other group for that matter, out of the entire Nile valley. As resilient as Leopold was, a series of shuttle diplomacy between London and Brussels ensued, leading to the 1890 Anglo-Congolese Agreement. Two of the provisions provided the following concessions: Article II specified a lease to Leopold and his successors for the Bahr el Ghazal, along with a 25-km-wide corridor in the upper Nile. It also included the western bank that extends longitudinally 30 degrees to the east. Article III provided a lease to the British for a 25-km wide south–north corridor across the Congo Free State. The provision was later rescinded midyear without any further demands by the British (Taylor 1950, p. 58).

Given the potential commercial benefits of the Nile valley, and despite earlier confrontations with the British in Fashoda, the French demonstrated resiliency in their imperialist maneuvers. This time, they focused more on diplomacy that revolved around meetings in Paris, Brussels, and London. Their colonial enthusiasts in the Foreign Office pushed for a settlement with the British, specifically to secure a piece of the pie in the Nile valley. The French likely learned from Leopold that resiliency pays off. It was in this vein that Gabriel Hanotaux, in the French Foreign Office, relentlessly pursued a deal with the British in order to get a piece of it. Hanotaux is recognized for championing the expansion of French colonialism in Africa (Spencer-Churchill 1989). Article III of the Anglo-Congolese Agreement that provided a leased portion of the Congo Free State was subsequently withdrawn.

The French, typically interested in Egypt and parts of the Congo, including parts of Uganda, engaged in relentless diplomacy to get the British to yield to an agreement. However, the latter insisted that that could only happen at a price. Subsequently, in 1898, the British obliged the French to recognize their existing sphere of influence without acquiescing to the demands of Paris and their broader interests in the Nile basin. Such were the initial political maneuverings after the 1884 Berlin Conference that partitioned African into colonial enclaves (Taylor 1950).

Although the events at the start of the twentieth century symbolized the politicization of this great river, it also marked the beginning of a new trajectory of the dams in the Nile Basin.

20th Century: Second Critical Juncture

This period represented an intensified drive to actualize colonial and administrative controls of the Nile through water storages and institutional measures. The purpose was to improve the ease of exploiting the resources above and under the ground. Africa then had substantial resources including the Nile ready for navigational and agricultural exploitation. To formalize such controls, the British and Italians brought the leaders of occupied territories to the Nile basin to sign a series of treaties. Ethiopia, however, proved difficult while upper riparian nations were not directly engaged as they remained colonial subjects to the British; Ethiopia was not.

The following steps are reviewed to showcase the colonial ingenuity to fully master and exploit the waters of the Nile. It is to be recognized that those actions coincided with the Mercantilist period in Europe that sought to acquire foreign territories for cheap resources and to engage in triangular trade that sent cheap raw materials from the colonies back to Europe for processing and then sold them to the colonies at a high cost. It was through such activities that the colonizers accumulated wealth and power. The first step was the commissioning of studies to assess how to exploit the Nile waters.

a) *Commissioned Studies*: The first study was assigned by the British in 1904 through Lord Cromer, Governor of Egypt. Completed by William Garstin, "the Report on the Basin of the upper Nile" recommended three strategic actions that could be taken to control and use the Nile for the benefit of their most cherished protectorate, Egypt (Okidi 1995; Tvedt 2004). One, was the strategy to regulate and control the lakes in East Africa from where River Nile emanates. Two, the desire to utilize the Blue Nile (in Ethiopia) for irrigation. Three, was the strategy to put into place structures and mechanisms that would ensure stable water supply to Egypt and at the same time control seasonal flooding.

b) *Treaties*: Upon the recommendation of the Garstin study, the British engaged Ethiopian Emperor Menelik II over possible control and regulation of the Blue Nile waters (Tvedt 2004). It is noted that it was during the same period that Mussolini's Italy expressed similar interests in the Nile. The Exchange of Notes led to two treaties signed on March 15, 1902 (Treaty Series, No. 16, 1902). The first one was between the United Kingdom and Ethiopia, and the second one between United Kingdom, Italy, and Ethiopia. Of interest is the pact between Britain and Ethiopia that validated Her Majesty's claim on the Nile Basin. Article 3 of that agreement read, in part:

His Majesty the Emperor Menelik II, King of Ethiopia, engages himself towards the Government of His Britannic Majesty not to construct or allow to be constructed, any work across the Blue Nile, Lake Tsana, or the Sobat which would arrest their waters into the Nile except in agreement with his Britannic Majesty's Government and the Government of Soudan.

As the provision of the treaty implies, Britain had the powers to obstruct any waterworks by Ethiopia that could impede regular water flow from the Blue Nile to Egypt. It should be noted that the 1902 Exchange of Notes was the first formal diplomatic undertaking between a foreign occupier and a local leader regarding the Nile Basin. Tvedt (2004) has noted that Emperor Menelik II was offered monetary compensation which he refused to accept. It has been insinuated that by refusing the offer, the king never signed the pact. Whether this is true or not, the provisions of that treaty remain the most detested legal documents by Ethiopia in the twenty-first century. As will be discussed in Chapter 3, the provisions of that treaty began an uneasy relationship between Cairo and Addis Ababa.—the effects of which are the subject of this book.

Following that initial treaty with Ethiopia, three others that relate to the Nile water use were developed and signed; see Table 2.2. The second treaty that followed, signed in 1906, was between Britain, France, and Italy. Although part of the agreement focused on the spheres of influence over Ethiopia, the rest of it, as spelled out in Article 4 (a), emphasized the requirement of consultations on any project that threatened the interests of Egypt and Britain. Intriguingly, Ethiopia was never a party in the agreement, nor was it a direct beneficiary. Behind those efforts was the desire of the British to construct a dam on Ethiopia's Lake Tana in order to hike up cotton production in Sudan's Gezira region. However, as events unfolded, the project never took off for two reasons: One, King Menelik

Table 2.2 Summary—Colonial Nile Agreements and Treaties, 1902–1959

Date	Basin	Treaties	Treaty Name
Nov. 1959	Nile	Egypt, Sudan	Agreement for the Full Utilization of the Nile Waters
May 7, 1929	Nile	Britain, Egypt	Exchange of Notes between United Kingdom and Egyptian government
1906	Nile	Ethiopia, Britain	Agreement between Great Britain, France, and Italy respecting Abyssinia
May 15, 1902	Nile	Ethiopia, Britain	Treaties between Great Britain, and Ethiopia, relative to the frontiers between Anglo-Egyptian Sudan, Ethiopia, and Erythroea
March 18, 1902	Nile	Ethiopia, Britain	Exchange of Notes between Great Britain and Ethiopia

Adopted from: Transboundary Freshwater Conflict Database, Oregon State University, 2007.

II of Ethiopia died after failing to acquiesce to the proposed dam. Two, the prevailing political instability in Egypt that led to its independence in 1922 made it harder to pursue the project. Moreover, they were unable to forge an agreement with Ethiopia's new leader, Emperor Haile Selassie. Although Italy saw Britain's weakened position as a window opportunity to institutionalize its interest in Ethiopia, the subsequent incursion was forcefully repulsed by Ethiopia in a major battle. In fact, the previously referenced mentioned window proved advantageous to Emperor Haile Selassie who opted to construct a dam with the help of an American firm. But that initiative placed the British against the Americans, thereby forcing the abandonment of the project (Tvedt, 2004).

With the failures in Ethiopia, Britain veered upstream to East Africa to develop storage facilities on the White Nile. Access to stable water flow was crucial for increasing cotton production in Sudan. The supply of cotton was required to uplift the failing textile industry back in England. Therefore, to achieve their objective, Britain worked behind the scenes with Egypt to form two commissions—the 1920 Nile Projects Commission and the 1925 Nile Water Commission—whose study recommendations focused on how best the Nile waters could serve the interests of Egypt. The negotiation that ensued led to the Exchange of Notes in May 1929 (Okidi 1994; Klare 2001). Signed by Egypt and Britain, with the latter representing upstream colonies, the contents of the treaty remain contentious, similar to the 1902 one. The most important clause to that accord read, in part:

> Save with the previous agreement of the Egyptian Government, no irrigation or power works are to be constructed or taken on the River Nile or its branches, or on the lakes from which it flows so far as these are in the Sudan or in countries under British administration, which would, in such a manner as to entail any prejudice to the interests of Egypt, either reduce the quantity of water arriving in Egypt, or modify the date of its arrival, or lower its level (Howell & Allan 1994, p. 84).

Judged by their contents and the limited signatories, both the 1929 and 1902 treaties could be considered prejudicial and pervasive in their effects; of course, that depends on where one stands. Ethiopians and other upstream states will consider the assertion positive while Egyptians and Sudanese will view it as negative. However, it is to analyze the causes of the present conflict between Egypt and Ethiopia that the statement is posited.

Notwithstanding, the first reason for considering the 1929 agreement prejudicial was the prohibition of any project that could potentially reduce the amount of Nile waters or its time of arrival to Egypt. Although signed about 30 years after the 1902 one, the agreement proved more pervasive because it detailed the prohibited effects of any waterworks undertaken upstream. Second, it restricted the distribution of water rights to only two riparian states, with Egypt-48 BCM and Sudan- 40 BCM annually. The remaining 32 BCM was considered lost to evaporation and seepage (Swain 2004). Thus, by allotting most of the water to Egypt and a smaller amount to Sudan, the treaty had failed the test of equity (Okoth 2009). Quintessentially, Egypt was bestowed monopoly rights over Nile water use (Calabresi & Melamed 1972). Third, the agreement was inequitable because it considered Egypt's historic rights and not Ethiopia's or any other upstream countries' territorial rights (Kliot 1994). Fourth, it failed to specify the treaty's expiration date (Hefney & Amer 2005).

The highly skewed allotment against Sudan was not well received by its leaders. With constant diplomatic wrangling, Egypt and Sudan entered another pact, the 1959 Agreement for the Full Utilization of the Nile Waters (Waterbury 2002). Signed at a time when Egypt was preparing to construct the Aswan High Dam, which Sudan opposed because of its potential environmental effects and the displacement of indigenous people to the north, a compromise had to be made. Sudan acquiesced to the dam construction and, in return, it could begin building the Roseries Dam on the Blue Nile. The reservoir was critical to Sudan's irrigation activities at the time. But like the previous treaties, it had some flaws. Foremost, Egypt upped its water allotment to 55.5 BCM while Sudan received 18.5 BCM, with 10 BCM lost to evaporation and seepage (Allan 1990; Hillel 1994; El Fadel et al. 2003; Swain 2004). Second, no water was allocated to other riparian states. Their position was worsened by denied rights to use the Nile headwaters for any waterworks, including irrigation and hydropower projects. As some have argued (Okidi 1994), it is hard to appreciate the concept of "full utilization" when many of the riparian states that contribute most to the water flow were excluded from the legal arrangement. Moreover, that exclusion planted the seeds of hostility that have grown over the years between upstream and downstream states, albeit much more intensified between Egypt and Ethiopia (Godana 1985). How that hostility has transformed over time, especially from the 1960s to the present, and what actions have been taken to address it, is the focus of the next section.

Creation of the Nile Basin Initiative

The attainment of political independence by upstream states in the early 1960s provided a critical juncture for the possibility of asserting their claims to the River Nile. Being politically sovereign meant that they could create institutional arrangements for more inclusive and fair uses of the Nile waters. As will be shortly discussed, local leaders joined hands to reject the validity of the colonial treaties to which they did not support, as they denied them any share in water allotment. It was from this premise (i.e., exclusionary colonial policy) that the upstream states seized the chance to work towards an institutional arrangement that would enable them to be equal partners when it came to shared water usage. Hence, the step towards the creation of the Nile Basin Initiative and the Nile Cooperative Framework Agreement was birthed.

The belief in the efficacy of institutions in general is nothing new. Ancient empires and civilizations survived because of the political, economic, and legal institutions they put in place and enforced. Those institutions that many nations today have either replicated or improved upon continue to guide how we manage our relationships with governments and with other nations. Undoubtedly, institutions are critical because they provide rules and regulations that prevent abuse or harm, property rights protection, rules for inclusive participation, and checks and balances (Acemoglu & Robinson 2012). As noted with the British colonial government, their ability to control, manage and allocate water rights would not have been possible without the development and implementation of political and legal institutional mechanisms. In fact, the resiliency of the 1929 and 1959 treaties into the twenty-first century lend credence to the argument advanced by Acemoglu and Robinson that institutions, by default, can have lasting (whether desired or undesired) effects. However, it ought to be recognized that the real efficacy of an institution, especially in a democracy or in situations where there is a common resource rests in its inclusive attributes and the degree of enforcement. This further suggests that institutions by themselves do not guarantee a path to equitable access or progress for all. That is why it is important to create an inclusive process that will produce an all-encompassing outcome. The establishment of the Nile Basin Initiative exemplifies the change in this institutional trajectory.

History of NBI Formation

At the dawn of independence and soon thereafter, the Nile upstream states that they were excluded by the colonial water use regimes began to challenge the status quo. The first formal calling for a new regime was made by Tanzania's premier Julius Nyerere. Faced with his country's need for economic progress and the concern about other independent states in the East African region, Nyerere called for a rejection of colonial agreements that denied them water rights. In a terse statement addressed to Egypt, Sudan and Britain on July 4, 1964, Nyerere made clear his country's stand on the 1929 Agreement:

> The Government of Tanganyika has [concluded] that the provisions of the 1929 Agreement purporting to apply to the countries 'under British Administration' are not binding on Tanganyika. At the same time, however, and recognizing the importance of the waters of the Nile that have their source in Lake Victoria to the Government and peoples of all the riparian states, the Government of Tanganyika is willing to enter into discussions with other interested Governments at the appropriate time, with a view to formulating and agreeing on measures for the regulation and division of the waters in a manner that is just and equitable to all riparian states and of the greatest benefits to all their peoples (quoted in Mekonnen 2010, p. 434).

Nyerere felt it unjust for the agreements to place his country at the mercy of Egypt, as they mandated consultation before any waterworks could be initiated upstream. Such a requirement, he contended, was inconsistent with the sovereign status that his country had attained. The Nyerere Doctrine, as it later became to be known as, turned into a rallying point to create a new water regime in which all the riparian states had the right to access and use. From there, the idea for a basin-wide institutional framework was conceived. Nyerere's call instantly attracted two other East African countries—Kenya and Uganda—because they were already part of an existing pact: The East African Community formed in 1967 as a loose federation. Thus, the Nyerere Doctrine served as the first force for introducing an inclusive institutional arrangement across the Basin.

The second force was a combination of international water laws and experiences. The Mekong Committee, for example, had already been set up in 1957 to address water sharing and management with the lower riparian states. Even much earlier, in 1944, the United States had also entered a pact with Mexico regarding the utilization of the Rio Grande, Colorado, and Tijuana Rivers. Equally important was the degree to which becoming members of the United Nations provided the opportunity to learn about existing international laws that governed international water systems.

A third force that provided momentum towards a new water-sharing arrangement was the changing socioeconomic imperatives within the basin countries. Specifically, the drive towards rapid economic growth and an increase in population meant that the status quo had be disposed of. The upstream states, therefore, needed to exploit their water resources including Lake Victoria and tributaries, for power generation and irrigation. Another important factor was external pressures by institutions, such as the World Bank, for Egypt and Sudan to cooperate with the upstream states and brainstorm ways to bring about shared benefits from this critical resource (Swain 2002a, b). Then came a breakthrough: a series of substantive activities that led to the founding of the Nile Basin Initiative in 1999.

The first formal activity was the formation of the Hydromet regional project in 1967 (Hefney & Amer 2005). Spearheaded by Egypt and Sudan, the project was created to conduct hydrological studies, establish a database for the exchange of information and to identify measures for further governance of the Nile waters. Though most of its tasks were primarily technical, it brought together experts from the participating states which, in turn, encouraged cooperation over Nile water management. The two countries further explored plans for setting up a body that would facilitate development within the basin. Interestingly, the offshoot was two instead of one. The first was the formation of Undugu (meaning brotherhood in Swahili) to coordinate basin-wide economic development. It, however, failed in its mission due to lack of commitment by other Nile Basin states. That led to the formation of The Technical Cooperation Committee for the Promotion of the Development and Environmental Protection (TECCONILE) in 1992, with a secretariat placed in Entebbe, Uganda (Mohamoda 2003). Only six countries—Uganda, Democratic Republic of Congo, Rwanda, Egypt, and Tanzania—were involved. The primary goal of TECCONILE was to harmonize basin-wide activities until a more permanent institutional framework was established.

After a series of conferences between 1993 and 1994, the Council of Ministers instituted, in 1998, an action plan proposed, inter alia, numerous projects (Tesfaye 2012). That action plan translated into the establishment of the Nile Basin Initiative (NBI) on February 22, 1999. Figure 2.1 (below) shows the geographic coverage of the Basin as well as constituent riparian states.

The formation of NBI was an important achievement, especially for the upstream states. For one, the NBI provided a forum in which they felt included in the Nile water affairs. Second, it signaled to both Egypt and Sudan that it would no longer be business as usual. Therefore, they recognized the need for join collaboration with co-consumers upstream to find effective ways for shared water use. For external donors and other friendly nations, the formation of the NBI was a milestone that deserved their technical as well as financial support. So, when the World Bank was asked by the newly formed body to assist with the coordination of its activities, they readily accepted. Moreover, the excitement about its creation attracted generous funding from numerous sources, including the World Bank, the European Union, and international development agencies (Waterbury 2002; Mohamoda 2003; Hefney & Amer 2005). With the NBI formation, the Nile River had joined 61 other international river basins that had formal organizations. There are a total of 276

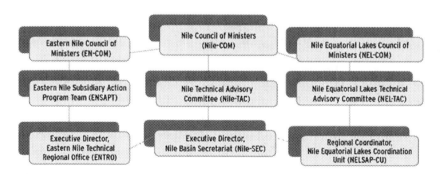

Fig. 2.1 Nile Basin Initiative Organization Structure (*Source* https://images.search.yahoo.com/; with permission)

international river basins shared by two or more countries, of which 59 are in Africa (Rieu-Clarke & Pegram 2013; UNEP 2013).

Goals and Objectives
Upon establishment, the NBI's primary aim was to institute activities that would ensure the socioeconomic development of all Nile states through equitable water utilization. Over time, the achievement of that goal broadened its functions to include (1) facilitation of cooperation within the basin, (2) management of local water resources by providing technical support, and (3) the development of water resource projects from which member states can benefit ("Cooperate Report 2019"). Beyond these functions are six strategic objectives: achieving water security, energy security, food security, environmental sustainability, climate change adaptation, and transboundary governance. Obviously, the attainment of these long-term goals in such a geographically diverse basin requires a more diffused structure to facilitate a smooth implementation.

The Structure
Structurally, the NBI, with headquarters in Entebbe, Uganda, is headed by an executive director who coordinates all activities on behalf of the Council of Ministers (Nile-COM). Nile-COM is composed of water affairs ministers from all member states. Below the Nile-COM are two subsidiary regional offices that coordinate specific projects to ensure NBI's strategic goals are achieved. The first is the Eastern Nile Technical Regional Office (ENTRO) based in Addis Ababa, Ethiopia, and the second is the Nile Equatorial Lakes Subsidiary Action Program Coordination Unit (NELSAP-CU), based in Kigali, Rwanda.

Besides the regional activities coordinated by such an elaborate structure, one issue that is not presently clear is what role, directly or indirectly, the NBI has played is addressing the conflict between Egypt and Ethiopia over the Renaissance Dam. As previously stated, one of the major functions of the NBI is the facilitation of cooperation among all members of the basin. However, over the past nine years (2011–2020) the conflict has escalated regardless of the efforts by the Secretariat. Although most upstream states have an interest in shared water arrangement, this, however, does not preclude making a good faith effort to mediate. But even more critical to this work is understanding the extent to which NBI's pursuit of six strategic goals, water security, energy security, food, and transboundary governance, played into the current conflict that has generated political polarization within the basin and the MENA Region. These are discussed briefly to provide further backdrop for the conflict.

NBI and Water Security Goal

The World Bank estimates that the average water use per person per year is 1,000 cubic meters (Levy & Sidel 2011). This desired water availability and use per person, of course, differs within each Nile riparian state. In Egypt, for example, the desired amount is 579 cubic meters per year while Ethiopia it is 125 cubic meters (Mabrouk 2019). This figure is surprisingly low despite its upstream location. The amount for Egypt is among the lowest in the world. Considering three composite indicators of water stress (environmental, human, and agricultural), Egypt is ranked exceedingly high, Sudan moderate and the rest of the upstream states low stress. Therefore, the inclusion of water security as one of NBI's strategic goals is warranted. The goal is to ensure the water security of its member states downstream and to some extent to the upper riparian states. To achieve this goal, the NBI supports the increase of water storage capacities within each member state. This indirectly justifies Ethiopia's dam (GERD) construction.

GERD Ignites Conflict

Chapter 1 addressed how the construction of Ethiopia's dam (GERD) triggered the conflict between Egypt and Ethiopia. Sudan was drawn into the feud, albeit lukewarmly. Thereafter, the Khartoum government took up the mediation role after shifting its political and hydro-alliance from Cairo to Addis Ababa. This brief section emphasizes three important triggers to the conflict.

One, the unilateral declaration by Ethiopia to construct the dam sparked the conflict. Two, the belligerent reactions of Egyptian leaders, combined with perceived harm not backed by facts, further fueled the confrontations. Third, the failure of the 2015 Declaration of Principles (Deal #1) to forge a lasting solution took the conflict to the next level. Fourth, the unwillingness of Ethiopia to agree to the middle-ground reservoir filling period (i.e., staggered filling) suggested by the United States mediators reduced the chances of reaching a solution sooner—as the two warring nations reached out to allies in the MENA Region in the African Union.

Looking back at the provisions of these earlier treaties, it seems they are mirror images of each other. Each treaty rejects any waterworks in the upstream. However, the revision of the 1902 treaty, codified in the 1906 accord, indirectly acquiesced to some waterworks by making consultations a requirement. Undeniably, those restrictions imposed by the treaties have acted as triggers to the conflict between upstream and downstream states over the Nile Basin. It is, therefore, understandable why upstream states have continuously defied the two treaties. For one, most of those countries were not partied in the negotiations that led to the signing of the 1929 treaty. Under the Nyerere doctrine (named after President of Julius Nyerere of Tanzania, 1962–1985), upstream countries have fervently opposed the agreement because, as colonial subjects, they were by *de jure* deterred from negotiating Nile water rights. The efforts to create programs such as Hydromet followed by a basin wider body, the Nile Basin Initiative, illustrates the commitment to cooperation in order to equitably share the Nile waters. The commendable teamwork that produced a new legal architecture, the 2010 Cooperative Framework Agreement and, later, the Declaration of Principles in 2015, signifies the desire for a lasting resolution to the conflict.

References

Acemoglu, Daron, and James A. Robinson. 2012. *Why Nations Fail: The Origins of Power, Prosperity, and Poverty*. New York, NY: Crown Publishing Group.

Allan, J. A. 1990. "The Nile Basin: Evolving approaches to Nile waters management." Occasional Paper 20, June. *SOAS Water Issues Group*. University of London.

Calabresi, G., and D. Melamed. 1972. "Property Rules, Liability Rules and Inalienability: One View of the Cathedral." *Harvard Law Review* 85:1089, 1092–1093.

El Fadel, M., Y. El-Sayeg, K. El-Fadl, and D. Khorbotly. 2003. "The Nile River Basin: A Case Study in the Surface Water Conflict Resolution." *Journal of Natural Resources and Life Sciences Education* 32.

Godana, B. 1985. *Africa's Shared Water Resources: Legal and Institutional Aspects of the Nile, Niger, and Senegal River Systems*. Geneva: Graduate Institute of International Studies.

Hefney, M., and S. E. Amer. 2005. Egypt and the Nile Basin. *Aquatic Science* 67:42–50.

Hillel, D. 1994. *Rivers of Eden: The Struggle for Water and the Quest for Peace in the Middle East*. New York: Oxford University Press.

Howell, P. P., and J. A. Allan. 1994. *The Nile: Sharing a Scarce Resource. A Historical and Technical Review of Water Management and of Economic and Legal Issues*. Cambridge: Cambridge University Press.

Klare, Michael E. 2001. *Resource Wars: The New Landscape of Global Conflict*. New York: Metropolitan Books.

Kliot, N. 1994. *Water Resources and Conflict in the Middle East*. New York: Routledge.

Mabrouk, Mirette. 2019. "Events at MEI." *The New Arab*, December 3. https://www.mei.edu/events.

Mohamoda, D. Y. 2003. "Nile Basin Cooperation: A review of the literature." *Current African Issues* 26. Nordiska Afrikainstitute.

Mekonnen, D. Z. 2010. "The Nile Basin Cooperative Framework Agreement Negotiations and the Adoption of a 'Water Security' Paradigm: Flight into Obscurity or a Logical Cul-de-sac?" *The European Journal of International Law* 21(2).

Levy, Barry S., and Sidel W. Victor. 2011. "Water Rights and Water Fights: Preventing and Resolving Before They Boil Over." *American Journal of Public Health* 101(5) (May):778–780.

Okidi, O. 1994. "History of the Nile and Lake Victoria Basins through Treaties." In *The Nile Sharing a scarce resource*, edited by P. P. Howell & J. A. Allan. London, UK: School of Oriental and African Studies.

Okidi, C. O. 1995. *Environmental Legislation in Africa: Some Recent Rrends*. IUCN (ID: MON- 054562).

Okoth, Simon. 2009. A 'Seat at the Table': Exploring the Relationship between Pluralist A 'Seat at the Table': Exploring the Relationship between Pluralist Structures and Involvement in Decision-Making—The Case of the Structures and Involvement in Decision-Making—The Case of the Nile Basin Initiative Nile Basin Initiative. PhD Dissertation, Virginia Commonwealth University.

Rieu-Clarke, Alistair, and Guy Pegram. 2013. Impacts on the International Architecture for Transboundary Waters. In *The UN Watercourses Convention in Force: Strengthening International Law for Transboundary Water Management*, edited by F. Rocha Loures and Alistair Rieu-Clarke, pp. 67–76. London and New York: Routledge.

Spencer-Churchill, Lieutenant Winston. 1989. "The Fashoda Incident." *The North American Review* 167(505) (December):736–743.

Swain, Ashok. 2002a. "The Nile River Basin Initiative: Too Many Cooks, Too Little Broth." *SAIS Review*.

Swain, Ashok. 2002b. "Managing the Nile River: The Role of Sub-Basin Cooperation." In *Conflict Management of Water Resources*, edited by Manas Chatterji, Saul Arlosoroff, and gauri Guha. Aldershot: Ashgate.

Swain, A. 2004. *Managing Water Conflict: Asia, Africa and the Middle East*. New York: Routledge.

Taylor, A. J. P. 1950. "The Question of the Upper Nile 1894–5." *The English Historical Review* 65(254) (January):52–80.

Tesfaye, Aaron. 2012. "Environmental Security, Regime Building, and International Law in the Nile Basin." *Canadian Journal of African Studies* 46(2):271–287.

Tvedt, T. 2004. *The River Nile on the Age of the British: Political Ecology and the Quest for Economic Power*. New York: I.B. Tauris & Co., Ltd.

UNEP. 2013. Annual Report-2014UNEP AR 2013-LR(1).

Waterbury, J. 2002. *Nile Basin: National Determinants of Collective Action*. New Haven, CT: Yale University Press.

CHAPTER 3

The Response

Responding to the conflict between Egypt and Ethiopia presented itself in different dimensions between 2011 and 2020. Starting with rage and threats of a military faceoff, the reactions transformed into shuttle diplomacy between Addis Ababa and Cairo, shifts in political alliances, technical assessments of the dam vis-à-vis potential effects and engagement of third-party mediation. Despite the efforts, it is important to recognize the work previously done by the riparian states to create a river basin organization: the Nile Basin Initiative (NBI). The NBI was created to forge basin-wide cooperation, to develop and manage water resources and to foster peace. More importantly, it was expected to set up rules and methods for more equitable sharing of the water. That meant negotiating a new agreement to replace the colonial treaties of 1929 and 1959. The Nile Basin countries were successful in doing so after nine years of effort. The signing of the Cooperative Framework Agreement in 2010 was, therefore, a milestone that was expected to change the Nile water regime for the better. But there was a setback: Egypt and Ethiopia did not endorse the document because of disagreement in the wording of Article 14 (b)—to be reviewed shortly. The failure to sign the new agreement exacerbated the already existing mistrust and hostility towards the two countries by upstream states. Therefore, it was not a surprise when the following year, 2011, Ethiopia's Prime Minister Meles Zenawi

© The Author(s), under exclusive license to Springer Nature Switzerland AG 2021
S. H. Okoth, *The MENA Powers and the Nile Basin Initiative*, https://doi.org/10.1007/978-3-030-83981-9_3

declared the construction of Africa's biggest dam, the Grand Renaissance Ethiopian Dam (GERD).

To better understand the responses that declaration elicited for the past eight to nine years, we focus not on the verbal exchanges but also on the formal approaches by the parties to address the problem. But first is a review of the systems that were put in place before the eruption of the conflict. The second section of the chapter examines initiatives that were instituted to address the conflict that erupted after the declaration was made to build the dam. The challenges experienced in that effort, to achieve desirable outcomes, are identified and explained.

The NBI and Its Limitations

Efficacy of Water Institutions

The efficacy of established institutions in governing shared water systems is well known. The Israeli–Palestinian Joint Water Committee (JWC), the Mekong River Commission, the 1889 International Boundary and Water Commission between Mexico and the governing waters of Rio Grande, the Permanent Okavango River Basin Commission (South Africa), the Commission of the Danube River and the Permanent Indus Commission between India and Pakistan are some examples. Overall, these institutions provide mechanisms for cooperation in water sharing and management, along with issues over conflict resolution, access and use.

The Nile Basin Initiative (NBI) was created in 1999 to address an imbalance in water allocation initiated by the colonial administration and to devise ways for efficient water use. As discussed in Chapter 2, the 1929 and 1959 treaties allotted Nile waters to Egypt and Sudan, thereby excluding eight upper riparian states. The efforts by those riparian states to redress past colonial arrangements over water use resulted in the launching of various programs by the NBI, in which cooperation and conflict mitigation were primary. Hence, what follows is an assessment of those various programs and their degree of effectiveness. Specifically, the success in implementing three relevant strategic goals—water security, energy security, and transboundary governance—is scrutinized. Also important is the role that the Secretariat (Nile-SEC) and its subsidiary entities (Nile Equatorial Lakes Subsidiary Action Program Coordination Unit, NELSAP-CU and Eastern Technical Regional Office, ENTRO) play towards these goals.

Suffice to say here that the Secretariat was primarily tasked to facilitate cooperation and ensure joint water development and management. The effort towards these objectives began by founding Hydromet in 1967 take out to conduct hydrological studies, create a central database and exchange information. Another function was to institute participation mechanisms. Although initiated by Egypt and Sudan, other basin countries later streamed in and enabled the body to transform into TECCONILE and, subsequently, into the Nile Basin Initiative (NBI) in 1999. To assess the degree of success as well as limitations of achieving cooperation and strategic goals prior to the eruption of dam conflict, relevant evaluative criteria has been developed and discussed vis-à-vis each goal. This is also examined from the perspectives of states' ability to mitigate conflict over the water resource.

Successes and Limitations

The NBI has undoubtedly provided an enabling environment for dialogue and cooperation among the Nile states. Fostering transboundary cooperation is linked to governance. According to the United Nations Environmental Programme (UNEP) (2013), indicators of transboundary water governance include the presence or absence of legal framework, hydro-political tensions and enabling environment. The United States Agency for International Development (ReWaB Project) identifies governance, functions, and decision-making processes as essential elements for assessing the effectiveness of river basin institutions (2010). Saleth and Dinar (1999) in the World Bank Technical Report, list water law, water policy, water administration and linkages as critical variables when assessing the performance of water institutions. For this analysis, the fusion of some elements leads to three concise evaluative criteria (Structure, Governance, Processes; see Table 3.1) that can be used to assess the strengths and limitations of NBI's strategic goals. This should inform our overall assessment of the institution's contribution, directly or indirectly, to the conflict between Egypt and Ethiopia.

Structure

The purpose of an institutional structure is to organize activities and responsibilities so that there is a smooth flow of responsibilities. To better serve the interests and goals of stakeholders, an organization will either institute a centralized or decentralized structure. Considering the size and

Table 3.1 Evaluative criteria for water institution effectiveness

Evaluative criteria	Detailed elements	Yes/No
Structure	Secretariat	Yes
	Council of Waters Affairs Ministers	Yes
	Ministers; diffused (sub-basin/regional units)	Yes
Governance	Water laws and policies	Yes
	Presence of treaty	Yes/No
	Water allocation	No
	Conflict prevention and resolution mechanisms	Yes/No
Processes	Administrative procedures (planning)	Yes
	Inclusive participation	Yes/No
	Implementation	Yes
	Monitoring and evaluation	Yes
	Enforcement	No
	Communication system	Yes
	Flexibility and adaptability	Yes
Outcomes	Subsidiary programs and benefits	Yes
	Enhanced cooperation	Yes/No

Source Adapted from UNEP (2010), Saleth and Dinar (1999) and personal additions including the level of performance (Yes/No) based on literature review and analysis

scope of its mandate for implementing projects covering 10 countries, the NBI instituted a diffused power structure with a Secretariat and regional bodies (NELSAP-CU and ENTRO) as well as national offices placed in member countries. The organization is led by the Council of Ministers drawn from each member state; this criterion has therefore been met (see Table 3.1).

Governance
Another criterion is governance. This can be defined as systematic political processes that establish policies, legal frameworks, and administrative laws and created an environment that encourages cooperative implementation of institutional activities. For each of these elements, the NBI has created specific and broad policies for governing water resources, water resource development and facilitation of peace and cooperation within the basin ("Cooperate Report 2019"). An additional element is the presence of a treaty. In 2010, the riparian states concluded the Cooperative Framework Agreement, which had been in the works for 10 years. Egypt and Sudan declined to sign the accord over the wording of Article 14 (b)

that reads: "not to significantly affect the water security of any other Nile Basin States." Instead, they preferred "not to adversely affect the water security and current uses and rights of any other Nile Basin State." The riparian team agreed to remove the wording and placed it in the Annex section until the problem was resolved at a later meeting.

By 2020, the conflict over wording had not been resolved, most likely overshadowed by the Renaissance Dam Conflict. What, then, does the presence of the treaty tell us? To the upstream states, the criteria is met while the opposite is true for Egypt and Sudan. The two downstream states do not recognize the presence of CFA as meaningful and, therefore, not a good measure of governance.

The other element that supports the efficacy of governance criteria is water allocation. Transboundary water that is equitably shared among members is key to the resiliency and effectiveness of a river basin organization. This is consistent with the 1997 Water Convention that underscores the importance of "reasonable and equitable utilization" for a shared water system. Fair allotment, with adjustments based on sound hydrological data, can yield peace and further cooperation. On this attribute, the NBI rating is a negative ("No"). However, this does not mean that the merits of the joint benefits approach, currently in practice, should be discounted. In fact, studies by Sadoff and Grey (2002) demonstrate that the sharing benefits approach has substantive gains, including enhanced cooperation in the management of water affairs as well as in other non-water issues. Such cooperation reduces conflicts and provide an environment that encourages increased incomes.

Given the paucity of information regarding actual benefits derived from each riparian state originating from joint projects (i.e., NELSAP-CU and ENTRO), further empirical assessments are needed to establish net gains Also significant is the determination of whether the approach has promoted or failed to promote cooperation, especially among the three warring states (i.e., Egypt, Ethiopia, and Sudan) regarding the Renaissance Dam.

Relating to conflict prevention and resolution mechanisms, and in-between assessment (Yes/No) is recorded as shown in Table 3.1. The affirmative stance is supported by, first, the stance that fostering cooperation and peace is a core function of the NBI. Second, Article 3 (#12) under the General Principles of the 2010 Cooperative Framework Agreement states that members shall uphold the "principle of the peaceful resolution of Conflicts" ("Agreement on the Nile River Basin Cooperative Framework" 2010, p. 8). To institutionalize this activity, Article 15 of the same agreement formalized the establishment of the Nile River Basin Commission to replace the NBI, which was considered a transitory institution. The negative stance ("No") is corroborated by NBI's failure to prevent or resolve the feud between Egypt and Ethiopia. It can similarly be argued that either the upstream majority states neglected to take on negotiating roles or quietly took sides without declaring their stand. It is also fair to suggest that the NBI, whose majority members are in the upstream, supports Ethiopia's position given the history of acrimony between them and Egypt.

Processes
Structures, however well designed, cannot guarantee desired outcomes. Like constitutions, they delineate functions and responsibilities and, to some extent, decide who shall take on those responsibilities. Governance refers to systematic arrangements including policies, agreements, and conflict resolution requirements. But they, too, cannot guarantee the success of a River Basin institution. As Fig. 3.1 illustrates, a model that ensures the attainment of desired outcomes, such as peace, cooperation, and shared benefits, should ideally begin with a carefully designed structure, followed by systematic policies (governance) and end up with processes for implementation. Such processes include, but are not limited to, administrative procedures, planning, staffing, training,

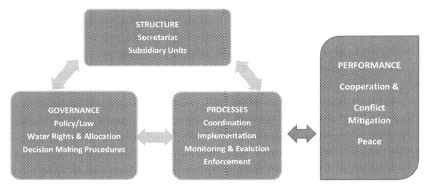

Fig. 3.1 Structure-governance-process model

organizing, directing, coordinating, budgeting, and ensuring inclusive stakeholder participation, program implementation, monitoring and evaluation, enforcement and maintaining regular and open communication.

Presently, all procedures except enforcement seem to be in place. Generally, and in practice, it is easier to focus on monitoring and evaluating to ensure things get done. Weak areas are addressed by taking corrective actions. But to have a sanction system is not only cumbersome in a transnational organization but also vulnerable to hostility and geopolitical polarization.

Inclusive participation has been somewhat elusive under the current institutional architecture. Field research conducted by this author in 2008–2009 at the NBI Secretariat in Entebbe, Uganda and ENTRO offices in Addis Ababa, Ethiopia, showed that non-official stakeholders (e.g., NGOs) were either denied participation or invited only as observers. Consequently, their presence merely fulfilled donor requirements even though their opinions were not considered in decision-making.

Achievement of desired outcomes is one of the primary measures of how effective and successful a river basin organization is. In this respect, the Nile Basin Initiative has been successful. For example, the Secretariat and its subsidiary offices have fostered improved cooperation within the Nile affairs and successfully implemented regional programs from which member states can derive direct or indirect benefits from the Nile.

CFA and Its Limitations

This is the second most important legal architecture instituted by the Nile Basin states to address the problem of Nile water sharing and management. Negotiating the agreement that started in 1997, but more concertedly in 1999, was concluded in March 2006. In June 2007, the agreement was submitted to the Nile Council of Ministers (Nile-COM) for deliberation and approval. By April 13, 2010, the agreement was ready for signatures. Table 3.2 shows the evolution of the agreement.

According to the Law of Treaties under the 1969 Vienna Convention, the formalization of an international treaty is a two-stage process. The first part requires signatures from all parties on the agreement after attaining a two-third majority vote as specified in Article 2 (1) of the Convention. The second requires ratification by each member state. Generally, this last stage requires the legislative body (e.g., Parliaments or Congress in some western countries) of each member state to review and debate

Table 3.2 CFA evolution

Dates	Activity/description
1999	NBI created; supported by all Basin countries
3/2006	CFA draft completed
6/2007	Draft submitted to Nile-COM for deliberation
3/2006–6/2007	Article 14 (b)-regarding water referred to Heads of State following contestation by Egypt and Sudan
4/13/2010	CFA open for signatures; rejection by Egypt and Sudan
5/2010–2/2011	CFA signed six countries; others promised to sign at a later date

Adopted from Nile Basin Initiative website: https://www.nilebasin.org/nbi/cooperative-framework-agreement

the merits of the signed document and then, through voting, decide to approve or reject. Because the process can take time depending on the issues each country considers a priority, only four out of the six who had appended their signatures have ratified the Cooperative Framework Agreement (CFA). Article 42 requires that all signatories ratify, but only comes into force 60 days "after the sixth instrument of ratification with the African Union." The treaty can only be applied only after ratification. Table 3.3 provides the list of countries that have signed and ratified the Agreement.

Table 3.3 Endorsement and ratification

Signatories	Date	Ratification date
Ethiopia	5/14/2010	6/13/2013
Rwanda	5/14/2010	8/28/2013
Tanzania	5/14/2010	3/26/2015
Uganda	5/14/2010	n.d.
Kenya	5/19/2010	N/A
Burundi	2/28/2011	N/A
Congo DRC	n.d.	N/A
South Sudan	n.d.	N/A
Sudan	n.d.	N/A
Eritrea	5/19/2010	

Adopted from JournalduCameroun.com (April 7, 2020) and Nile Basin Initiative. https://www.nilebasin.org/nbi/cooperative-framework-agreement

The aims of this agreement are to (a) stimulate cooperation among all the basin states, (b) accelerate integrated and sustainable development, (c) foster peaceful use of Nile water resources, and (d) safeguard basin-wide environment (Cooperative Framework Agreement 2010). One other goal as stated in Article 4 of the agreement, is to facilitate equitable and reasonable use of the Nile water.

In principle, the CFA aimed to address the imbalance of Nile water allocation. In fact, the ability of treaties to foster peaceful resolution of water rights conflicts is supported by previous studies as well as international experiences (Zawairi et al. 2016). Hence, the likelihood of negotiating conflicts increases with treaty formation.

A combination of factors contributes to the efficacy of international water treaties and agreements. These factors (in Table 3.4) also serve as indicators with which to assess whether a shared water agreement will either restrain or provoke further water conflict. Given the importance of CFA for the future of the Nile Basin cooperation and it being first to replace colonial agreements, assessing its effectiveness can assist the Nile countries is identifying specific limitations. The same indicators are used in subsequent sections of this chapter to analyze the effectiveness and limitations of other formal arrangements to address the conflict between Egypt and Ethiopia.

Table 3.4 Indicators/evaluative criteria for effectiveness of international water frameworks

Indicator/criteria	Elements/description
Ratification	Treaties/agreements come into force after ratification by signatories
Permanent institution	Inclusion of a permanent basin organization (implement, monitor, regulate, enforce)
Water security	Right of access and use; Water allocation (equitable and reasonable utilization; obligation not to cause significant harm)
Conflict resolution mechanisms	Negotiation, mediation, third-party arbitration
Adaptability	Considers changes in hydrology, population, and Economic development requirements; adjustments to water allocation; modifications to the framework
Pluralistic in decision-making	Mechanisms and actual engagement of all member states by considering competing interests. States consult with riparian communities

Treaty Ratification

As already discussed in the previous section, an international treaty comes into force after its formal ratification by the signatories. This requirement is embedded in Article 26 of the Laws of Treaties under the 1969 Vienna Convention which states that "every treaty in force is binding upon the parties to it and must be performed by them in good faith" (Roberg 2007, p. 182). The strength of a ratified treaty lies in the commitments as well as constraints placed on each member. This legal requirement for Egypt implies that it is not bound by its mandates. Moreover, it gives Egypt the right to continue deferring its water rights based on the 1929 and 1959 treaties. Although Egypt and Sudan rejected the CFA because of the wording of Article 14 (b), namely: "not to significantly affect the water security of other Nile Basin States," Mitchell and Zawahri (2011) have argued that prevailing factors (political and economic) over which riparian countries have less control can inhibit opportunities to sign and ratify a treaty. Arguably, months after the CFA was ready for signatures in 2010 the Arab Spring had started gaining momentum in Tunisia not far to the west. By January 2011, protests in Cairo's Tahrir Square had signaled a major revolution would destabilize the country's governing apparatus and credibility. Therefore, to expect Egypt to think about CFA in the face of internal political instability is to demean the destabilizing effects of a political revolution. So, how does the CFA take into account this attribute? In terms of approval by members, it has been successful; four out of six countries, or 67%, have ratified the agreement (see Table 3.5). However, in the absence of ratification by all the ten countries for the agreement or its proxy, the Nile River Basin Commission, cannot expect full cooperation nor to attain lasting peace.

Permanent Institutions

One of the requirements for most shared international river basin treaties (or agreements) is the inclusion of a permanent institution. Such institutions provide structures, rules, and resources (human and financial) in order to execute the mandates of the treaty. Moreover, they provide mechanisms for the implementation and monitoring of subsidiary projects and programs across member states (Barrett 1994). Although the institutions and their rules should enforce obligations on each treaty signatory, this can be daunting for two reasons. One, each country is a political sovereign and can only respond to the interest of its leaders and citizens—which are dynamic. Two, technically states are bound by treaties to which they are signatories but in practice, they do so as a matter of good faith and not by legal obligation.

Study after study demonstrate that transboundary institutions are critical to the survival of multilateral treaties because they possess mechanisms that govern riparian relations and the implementation of treaty provisions (Wolf 2007). For example, the institutionalization of the International Joint Commission (IJC) by Canada and the United States has succeeded in coordinating and implementing "The Treaty Relating to Boundary Waters" (of Columbia River). The treaty was signed in 1909 between the United States and the United Kingdom (acting on behalf of Canada) ("Columbia River" 2003). The IJC continues to coordinate flood control, hydroelectric and oversees pollution issues. Another example is the OKACOM Agreement signed in 1994 by Angola, Botswana, and Namibia to coordinate equitable utilization of the Okavango River (OKACOM 2020).

Similarly, such institutions enhance the capabilities of the states in the agreement to share information, interact more frequently and to comply with the stipulations of the pact (Abbott and Snidal 1998).

To fulfill the treaty requirement, the CFA established the permanent Nile River Basin Commission (NRBC) to replace the Nile Basin Initiative (NBI). The transitioning of the NBI into the current Commission is provided for by Articles 15–21 of the CFA. Article 16 stipulates three objectives for NRBC as follows: to implement "the principles, rights, and obligations provided for in the present Framework; serve as an institutional framework for cooperation; (and) to facilitate closer cooperation" (Cooperative Framework Agreement 2010, p. 26). Hence, by instituting this legal body, CFA has met the requirements of a permanent institution.

Water Security

Though an essential element to transboundary agreements, institutions alone cannot guarantee the success or resiliency of water treaties. The inclusion of water security and how it operates can ensure the survival of any international water treaty.

The concept of water security in relation to shared water use can be complex in meaning and through practical application. According to "The 1997 U.N. Watercourses Convention" (UNWC), water security should be viewed in terms of availability, access, and use. Missing out on any or of the three can cause undue water stress that would undermine human survival. Water, with no known alternative, is linked to the economic, political, and social security of any state (Wouters and Moynihan 2013). It supports agricultural production, public health, industries, and energy production. It is, for this reason, the United Nations General Assembly adopted "water for all" under its Millennium Development Goals. In 2015 this was revised to "Water and Sanitation for All" by 2030 under the Sustainable Development Goals (SDG#6).

Achievement of "water security for all" deserves greater attention as the demand for the available 1.7% of global freshwater is increasing exponentially. The resulting water stress is affecting some 80% of the human population worldwide (Wouters and Moynihan 2013). The MENA Region, of which Egypt is part of, is already water-stressed than take out the Nile Basin. Matters will worsen as the consequences of climate change take effect. Adding to this dismal water security outlook is the spike in the human population. By 2018, for example, the population of the MENA stood at 448.9 million (World Bank 2020) and the Nile Basin 257 million (NBI 2021). The numbers are projected to increase by 2030, straining the dwindling water resources.

With these increased pressures on shared international freshwater systems, the discourse on the securitization of water is also on the rise. The situation is direr for the Nile downstream states for which water security is a matter of life and death. By being at the end of the pipe, anxiety about potential harm regarding actions by those who control the tap upstream often elevates water security to national economic and political existence. It is, therefore, logical from this perspective, why Ethiopia's decision to construct a dam upstream was immediately treated as a security threat by the Cairo government.

When, for example, this author conducted field interviews at Cairo University and with people on the streets between May and June 2014, the often-repeated phrase was—"this is a matter of existence." In fact, previous Egyptian presidents Anwar Sadat (1970–1981), Hosni Mubarak (1981–2011), Mohamed Morsi (2012–2013) and General Al Fattah Sisi (2014–present) have all been in unison when it came to securitizing the waters of the Nile as they saw it as a matter of life or death. This is supported by the fact that 95% of the Egyptian population lives on the banks of The River Nile—making it one of the world's most densely populated regions of the world, at 3,820 persons per square mile (Hoyt 2020).

Ethiopia has similarly securitized the waters to justify the construction of Africa's biggest dam on the Blue Nile. The pressure on water needs is increasing with a population that had surpassed 100 million by the end of 2019. Moreover, 40% of its population depends on rainfed farming. Therefore, to steer away from unpredictable seasonal rains, Ethiopians bank on the Renaissance Dam to store and provide steady water supply. Similarly, in the MENA Region, Israel has had hostile relations with their Arab neighbors, Syria, and Palestine, which were both deemed a threat to water security and national survival. In fact, the Israeli occupation of the Golan Heights (northeastern border with Syria) and the West Bank in 1967, along with their unwillingness to relinquish the territories, were purposely made to protect the headwaters of River Jordan and the Mountain Aquifer—both key to their water security (Wolf 1995). Undoubtedly, in both the Israeli and Egyptian cases, the rationale for integrating the securitization of water into national discourse is to win national as well as international support (El-Sayed and Mansour 2017). As will be addressed shortly, by securitizing the Nile waters, Egypt has not only attracted sympathy beyond its borders, but also attracted broader international support for more flexible filling and operations of the Renaissance Dam to prevent any potential harm. But as Egypt continues to securitize water, so does Ethiopia. Addis Ababa government, for example, continues to rally support in the Sub-Saharan and MENA Region to defend its sovereign right to use water resources within its territory. In both situations, each country seems to associate water security with external military threats, which must be concertedly defended.

Considering the above, the CFA has included security criteria in its Article 14. By doing so, it underscores the need to cooperatively develop the Nile River system to ensure water security for its members. Second, the Nile River Basin Commission birthed by the agreement is tasked with implementing equitable and reasonable water use processes by each riparian state. Additionally, Article 5 of the Agreement stipulates that each riparian state must, in developing waterworks within its territory, take measures not to cause significant harm to any other member. To abide by these international rules (i.e., equitable use and not to cause significant harm), member states are expected to consider the following factors consistent with Chapter 2, Article 5 (2) of the 1966 "Helsinki Rules on the Waters of International Rivers" (River Nile Basin Cooperative Framework 2010, p. 12). This is a partial list:

1. Geographic, climatic, and hydrological factors
2. Economic and social needs of relevant riparian states
3. Percent of population directly (or indirectly) dependent on the water
4. Availability of alternatives for existing or planned uses
5. Contribution of each riparian state to the shared water system
6. Proportion of the river drainage area in each of the concerned basin state.

However, abiding by these requirements, in full or in part, can be problematic. First, the general rule of "equitable and reasonable utilization" for a river system raises obvious questions: What is considered equitable? And what is "reasonable"? Each country's needs are different; some will require more water per capita than others. Second, although these factors offer the guideline for equity both in access and use, it is unreasonable to assume that a riparian state planning waterworks will first weigh in on each of the factors and take actions that protect the interests of other riparian states. Moreover, there is no clear operational definition or meaning attached to the phrase "significant harm." Therefore, by simply replicating these two principles (i.e., equitable utilization and no significant harm) into the Agreement without deconstructing and spelling out what they really mean in the application, the CFA fell into the trap of vagueness akin to most international treaties.

Another challenge to the CFA provisions concerning water security is the failure to address water allocation. As will be explored further in Chapter 8, failure to include the provision for a water allocation is a fundamental weakness to the agreement. To date, the NBI, and presently the NRBC, have preferred and operationalized the shared benefits approach through regional subsidiary programs. However, this work contends that until the Nile water is apportioned using either all or modified factors developed by the 1966 Helsinki Rules, the Nile Basin states will continue to experience an intermittent resurgence of conflicts. This will become even more compelling as increased demand for freshwater occurs due to a surge in population, economic growth and climate change. The envisioned competition for this vital resource requires a system in which each state knows how much it has the right to use. The British colonial government was able to use a group-based approach to quantifiably allocate water between Egypt and Sudan, albeit inequitably. With a new legal framework in place, supported with more accurate data and sophisticated models, the Nile Basin countries can reallocate the water more equitably.

Conflict Resolution Mechanisms

It is easier to mitigate than to resolve conflicts. Though resources designed to develop and operationalize mechanisms to mitigate potential conflicts can be substantial at first, failure to do so can be more expensive and overwhelming in the long run. That is why it is an issue where the UN Watercourses Convention (UNWC) underscored the importance of institutional mandates that includes inbuilt rules, and promoting trust and cooperation. To mitigate potential conflicts, several provisions (Articles 12–16 and 18–19) clarify actions a riparian state needs to take prior to engaging in any waterworks. For example, Article 12 of the Convention regarding "Notification Concerning Planned Measures with Possible Adverse Effects" states that:

> Before a watercourse state implements or permits the implementation of planned measures which may have a significant adverse effect upon other watercourse states, it shall provide those states with timely notification thereof. Such notification shall be accompanied by available technical data and information, including the results of any environmental impact assessment, in order to enable the notified states to evaluate the possible effects of the planned measures. (UNWC Online User's Guide 2020)

In addition to prior notification (or consultation), Article 33 identifies specific approaches to mitigating and resolving water conflicts. These include negotiation, mediation by a third-party, and arbitration by a tribunal or litigation through an independent court system such as the Internal Court of Justice. If not, the agreement is reached either by negotiation or mediation; it is suggested that a fact-finding body is established.

To what extent are these provisions included in CFA's Charter? Article 5 of the CFA addresses consultations regarding any planned measures by a co-riparian to evaluate any potential harm caused. Article 34, "Settlement of Conflicts," is a mirror image of UNWC's Article 33 that requires conflicts be resolved peacefully. Sections (a) and (b) of Article 34 recommends the use of negotiation, mediation, conciliation and, when necessary, arbitration by the courts. Impartial fact-finding by the established commission is also included in Article-34(b) ("Agreement on the NRBC Framework" 2010, p. 52).

Adaptability
Legal frameworks are politically constructed to assist nations that share transboundary water systems in allotting this vital resource equitably and peacefully. But, given the dynamic socio-economic and physical conditions within which these frameworks operate, it is important to dictate the framework with a language that adaptable to those changes. For example, shifts in hydrology due to changing climatic conditions, population growth and economic growth will prompt increased uses of available water and unprecedented stress. Therefore, water allocation arrangements should, at the least, include a provision for adjustments based on changing data. Article 26 of the CFA has considered the need for adaptability as reflected in Article 26 (9). It empowers the Technical Advisory Committee (TAC) to recommend any modification to the framework (or to expand on existing protocols) but only if instructed to do so by the Council of Ministers. This assumes that the Council or its members can bring to the table the need for modification before the Advisory Committee works out the details for further discussion prior to ratification.

For a transboundary legal framework to easily adapt to changes necessitated by uncertainties in the external and internal environment, two approaches must be followed. First, the framers should include ambiguities into the language of the treaty (Driechova et al. 2010). The aim is to make it flexible to allow varied interpretations and adjustments to meet changing conditions and dynamics coming from within and outside of the basin. That way, those charged with governing the river basin organization have wiggle room for consultations and modification. True to all international water treaties, there is always a need to adjust, either due to changes in water use behaviors or external factors difficult to predict or control like climatic inconsistency and water use intentions by riparian states. The second option to address the adaptability of transboundary water agreements is to seek clarity and directness by including provisions that are action-oriented, measurable obligations, and legally binding. Additionally, it is important to include institutions with the capacity for data collection, strategic planning, implementation, monitoring, enforcement, and enforcement capability. Although the former is ideal, the latter is much more practical in the bilateral framework because of simple follow-up due to the limited number of states involved. In the case of the Nile CFA with ten countries involved, it would be ill-advised to seek this second approach because of the difficulty of obtaining consensus and constraining diverging behaviors and interests. It, therefore, seems logical to suggest that the CFA incorporate the first track when dealing with adaptability—with some ambiguity and flexibility to allow for adjustments. This is quite relevant when it comes to water allocation, as it is determined by unpredictable climatic and weather patterns.

Pluralistic Decision-Making

Decision-making for shared water systems should, ideally, be pluralist and involve all riparian state member stakeholders in the process. The concept of pluralism refers to different interest groups (e.g., Nile Basin countries) competing to push their interests for consideration in decision-making. For example, in the formulation and drafting of the final CFA, each Nile State pushed their agendas by considering national interests and how they are to benefit from the new legal regime. The outcome of the new regime demonstrates the degree to which pluralism has been exercised in the Nile basin. All nations participated in the process. However, as is expected in pluralism, the position taken by some—Egypt and Sudan—on one of the provisions, Article 14 (b) regarding water security, exhibited the power of the democratic process. The majority won and the minority lost. It should also be added that this conclusion does not imply that the Nile Basin, in preparing the CFA, engaged all relevant stakeholders. The December 2008 study conducted by this author at the NBI Secretariat to determine the degree of stakeholder (especially NGOs) involvement in the Nile affairs decision-making, disclosed that a select few were invited but only as observers. Moreover, the meetings involved only high-level officials from the Nile Basin, including the Nile Council of Ministers. The concern here is not the completeness of inclusion but whether the pluralist approach was exhibited, which it was.

International Panel of Experts

Soon after the diplomatic standoff between the two countries, the government of Ethiopia instituted the International Panel of Experts (IPoE).

The goals were to assess the potential impacts of the dam on downstream states, foster cooperation and determine ways for joint benefits from the dam. To achieve these goals, each country was asked to assign two members to the panel, with additional four international experts added to the team. The four included an environmental expert, socioeconomic expert, dam engineering expert and water resources, and hydrological modeling expert. The four group of experts were nationals of Britain, France, South Africa, and Germany (Berhane 2012). In the subsequent months, the ten-member Tripartite Panel visited the project site four times and held a total of six meetings. Those meetings rotated between each capital, Cairo, Khartoum, and Addis Ababa. Although initially projected to take nine months, an extension of three months was granted due to the complexity of the work.

The final report which was concluded, signed, and presented on May 31, 2013, was divided into three areas: Dam Safety and Engineering, Water Resources and Hydrology, and Environmental and Socioeconomic. Of these, the most substantive finding was regarding hydrology. The simulated effects were analyzed from three different scenarios. First, when GERD is filled during the wet season, no effect on Egypt's water supply is expected. The only effect would be a decrease in AHD's power generation by about 6% (IPoE 2013, p. 36). This is because the filling of GERD's reservoir upstream would reduce Lake Nasser's water level. Second, if the impounding were to occur during droughts, AHD's minimum operating level would be affected for four consecutive years. This has serious negative effects on power generation capacity and the amount released for irrigation substantially reduced. On environmental assessment, the report identified two benefits to both Sudan and Egypt as regulation of water flow would substantially reduce the level of sedimentation in Lake Nasser and the two dams in Sudan—Roseries and Sennar. The other benefit noted is a reduction in flooding in both countries. Socioeconomic impact studies were not conducted, hence the necessity for conducting a future study to determine from precise effects on crop production and household income levels. The report further suggests a comprehensive assessment of the impacts on biodiversity, such as fish stocks.

Although the IPoE is credited for laying out the technical details of the project as well as potential effects downstream, the modeling scenarios did not extend to environmental and socioeconomic implications. One reason could be limited time and the pressure from Egypt to get the results as soon as possible. If anything, the findings on the potential effects of the Aswan High Dam (AHD) and its capacity to generate energy and supply water to farmers was the single most important element at the time for Cairo policymakers. Another reason was the failure of the three countries to project the timeline based on the complexity of the work. The consequence was a false budget estimate for the exercise. Despite this shortcoming, the panel laid out an important groundwork for the ensuing negotiation activities by providing data that states could use to make informed bargaining and mediation decisions.

Mediation-1: The Declaration of Principles
As soon as the International Panel of Experts submitted their report on the technical design and possible impacts on downstream states, the formal negotiation process started. As Table 3.5 illustrate, the first negotiation to secure a long-term solution started with the meetings of ministers for water affairs from each of the three countries. This, and meetings that followed, came to be known as the Tripartite Ministerial Meetings. The first through the fourth meetings took place in the Sudanese capital of Khartoum, the fifth in Addis Ababa, the sixth in Cairo, and the final in Khartoum.

We can see from Table 3.5 that the three countries successfully formed representative Ministerial meetings to address the demands of Egypt.

Although initially the Republic of Sudan enlisted its reservations about the dam, by December 4, 2013, it declared its support and subsequently took up the mediating role. Unfortunately, the first, second, and third meetings ended in failure because, as would be expected, the tensions were still high as Egypt and Ethiopia maintained their positions. Matters, however, improved after President General Sisi (Egypt) and Hailemariam Desalegn (Ethiopia) struck a deal at an African Union Summit in Malabo, Equatorial Guinea, June 26–27, 2014 (Hassen 2014). Three successive meetings between August and October of the same year produced a compromise for the future. That compromise, "The Agreement on Declaration of Principles," was finalized at the Seventh Meeting, held between March 3 and 5, 2015, in Khartoum. The document was signed by the three parties on March 23, 2015.

Sudan's mediation role deserves further scrutiny as alluded to earlier, as sometimes the choice of a mediator is dictated by the urgency of an issue at hand, the degree of tension, familiarity of the issues, and the willingness to take up that responsibility. But equally important is the timing and accessibility of the mediator. Fortunately, Sudan is next door to Ethiopia.

Table 3.5 Negotiation timeline for dam project—success or failure

Date	Description	Success/failure
May 2012–May 2013	Join study by International Panel of Experts on design and potential impacts. Six meetings held and the final report signed May 31, 2013	Success
November 4, 2013	First Tripartite Ministerial meeting in Khartoum. Egypt demands construction suspension and studies	Failure by independent international experts. Ethiopia disagrees
December 4, 2013	Second Tripartite meeting. President Al-Bashir announces Sudan's support for GERD, breaking a half-century alliance with Egypt. Ethiopia suggests joint further studies. No compromise	Failure
January 2014	Third Meeting in Khartoum; no compromise. No official communication between Cairo and Egypt for five months	Failure
June 26–27, 2014	Egypt's President El-Sisi meets with Ethiopia's Prime Minister Delasegn at African Union summit, Equatorial Guinea. Agrees on continued meetings	Success
August 25–26, 2014	Fourth Meeting in Khartoum. Parties agree on two studies by international consultants selected jointly	Success
September 22–23, 2014	Fifth Meeting in Addis Ababa. Agreements on the selection of consultants by a panel from each country (i.e., Tripartite National Committee, TNC). TNC to be rotational	Success
October 16, 2014	Sixth Meeting in Cairo. The agreement that studies to be completed in six months	Success
March 3–5, 2015	Seventh Meeting in Khartoum. Ministers of Water Affairs, Foreign Ministers, and respective Heads of State sign "Agreement on Declaration of Principles"	Success

Both share common boundaries as well as the Blue Nile tributary, which is at the center of contention. Geographically, Sudan is located between Ethiopia and Egypt. Moreover, Sudan's leader Al-Bashir, who served for 30 years (1989–2019), was more knowledgeable about the conflict than either El-Sisi or Desalegn. Although Sudan's Al-Bashir may have met the stated conditions, it is not clear how he stepped into that role. Was it a joint decision by either Egypt, Ethiopia or both? Or did Sudan voluntarily step in?

Regardless of the mediation outcome, there are few reasons why Sudan should not have stepped into that role. First, in 2010, Sudan joined Egypt in rejecting the Nile Cooperative Framework Agreement because the framework failed to address its water security concern. Second, it was based on the same agreement that Ethiopia later decided to build its now controversial dam. Third, for the last 50-plus years, Egypt and Sudan have been close allies. They both had exclusive Nile water rights protected by colonial treaties. Moreover, both belong to the 22-member Arab League. So, it seemed curious for Sudan to play a neutral role in mediating the conflict. It can be argued that the sudden about-turn by Sudan was driven solely by national self-interest. This is supported by a study that suggested that the country stood to benefit from the dam through cheap power imports and reductions in perennial floods. Another indicator was exhibited in March 2020 at the Arab League Summit in Cairo. At that meeting, Sudan failed to make its support known even though all other members sided with Egypt on the dam conflict. Additional justification is the unresolved conflict over the Halayeb territory, which is to the northeast of the country. Although this will be discussed further in Chapter 6, historically, the British colonial government provided both countries divided rights—with control over the inhabitants to Sudan and territorial administration to Egypt. Though Sudan took the matter to the United Nations for arbitration in 1986, no significant action has been taken. Clearly, the protection and fulfillment of national interests by Sudan explains its support for the dam, as well as their mediation role. While there is no reason to generalize about whose side Sudan is on with the negotiation outcome, the above testimony suggests that Khartoum would rather see Ethiopia prevail in the conflict.

Despite these questionable inclinations, Sudan ought to be credited for successfully bringing the two warring states to the table and producing the Agreement on the Declaration of Principles on March 23, 2015. However, what remains to be understood is the effectiveness of that declaration. Two things stand out in making the assessment: (1) the perceptions of Egyptian and Ethiopian citizens and (2) the strengths and weaknesses of the resolution for the conflict. These two areas are explored first by explaining what mediation is and under what conditions mediation is necessary. Second, criteria for assessing mediation are developed, followed by the analysis of the declaration vis-à-vis each of the criterion.

Mediation

Mediation can be defined as the involvement of a third, neutral party in a conflict between two parties to bring about a negotiated settlement. Generally, the engagement of mediators in a conflict between two parties is necessary when the following conditions exist. One, an interstate conflict has erupted, and neither side is willing to sit and discuss their differences. Two, when tensions remain high in a conflict that has persisted for a long time but with no solution in sight. Third, when the warring parties have previously negotiated but thorny issues persist. Only then do the parties then agree to invite a third-party mediator.

The preference for third-party mediation in resolving interstate conflicts is supported by literature. Hoeffler (2014, pp. 81–82) reports that mediation attempts represent 82% of all coded interventions. Despite this frequency in use, mediation tends to focus on immediate agreements. This can problematic because failure to address possible long-term issues can result in relapses. Another limitation is partiality. We live in an era where national self-interests dominate international relations. This constrains the ability to find individual mediators who are completely neutral. But this does not mean it is impossible to find one. Rather, what seems to determine the choice of mediator is the degree of tension, urgency, and familiarity with the issue. The willingness of the mediator, along with other factors not identified here, are equally important.

To determine the effectiveness of a mediation outcome, the following evaluative criteria, as shown in Table 3.6, has been developed.

a. Occurrence

A significant result of any mediation is its occurrence. When Egypt and Ethiopia failed to find the way forward, the worst outcome was expected as each side hurled accusations and counteraccusations. But, when a formal mediation brought them to the table to discuss their

Table 3.6 Evaluative criteria for effective third-party mediation

Criteria	Description	Success/failure
Occurrence	Mediation has taken place	Success
Competency	Mediator has requisite knowledge and skills neutrality	Partly
Process	Willingness of both parties Timing; location; input Absence of duress	Success
Outcome	Agreement/settlement is reached	
Compliance and implementation	Both parties comply Settlement implemented	Failure
Client satisfaction	Concerns and interests addressed Fairness on both sides	Failure

Developed from: Sandu (2013), Hoeffler (2014) and personal knowledge

differences that was considered a success (Hoeffler 2014). Therefore, the seven Tripartite Ministerial meetings that produced the Declaration of Principles in March 2015 can be viewed in this same light.

b .**Competency**

Ideally, the effectiveness of any mediation should begin with the mediator's competency level. Foremost, it requires considerable knowledge. This implies a deeper understanding of the conflict, the context, causes, and prior attempts to address it and why they have not worked. The mediator must also understand the roles that domestic and international dynamics play in the conflict. Moreover, knowledge about the individual actors in the conflict (e.g., presidents), their behaviors, preferences, and ideological inclinations have all contributed to the state of affairs.

Equally important is the skill set of the mediator. Communication skills stand out because without them, the mediator cannot easily build trust and rapport. Additionally, with good communication skills, the mediator can listen and, at the same time, read the reactions and feelings of the parties involved in mediation discussions. This ability is what academics call hermeneutics; interpretation of the undercurrents—what is not said or obvious. To successfully engage in hermeneutics, one must employ intuition and judgment, or analytics. Therefore, a mediator equipped with these attributes will skillfully navigate reasons for expressions of anger or why negotiating party would get angry, bang the table and walk out during a discussion.

Being able to maintain neutrality is instrumental to the process, as well as the outcome of the mediation. Any bias will immediately affect the talks as well as the outcome. Therefore, whenever a mediator is identified, he must be free from bias. Consequently, in a high-stakes conflict such as the one between Egypt and Ethiopia, the mediator must have no personal interests nor be politically inclined to act in the interest of one party over the other. The information reviewed tells us that Sudan's neutrality was in question for two reasons. One, it declared the change in political alliance from Cairo to Addis Ababa in order to safeguard its national interest in cheap power trade with Ethiopia and the potential reduction in floods through regulated water flow by the dam. Two, the hostility between Khartoum and Cairo over the contested Halayeb territory remained unsettled. These two narratives could have skewed Al-Bashir's position as the mediator even though they (Sudan and Egypt) both share Arabic culture, language and members of the Arab League. Knowing these facts, should Sudan have stepped into the mediation role or not?

c. **Process**

There is little doubt that the process of mediation will determine the dam's outcome. Typically, the structure of the mediation process includes the following: location, rules and procedures, timeframe, goals and objectives, statement of positions, discussions and resolution. As shown in Table 3.5, the location of the meetings over the Renaissance Dam rotated between the three capitals—Khartoum, Addis Ababa, and Cairo. Upon agreement for the rules and procedures, the interlocutors review the objectives before each party expresses its position. The mediator then institutes individual caucusing as well as joint sessions to explore alternative solutions. At this point, the team can either employ SWOT analysis (i.e., Strengths, Weaknesses, Opportunities, and Threats) or any other approach acceptable for both parties. This will be explored further in Chapter 6, which addressed short-term solutions.

Regardless of the process chosen, what seems important to mediators is the outcome, successful implementation and the sustenance of peace. To avoid possible relapse, the mediator should steer the parties towards an agreeable solution. This, however, does not mean that each party arrives at their desired solution. As I will argue in Chapter 6, the goal of conflict resolutions differs by case. Sometimes, the goal is about reaching a satisfactory solution rather than an optimum one.

Although, for the most part, conflict resolutions focus on win-win outcomes, the difficulty of this desired outcome is the ambiguity of the very minimum appeal to either party. Egypt might, for example, insist on ten or more years of the reservoir filling and, yet their "unrevealed" acceptable minimum years are five. Ethiopia, on the other hand, might similarly not reveal the precise maximum years acceptable to fill the reservoir, but instead will push for one to two years. What this game demonstrates is the difficulty in defining what win-win means at the mediation table. Therefore, to hedge against future contestation, it is important for the mediation party to agree first on what constitutes a win; the very minimum one is willing to accept. It is also critical to identify what each party is willing to give up for any desired gain. Although win-win solutions are feasible in certain conflicts, it is presumptuous to believe that its strict guidelines will apply to water rights conflicts. That is why warring parties should not approach mediation with a something-or-nothing attitude. It is in this light that a study participant in Cairo remarked that it is better for Egypt to acquiesce to the mediation agreement, which in principle minimizes potential risks (e.g., war, water shortage) to maximize gains in the long term.

Although the mediation outcome (The Agreement on the Declaration of Principles) signified the success of the process, the resurgence of tensions between 2016 and 2020 lends credence to the highlighted weaknesses. Until Egypt and Ethiopia can agree on the definition of a win-win solution, the conflict will take even longer to resolve.

d .Implementation and Compliance

Another important measure of mediation effectiveness is compliance with an agreement. Foremost, the signing of the document is an indicator of the willingness by each party to comply with the wordings, obligations, and rules as stipulated. This means that each party understands the implications of the language used and meanings of the demands. More importantly, compliance should be reflected in the actual implementation of stated activities. To do the opposite renders previous work invalid.

The Agreement on Declaration of Principles was formally signed on March 23, 2015, by the three leaders, Abdel Fattah El-Sisi of Egypt, Omer Hassan El-Bashir of Sudan, and Hailemariam Desalegn of Ethiopia. Generally, in international law, the Declaration of Principles implies that parties, regarding the legal framework agree on sharing values or what they believe in (e.g., rules, norms and procedures) and how those principles shall guide either future relations or the conduct of specific affairs. Alternatively, it suggests common understandings of the parties, broader goals and ambitions, and its conformity to international standards. It is not usually binding or mandatory but rather a confirmation of understanding and intention of parties. For example, the Declaration of Principles signed by the three countries contained ten of the following intentions: agreement to cooperate, push for regional development, not to cause significant harm to other riparian states, utilize water equitably and reasonably, support in first filling and operation of the Dam, build confidence, exchange information, ensure dam safety, respect territorial integrity, and peacefully resolve Conflicts.

To what extent have these principles been complied with and implemented by each party? Given the nature of politics and the importance of water rights to each of the nations involved, it would be presumptuous to think that every principle would be followed precisely. Politics is driven by interests and those interests are shaped by public opinion—domestic and international. It is no surprise that soon after it's signing, the contents of the agreement were received variedly in Cairo and Addis Ababa. The reactions in Cairo were mixed. To one group, it signaled the potential for a permanent resolution to the conflict and chances for the looming military face-off to become significantly reduced. To another group, the declaration was a mistake because it meant that Egypt, for the first time in history, acceded to Ethiopia's rights to the Nile waters. Before then, only Egypt and Ethiopia maintained monopoly backed by "historic" (or prior-in-use) rights enshrined in colonial treaties. To these skeptics, it was Ethiopia who won, while Egypt lost. But this opinion should be considered with caution because since the Declaration of Principles, Ethiopia seems to have backtracked on Article V(a) that states the three countries "agree on guidelines and rules on the first filling of GERD which shall cover all different scenarios, in parallel with the construction of GERD" (Declaration of Principles 2015, p. 209). Ethiopia's unwillingness to comply with this provision is the reason the conflict was, in November 2019, brought to the United States government to mediate.

e .**Client Satisfaction**

Satisfaction with mediation should assess in terms of its occurrence, neutrality of the mediator, objective process, acceptable outcome, compliance by all parties, and implementation of the mediated settlement. Although perceptions by citizens will differ depending on their normative and political inclinations, a combination of these factors indicate the extent to which interlocutors and all stakeholders are satisfied with the mediation. This, however, should discount segregated levels of satisfaction. Thus, rather than expressing whether they are satisfied or not satisfied with the mediated settlement by Sudan, it is entirely appropriate for states to find satisfaction or dissatisfaction in any of the measures in Table 3.6. Accordingly, Egyptians and their supporters find dissatisfaction in Ethiopia's compliance with the filling and operation measures, as stated in the Declaration of Principles.

As already discussed above, the durability of any mediated settlement depends on several factors. However, regardless of how many years it has taken to arrive at the agreement, the failure to strike a deal on an issue considered thorny by one party can undermine what has been achieved and take both parties back to the drawing board. This is the situation in which Egypt, Ethiopia, and Sudan found themselves in—almost five years after the first mediated settlement. The number of years or times it takes to reach permanent agreements to water conflicts can be lengthy. For example, the negotiation of the Columbia River between the United States and Canada was first signed in 1909 (Boundary Waters Treaty), with another in 1961 (Columbia River Treaty) and the ratification in 1964 (Protocol & Ratification)—55 years in total; La Plata (10 years), the Ganges (24 years), Indus (87 years), and Mekong (30 years). All involved more than two agreements. Table 3.7 demonstrates this trajectory of international water treaties.

Therefore, the resurgence of conflicts between Egypt and Ethiopia after the signing of the Cooperative Framework Agreement in 2010 and the Agreement on the Declaration of Principles in 2015 is not unusual.

The events leading to the second mediation attempt by the former United States President Donald Trump, between November 2019 and February 2020, further demonstrates the resiliency of international water rights conflicts. This is discussed next.

Table 3.7 International water agreements—number and duration

River	Countries involved	Years of agreements	Number of treaties
Indus	Pakistan, India, Britain	1960 (2), 1948 (1) 1892, 1873	5
Ganges	Bangladesh India	1996, 1982 1977, 1972	4
Columbia	United States, Canada	1909, 1961 1964	3
La Plata	Argentina, Bolivia Brazil, Uruguay and Paraguay; Brazil and Paraguay	1969, 1973 1979	3
Mekong	Cambodia, Laos Thailand, Vietnam; Thailand, Vietnam and Laos; Thailand and Laos	1995, 1978 1965	3

Developed from: Atlas of International Freshwater Agreements (2002)

Mediation-2: Trump's Deal or No Deal?
Although the negotiation discussed in this section is considered Mediation-2, it is a third attempt to strike an agreement over the Renaissance Dam conflict. The first was a negotiated settlement that produced the Nile Cooperative Framework Agreement in 2010. The second was a mediated settlement by Sudan; its outcome—the Agreement on the Declaration of Principles in 2015. Although both were a milestone for bringing about a cooperative approach to utilizing the Nile waters, non-compliance with some of the provisions was a setback. For example, the rejection of the Cooperative Framework Agreement by Egypt and Sudan opened fault lines that are difficult to fix. In effect, their stance indirectly triggered defiance by Ethiopia, which, in turn, declared the intention to fill up the reservoir as earlier planned, taking between three and seven years. Ethiopia's action thus contravenes Article 10 of the Agreement on the Declaration of Principles that stipulates that all parties shall abide by the rules and guidelines for the first filling, as shall be recommended by the joint Tripartite National Committee (TNC). Addis Ababa not only overlooked this legal provision but "jumped the gun" before the conclusion of the subject was agreed upon.

It is important to clarify why the filling and operation of the dam remain at the center of the contention. First, Ethiopia prefers that the filling be carried out between three to seven years to ramp up its demand for energy, which is presently estimated at an average of 25 per year (Tesfa 2013). This demand is projected to increase to 32% if the present economic growth rate is maintained and the population, currently 100 million-plus, continues to rise. Therefore, additional power is essential to fill this gap and to sustain the rapid economic growth of 10.3% achieved over ten years ending in 2016 (The World Bank 2018). Equally important is the projected annual revenues of about $1.1 billion from power sales, assuming a production capacity of 15,692 GWh is maintained by GERD (Bezabih and Tesfa 2019). This additional income promises to boost opportunities for development in a country that is still struggling economically. Also, by connecting electricity to 65–75% of households currently without any, the political benefits could be substantial. Therefore, for Ethiopia, the GERD project is not only timely but a strategic response to the realities on the ground.

Egypt's position is equally significant. They want the 74 billion cubic meter reservoir filling to be staggered in more than seven years and carried out only during Ethiopia's rainy season—between June and November. Although opinions differ, some experts contend that a shorter filling period (three to seven years) could have dire consequences for Egypt. Studies suggest that filling within six years could lead to a loss of up to 17% in agricultural land (Nader 2020). That loss could spike to 51% in a three-year filling scenario. Research by the Geological Society of America further predicts a water shortage of about 25% by Egypt should the filling take place between five to seven years. Although further studies are necessary to clear up the uncertainty surrounding the substantive effects, what is key to understanding the impact, if any, is to agree upon the amount of water release from the turbines during the filling periods. Egypt maintains a minimum release of 40 billion cubic meters per year while Ethiopia wants it at 31 BCM. Egypt's goal is to minimize losses because, without the dam, the water flow from the Blue Nile into their territory is about 50 BCM per year. Conversely, Ethiopia wants to release less so as not to endanger the dam's capacity. Also, what irks Ethiopia is the requirement by Egypt that Ethiopia seeks approval each time the filling is carried out throughout the life of the dam.

After reaching a deadlock following several meetings by the three parties at a bilateral level, Egypt turned to international third-party mediation. This is an approach Cairo had, since 2011, insisted on while Ethiopia preferred negotiation that was restricted to the three countries involved. Thus, for Cairo, the time was right to unilaterally invite an external mediator. Egypt subsequently chose the United States President Donald John Trump. In making the announcement, President Abdel Fattah al-Sisi stated that Trump possessed "unique standing with the power in dealing with conflicts… and finding solutions for them" (Reuters 2019). His decision found legal backing in Article 10 of the 2010 Nile Cooperative Framework Agreement that states, in part, "if the Parties are unable to resolve the Conflict through consultation or negotiation, they may jointly request for conciliation, mediation or refer the matter for the consideration of the Heads of State/Heads of Government" (Declaration of Principles 2015, p. 3). That decision, however, caught many by surprise for three reasons. For one, President Trump had not, since the beginning of his presidency, prioritized African issues on the White House Agenda. Secondly, the meeting was not on the president's public schedule, according to a Voice of America report (Widakuswara 2019). Another reason was the designation of the Secretary of the Treasury, Steven Mnuchin, as chief negotiator as opposed to Secretary of State Mike Pompeo for this issue.

Four subsequent meetings were arranged, beginning in November 2019 through February 2020. The goals were to (a) develop a plan for the filling and operation of the dam in conformity with the Declaration of Principles signed in 2015; (b) determine an agreeable timeframe within which the initial reservoir filling could begin. Ethiopia was then focused on July 2020 as the start of the filling—even before the joint TNC study report was complete and analyzed and (c) flesh out safety plans and Conflict resolution mechanisms. Consequently, the first meeting took place on November 6, 2019 in Washington with Treasury Secretary Mnuchin as Chair and World Bank President David Malpass as an observer. At the end of the meeting, the foreign ministers (Sameh Shoukry of Egypt, Gedu Andargachew of Ethiopia, and Asma Abdalla of Sudan) voiced their commitment to reaching an agreement on GERD's filling and operation. They further announced four separate technical meetings by the ministers of water affairs. Although considered a bit ambitious, the team targeted January 15, 2020 for the final agreement with the signing ceremony at the end of February.

This ambitious plan, however, never came to fruition after three additional meetings were held on December 9, 2019, January 13, 2010, and February 27–28, 2020. The outcomes of those meetings are summarized in Table 3.8.

Table 3.8 Outcomes of meetings with Trump administration

Date	Attendees	Issues/Agreement
November 6, 2019	President Donald Trump; Foreign Ministers meet with the United States Treasury Secretary and World Bank President Malpass	Issues clarified; process of filling and operations reviewed
December 9, 2019	Foreign and water affairs ministers	Meet in Addis Ababa
January 13–15, 2020	The United States, Egypt, Sudan, Ethiopia World Bank	Review results of ministerial technical meetings in Addis Ababa and Khartoum; finalize the agreement
February 28, 2020	The United States, Egypt and Sudan—Ethiopia skips meeting	Schedule for stage-based filling; methods for mitigating the filling and for annual operations during drought/dry years

The Department of the Treasury summarized the January 28–31 meeting with the following resolutions: (1) a schedule for staged filling of GERD reservoir, (2) a mechanism for reservoir filling during periods of drought and dry seasons and (3) a method for the operation of the dam during extended droughts. The team further agreed to explore the operations of the dam under different hydrological conditions, information sharing, and dam safety, mechanisms for conflict resolution, environmental impacts, and overall coordination. The mediation was constrained to some but not all the issues.

But as Table 3.8 shows, the Ethiopian delegation skipped the last meeting held between February 27 and 28, ostensibly to consult citizens before they could sign the document. As it later came to be revealed, Ethiopia alleged that they were being pushed into signing the document by the Trump administration. Moreover, the conditions directed at Ethiopia by the Treasury Secretary were apparently demeaning and undiplomatic (Maru 2020). Specifically, the conditions required the Addis Ababa government to (a) sign the draft agreement as soon as its consultation with citizens was complete, (b) refrain from testing or filling of the reservoir before signing the agreement, and (c) implement safety measures before the filling begins. As Maru (2020) noted, the conditions were directive and impartial in tone. Unmoved by those requirements,

Ethiopia restated their commitment to proceed with the initial filling as scheduled, beginning July 2020, following international principles of "equitable and reasonable utilization" and "causing no significant harm."

Accordingly, the Associated Press reported on July 14 the findings by the European Space Agency's Sentinal-1 Satellite imagery which showed increased water accumulation behind the dam (Associated Press 2020). This is consistent with a separate announcement by Ethiopia's Minister of Water, Irrigation and Energy Seleshi Bekele that the filling of the dam (with a formal agreement) had begun (Gebre 2020). The decision to go ahead came only two days after the latest mediation attempts by the African Union failed. The pace of filling the 74 billion cubic meter dam reservoir has been at the center of contention.

Twists and Turns
There is little doubt that the lack of endorsement of the agreement by Sudan and Ethiopia left Egypt unsettled over the dam's future effects. Even as Ethiopia remained unperturbed on its position, Egypt's restiveness took different turns and twists in its search for a resolution. Five days after the conclusion of the February 28 meeting, Egypt took the matter to the Arab League meeting held in Cairo on March 4, 2020. A ministerial-level resolution presented to the broader Council was framed specifically to seek support for its water rights to the dam conflict. All the 22 members, except Sudan, were in unison in their backing as reflected in the following joint statement: "The water security of Egypt is an integral part of the Arab national security" (ENA 2020). This securitization of [the Nile] water as an Arab (or MENA Region) security issue will be the subject of further discussion in the section of this chapter.

In what appeared to be "mediation-hopping," the Egyptian Foreign Minister Sameh Shoukry has since then engaged in shuttle diplomacy, trying to drum up support, and find an immediate settlement to the impasse. What makes the "mediation hopping" more apparent is Cairo's turn to the United Nations Security Council for intervention just over a month after presenting its case to the Arab League. The Foreign Minister announced that he had sent a formal letter to the world's specialized body the first week of May. But why the Security Council? The Council is the highest policymaking organ of the United Nations and consists of core five major powers—United States, Russia, China, Britain, and France—plus ten rotating members. The mandate of the Council is to maintain peace and security. Although the United Nations is generally considered powerless in its ability to enforce most of the resolutions passed by the General Assembly, it is the Security Council that has the upper hand because of its binding decisions. Consequently, it is armed with instrumental tools such as sanctions, peace operations and approval of military actions. Hence, the decision by Egypt to approach the Council is anchored on its legal mandate and ability to institute quick investigations on conflicts that are consequential. However, what is troubling about the Council's ability to mediate the Egypt–Ethiopia water rights conflict is the difficulty to reach a consensus. Even for major incidents with far-reaching consequences such as the Syrian War and ISIS terrorism events, it is extremely difficult to get a consensus on either military intervention or international sanctions. This is because each of the five members of the Council possess veto powers. Therefore, a veto or abstention by a member kills a proposal on the table, regardless of its urgency. Given this reality, it is inconceivable that Egypt would get the support of all the five members although the investigation into the conflict could be authorized. Also, to scale up its chances of support, Egypt would have to lobby the ten temporary members who, at the beginning of 2020, included Belgium, Dominican Republic, Estonia, Germany, Indonesia, Niger, Saint Vincent and the Grenadines, South Africa, Tunisia, and Vietnam (United Nations Security Council 2020).

Similarly, Ethiopia has been caught in the frenzy of "mediation-hopping." After missing the final round of meeting in Washington, DC, Prime Minister Abiy Ahmed approached South Africa's President Cyril Ramaphosa, who was then serving as African Union Chairman (February 2020–February 2021), to mediate. He succeeded Egypt's General, el-Sisi (February 2019–February 2020). By attempting to engage the South African leader in the mediation, Ethiopia exhibited its long-term commitment to finding African solutions to African problems. Since then, Ethiopian officials have increased their official contact with the African countries to drum up support for their position on the dam. Consequently, the hasty but calculated outreach from the two warring nations attracted the interests of MENA Powers, including Saudi Arabia, Turkey, Qatar, the United Arab Emirates, and Israel. The nature of their involvement and implication for the water rights conflict is discussed in the next section of this chapter.

Regional "Capillarity Effect"

The MENA Powers and the Nile Basin Initiative

The term "Regional Capillarity Effect" is used here to mean the extent and force of which (Nile) water rights issues involving two or more nations (Egypt and Ethiopia) spreads to secondary countries that do not share national boundaries with the riparian states. The conflicts over international rivers are to a large extent confined within the riparian basin states. Examples of rivers whose conflicts meet these criteria include Euphrates and Tigris (Turkey, Iraq, and Syria); the Mekong (Laos, Cambodia, Vietnam, Thailand, and China), Indus (India and Pakistan), Colorado (United States and Mexico) and Silala Rivers (Bolivia and Chile). The Jordan River and the iconic River Nile are the exceptions. International involvement in the River Jordan conflict could not be constrained because of international and geopolitical alliances that had been built over the years. Since the return of the Jews to Palestine and the subsequent political independence of Israel in 1948, geopolitical alliances have played a key role in shaping policy actions by the Tel Aviv government. For example, Western nations, especially the United States, have backed Israel's territorial rights and its water security. When Israel occupied Syria's Golan Heights in 1967 to the northeast to secure water flow of the Yarmouk River that feeds into the Jordan River, and later the control of Mountain Aquifers in the West Bank, the United States steadfastly offered its support. The same can be said of the 22-member Arab League's support for Palestinian water rights to the Mountain Aquifers.

It is thus undeniable that international river systems shape riparian politics. Rivers form national boundaries, some of which are subject to conflicts. Secondly, the relations between upstream states and downstream ones are often tenuous because geographical location provides each state with a varying level of power. The former derives more leverage because it controls the tap, while the latter possesses less clout due to its vulnerable tail end location. A third point to consider is the role that water plays in fueling economic activities such as agricultural production, commerce, and trade. When, for example, a country experiences prolonged spells of drought, less production will lead to scarcity, which in turn is reflected in high prices. Egypt, for example, experienced high food prices in 1977 and 2007 that gave rise to "bread riots." Although the shortage of farmland and inconsistent government policy on bread subsidies were to blame in

Egypt, the limited share of irrigated water also contributed to the situation. Fourth, water, like oil, structures international relations through conflicts and cooperation. Through the "capillarity effect," multi-member river basins such as the Danube (10 countries), the Mekong, (5) and La Plata (5) have forged cooperation in other areas (trade, tourism), other than water management alone. Therefore, the involvement of the MENA Powers in the River Nile Conflict is not unusual.

A relevant and popular theoretical framework that can be used to further analyze the escalation of water rights conflict beyond a river basin, is the "Regional Subsystem." Hence, it is a tool with which one can try to understand why the Nile Dam saga has attracted the attention of distant neighbors in the MENA Region.

Regional Subsystem
Regional Subsystem theoretical framework was first formulated by Johan Galtung (1966). It is based on the idea that the world's community of nations is divided into at least four sub-categories—size, wealth, military power, and degree of development—all of which shape interactional relations between and among nations. Accordingly, a country that ranks/scores high on one of these attributes also ranks high in other attributes; the converse is also true. A country that ranks low on any one of the variables also ranks low in others. This implies that a higher degree of interaction occurs among nations that score (or rank) high on the four attributes. This also means that the states that have formed a regional body such as the Arab League or the Nile Basin Initiative are assumed to interact frequently, and with some degree of intensity, on matters (e.g., economic, political, cultural, and tourism) that affect them (Galtung 1966; Zakhirova 2013). Typically, a subsystem such as the Arab League (or the Gulf Cooperation Council, GCC) cares most about the local or intra-regional issues than those to which they are remotely linked. Therefore, any development (political, economic, or social) that has the potential to destabilize a subsystem member must be quickly contained. Failure to do so, could enable the spread of the negative effects to member states.

Regional Subsystem, thus, explains the involvement of MENA Powers (Saudi Arabia, Qatar, United Arab Emirates and to some extent—Israel and Turkey) and the Nile Basin countries in the conflict between Egypt and Ethiopia. Theoretically and functionally, the Arab League (or the GCC) is an independent system of interaction that shapes the policies and behaviors of its members. But more importantly, the body is expected to intervene in consequential events—internal or external—that threaten political and economic stability or social cohesion. The Arab League members are tied together by the Islamic religion, the Arabic language and by trade. It is, therefore, no surprise that after the March 2020 meeting in Cairo, the League gave its unequivocal support to the General el-Sisi government by equating Egypt's water security to Arab national security. As it were, what affects Egypt, directly, or indirectly affects all Arab League members.

A subsystem, however, does not rule out the exercise of pluralist behavior in which individual countries and actors compete to influence policy decisions. In such competition, only those who wield more power by virtue of their numbers, financial resources or even history, can influence policy outcomes. In this light, Egypt, Saudi Arabi, Turkey, and Israel are the major power brokers with the least being Qatar and the United Arab Emirates. So, when Egypt, a major power, brought their case to the table about the Renaissance Dam, it received overwhelming support from the Arab member states. Sudan's failure to declare its support to Egypt during the Arab League meeting in Cairo can be interpreted two ways. One, it had already declared its support for Ethiopia because of potential cheap power imports once the dam is complete. Two, Sudan still had unresolved geopolitical issues with Egypt. Therefore, for Sudan, the protection of national interests comes first.

Both Egypt and Sudan have wrangled over the Halyeb Triangle ever since their border was formalized by the British colonial government in 1899. Although a framework for the administration of the territory was set up by the Anglo-Egyptian Condominium in 1902, in which Egypt exercised sovereign rights over the territory and Sudan over the residents, that arrangement obviously set both nations on a collision path. Ordinarily, it is not possible for a state to have sovereignty over a territory and not over its residents, or alternatively, or vice versa. Ethnically, the nomadic inhabitants of the contested territory are related to Sudan and, hence, the decision by the British to give Sudan the rights over the people and not the territory. There is no doubt that these conflicting rights contributed to the intensification of conflicts soon after Sudan's political independence from the British in 1956. Ethiopia's Emperor Haile Selassie attempted to mediate in 1958 but came up with little success as the Egyptian President Gamal Abdel Nasser and Premier Abdullah Khalil of Sudan claimed ownership rights of the territory (Caruthers 1958). The issue, however, took on a different dimension in the 1990s when Egypt established its presence by forcing Sudan's military out. By 2000, Sudan had pulled out all its military and officials from the territory. Egypt is reportedly looking into Manganese deposits, while Sudan had been interested in oil exploration with the contested territory. Halayeb is accessible to the Red Sea and, therefore, geopolitically strategic. This brief account of the territorial conflict further lends credence to Sudan's violation of the subsystem rule in which members of a cohesive group are assumed to protect the interests of fellow members. It also justifies the pluralist behavior in which members of a group openly compete to influence policy for their own benefit.

The second subsystem whose involvement has been expanding is the Nile Basin Initiative (NBI). Brought together in 1999, the eleven member states have forged improved cooperation through structural and operational programs to enhance joint benefits from the shared river. More importantly, they have worked together to produce the Nile Cooperative Framework Agreement as a replacement to the 1902, 1929, and 1959 colonial treaties—though Egypt and Sudan refused to sign the document. Even as downstream states battle over the Renaissance Dam, all the Nile Basin countries continue to be part of the subsidiary regional institutions—the Nile Equatorial Lakes Subsidiary Action Program (NELSAP) and the Eastern Nile Subsidiary Action Program (ENSAP). Therefore, the Nile Basin is the natural home to the conflict, hence the involvement in full or in part by member states should not be unexpected. Unfortunately, the NBI as a body, nor its upstream member states have been reluctant to get involved in the conflict deferring instead to the CFA provision in settling conflicts. Article 34 part (b) for example states that,

> If the States concerned cannot reach agreement by negotiation requested by one of them, they may jointly seek good offices, or request mediation or conciliation by the Nile River Commission or other third party, or agree to submit the Conflict to arbitration, in accordance with procedures to be adopted by the Council, or to the International Court of Justice. (CFA, p. 52)

Part (b) of the same article provides for the commissioning of fact-finding should the resolution to the conflict fail after six months, either by way of negotiation or arbitration. Whereas this approach to adjudicating conflicts is standard, the total silence of the NBI in the almost ten years of tensions and search for a solution is disturbing. At the core of the subsystem approach is the frequency of interactions among state members of a regional group. They are assumed to interact on more issues that affect group members and less on those that affect them only remotely. Therefore, the response to the dam conflict goes either way. Viewed as a holistic subsystem, the NBI ought to be involved in the conflict regardless of the avenues for resolving the conflict stated by Article 34 of the CFA. Alternatively, their lack of involvement is supported by the subsystem rule that there is a low degree of interaction (and, therefore, less influence) among those states that do not belong to the same subsystem. Although the NBI is theoretically a subsystem, functionally it has divided itself into two separate subsystems—NELSAP (upper Nile) and ENSAP (Eastern Nile). This means that the events in the Eastern Nile are viewed by the upper Nile as separate and, therefore, marked by the low degree of interaction. That is to say, "solve your own problems."

Ultimately, this led to formal Mediation-3 by the African Union. The involvement by the continental body was initiated by Abiy Ahmed, Ethiopia's President, when he requested South Africa's Cyril Rahomphosa mediate. Though Cyril used his position as the AU's Chair to get the issue mediated by the body, the impasse was never resolved. The mediation was conducted remotely between June and July due to COVID-19 pandemic.

Therefore, with or without the subsystem framework of analysis, Egypt and Ethiopia were stuck in panic mode. From engaging the United States as a mediator, Cairo engaged the Arab League and approached the United Nations' Security Council within the span of three months. Ethiopia, on the other hand, expanded its reach to the Nile Basin upstream states, South Africa and the African Union. Undoubtedly, each subsystem has its weaknesses. Regardless of the degree of interactions, high or low, what really shapes involvement in the affairs of other regional subsystems is national interests. What benefits will accrue to my country (or as an individual mediator)? That is the question.

Summary

As the Nile Basin states have found out, the process of resolving water rights conflicts is complex and daunting. First, it requires a lot of investment in time and resources (financial and human). For example, resolving the disagreements over monopoly rights by Egypt and Ethiopia began, in earnest, in early 1960. It was not until 1999 when the riparian a region-wide body, the Nile Basin Initiative, was formed to develop strategies for cooperation in the management of the Nile waters. It was also tasked to begin the process of negotiating a new legal regime to replace the controversial colonial Nile treaties. After ten years of negotiation, the Cooperative Framework Agreement came into being with initial signing taking place during May 2010. By incorporating pertinent elements of the 1997 Helsinki Rules, the new regime established a permanent institution—the Nile River Basin Commission—to foster cooperation and the implementation of its core principles and strategies. Although faces the agreement places more weight on cooperation, water security, shared benefits, and conflict settlement procedures, it fails to ensure water security for each member state through water allocation. Moreover, the reliance on the vague principles of "equitable utilization" and "significant harm" and if member states will determine what is equitable and significant harm to other members is unrealistic. As already noted from the discussion, these principles have not helped prevent or remedy the conflict between Egypt and Ethiopia.

The second reason why finding the solution to the Nile water rights has been complex is its political dimension. Dams are political projects because of the policies that establish them and budget allocation negotiations that go through the legislature. As we know, politics is about values and different interests. There are those who will support the dam and those who will not. Factions for and against inherently make dam projects political from beginning to end. In the case of the Renaissance Dam, we have seen the degree of politicization from the day of its declaration by Prime Minister Meles Zenawi of Egypt. The reactions by political leaders in Cairo and the ensuing hostile exchanges led to threats of a possible military face-off. This was followed by diplomatic talks that led to the appointment of a technical team, the International Panel of Experts, to study the project and its possible consequences downstream. Hence, the third reason is because of human and financial resources that enable a full assessment of the project.

We have also noted that the involvement of the International Panel of Experts was only for informed policy decisions and direction. Additional effort was by the formation of a Tripartite National Committee, involving water ministers from each of the three countries. After three years of meetings, between November 4, 2013 and March 5, 2015, the agreement on the Declaration of Principles was signed. But the agreement has been found to be deficient as well. For example, it failed to enunciate the substantive issue of water for each member by way of water allocation. Instead, it focused on the filling timeline and dam operations. By signing the agreement mediated by Sudan, Egyptians believed they had, for the first time, acknowledged Ethiopian water rights.

A fourth reason why is the number of negotiated settlements. Mediation One was initiated by Sudan. But that seemed not to have resolved the impasse. In November 2019, Egypt approached the President of the United States, Donald J. Trump, to mediate the conflict. That too originated a deal agreeable to all the three parties (Egypt, Ethiopia, and Sudan). From there, officials from Cairo and Addis Ababa have been scouting for support as well as a viable mediator. Egypt has reached out to the Arab League and the United Nations Security Council, while Ethiopia counts on members of the Nile upstream states and the African Union to stand on its side. Though these latest developments elucidate the panic mode in which Egypt and Ethiopia find themselves in, the latter is determined to continue with the filling of the reservoir. A timeline for all the negotiation efforts are listed in Appendices 1a and 1b.

References

Abbott, Kenneth W., and Duncan Snidal. 1998. "Why States Act through Formal International Organizations." *Journal of Conflict Resolution* 42(1): 3–32.

AP (Associated Press). 2020. "Egypt Supports Sudan's International Arbitration Proposal in Dam Dispute with Ethiopia." TheNationalNews.com.

Atlas of International Freshwater Agreements. 2002. United Nations Environment Programme. Retrieved from https://transboundarywaters.science.oregonstate.edu/sites/transboundarywaters.science.oregonstate.edu/files/Database/ResearchProjects/AtlasFreshwaterAgreements.pdf; September 22, 2021.

Barrett, S. 1994. "Self-enforcing International Environmental Agreements." *Oxford Economic Papers* 46:878–894.

Berhane, Daniel. 2012. "Nile: The Int'l Panel of Experts on Renaissance dam officially launched." Hornaffairs.com, May 22. Retrieved from https://hornaffairs.com/2012/05/22/nile-the-intl-panel-of-experts-on-renaissance-dam-officially-launched/.

Bezabih, Mitwab., and Tesfa, Belachew. 2019. "Grand Ethiopian Renaissance Dam (GERD) Filling Scenarios: Analysis of Energy and Revenue losses." *International Journal of Nile Basin (UNB)- Energy, Water, Environment & Economic* 3 (5):1–11. December.

Caruthers, Osgood. 1958. "Haile Selassie Mediating Sudan Dispute with Egypt." New York Times, February 22.

Cooperative Framework Agreement. 2010. Nile Basin Initiative. http://www.nilebasin.org/index.php/nbi/cooperative-framework-agreement.

Declaration of Principles. 2015. *Agreement on the Declaration of Principles between the Arab Republic of Egypt, the Federal Republic of Ethiopia and the Republic of the Sudan on The Grand Ethiopian Renaissance Dam Project (GERDP)*. Khartoum: State Information Service.

Driechova, Alena., Itay Fischhendler, and Mark Giordano. 2010. The Role of Uncertainties in the Design of International Water Treaties: An Historical Perspective. *Climate Change* 105:387–408.

El-Sayed, Mustapha, K., and R. Soheil Mansour. 2017. "Water Scarcity as a Non-traditional Threat to Security in the Middle East." *India Quarterly* 73(2):227–240.

ENA [Ethiopian News Agency]. 2020. "Sudan Refuses to endorse Arab League Resolution Over GERD Row." March 5.

Galtung, Johan. 1966. "East-West Interaction Patterns." *Journal of Peace Research* 3(2):146–177.

Gebre, Samuel. 2020. "Ethiopia to Press Ahead With Africa's Biggest Hydropower Dam." Retrieved from https://www.bloomberg.com/news/articles/2020-04-10/ethiopia-vows-to-press-ahead-with-hydropower-dam-despite-virus. April 10.

Hassen, Anwar. 2014. "The Geopolitics of Water Negotiations Succeeding the GERD Project in The Nile River Basin." Retrieved from https://www.academia.edu/31728758/The_Geopolitics_of_Water_Negotiations_succeeding_the_GERD_Project_in_the_Nile_River_Basin.

Hoeffler, Anke. 2014–03. Can Intervention Secure the Peace? *International Area Studies Review* 17(1):75–94.

Hoyt, Alia. 2020. "How the Nile Works: The Nile Today." Retrieved from https://adventure.howstuffworks.com/nile-river.htm. April 14.

IPoE. 2013. International Panel of Experts (IPoE) on Grand Ethiopian Renaissance Dam Project. Final Report. Addis Ababa. May 31.

Maru, Mehari. 2020. "Can Trump Resolve the Egypt-Ethiopia Nile Dam Dispute?" AlJazeera.com (OPINION). April 26.

Mitchell, S. M., and A. Nade Zawahri. 2011. "The Effectiveness of Treaty Design in Addressing Water Disputes." *Journal of Peace Research* 52(2):187–200.

Muckleston, K. W. 2003. *International Management in the Columbia River System*. New York: International Hydrological Programme, UNESCO, and PC-CP.

Nader, Mina. 2020. "Egypt, Ethiopia, Sudan at Loggerheads over Nile Dam Agreement." Retrieved from https://themedialine.org/top-stories/egypt. January 19.

NBI (Nile Basin Initiative). 2021. Demography: Estimated and projected total population in the Nile Basin Countries. Nile Basin Water Resources Atlas. Retrieved from https://atlas.nilebasin.org/treatise/estimated-and-projected-total-population-in-nile-basin-countries/. September 22.

OKACOM. 2020. The Permanent Okavango River Basin Water Commission. https://www.okacom.org/documents.

Reuters. 2019. "Trump Speaks with Egypt's Sisi, Back Talks on Disputed Ethiopia Dam." September 23.

River Nile Basin Cooperative Framework. 2010. Agreement on the Nile River Cooperative Framework (Accord-cadre Sur la Cooperation dans le Bassin du Fleuve Nil).

Roberg, Jeffrey, L. 2007. The Importance of International Treaties: Is Ratification Necessary?" *World Affairs* 169(4)(Spring): 181–186.

Sadoff, C., and D. Grey. 2002. "Beyond the River: the Benefits of Cooperation on International Rivers." *Water Policy* 4:389–403.

Saleth, R., and Ariel Dinar. 1999. Evaluating water institutions and water sector performance." *The World Bank Technical Paper*. Washington D.C.

Sandu, Antonio. 2013. Communicative Action and Philosophical Practice. *Romanian Journal for Multidimensional Education / Revista Romaneasca pentru Educatie Multidimensionala* 6(1):39–66, 28. June 2014.

Tekle, Tesfa-Alem. 2013. "Egypt to Establish Military Base in Eritrea." Sudan Tribune, April 18.

Tesfa, Belachew. 2013. "Benefit of Grand Ethiopian Renaissance Dam Project (GERDP) for Sudan and Egypt." Discussion Paper. *EIPSA Communicating Article: Energy, Water, Environment & Economic* 1(1). Available at http://eprints.hud.ac.uk/id/eprint/19305/. December.

The World Bank. 2018. Ethiopia Economic Update: The Untapped Benefits of Services Reforms. Press Release, June 11. Retrieved from https://www.worldbank.org/en/news/press-release/2018/06/11/ethiopia-economic-update-the-untapped-benefits-of-services-reforms.

United Nations Environmental Programme (UNEP). 2013. Annual Report-2014 UNEP Annual Report 2013-LR(1).

United Nations Security Council. 2020. Highlights of the Security Council. https://www.un.org/securitycouncil/.

UNWC Online User's Guide. Part III Planned Measures. Retrieved from http://www.unwatercoursesconvention.org/the-convention/part-iii-planned-measures/.

Widakuswara, Patsy. 2019. "Trump Meets with Egypt, Ethiopia, Sudan, FMs About Dam Feud." Voice of America. https://www.voanews.com/a/usa_trumpmeets-egypt-ethiopia-sudan-fms-about-dam-feud/6178950.html. November 6.

Wolf, Aaron T. 1995. International Water Dispute Resolution. The Middle East Multilateral Working Group on Water Resources. *Water International* 20(3):141–150.
Wolf, Aaron T. 2007. Shared Waters: Conflict and Cooperation. *Annual Review of Environment and Resources* 32:241–269.
World Bank. 2020. Population, Total—Middle East & North Africa. The World Bank. Retrieved from https://data.worldbank.org/indicator/SP.POP.TOTL?locations=ZQ.
Wouters, Patricia., and Moynihan, Ruby. 2013. "Water Security—Legal Frameworks and the UN Watercourses Convention." In *The UN Watercourses Convention in Force: Strengthening International Law for Transboundary Water Management*, eds. F. Rocha Loures and Alistair Rieu-Clarke, 336–351. London and New York: Routledge.
Zakhirova, Leila. 2013. The International Politics of Water Security in Central Asia. *Europe-Asia Studies* 65(10): 1994–2013.
Zawairi et al. 2016. Ariel Dinar and Getachew Nigatu. Governing International Freshwater Resources: An Analysis of Treaty Design. *International Environ Agreements* 16:307–331.

CHAPTER 4

Lessons Learned

INTRODUCTION

The last three chapters have explained the problem: a conflict over water rights prompted by Ethiopia's Renaissance Dam whose construction began in 2011. Egypt, in the downstream, has employed threats, diplomacy, and negotiations as the means to address this problem but with limited success. The sticky issues in the conflict, the speed of reservoir filling and dam operations, remain unresolved, at least for now. Egypt fears that if the dam is filled quickly, say between three and seven years, then the amount of Blue Nile water flow into Egypt's Lake Nasser, a reservoir behind it high Aswan Dam, will be reduced. The effect would amount to reducing power generation capacity and less water distribution to farmers. Egypt, as has already been noted, depends on the Nile (Blue and White Nile tributaries) for 90% of its freshwater availability. To Egypt, water security is synonymous to national security. Furthermore, as the Arab League pronounced at the 153rd meeting in Cairo on March 4, 2020, "Egypt's water security is [by extension] Arab national security." The degree of securitization of water in the MENA Region cannot be compared to the securitization of water in upper Nile riparian states because they receive relatively higher rates of precipitation than the MENA Region of Egypt (and sometimes Sudan) does. For Egypt, therefore, any waterworks in the upstream have potentially negative impacts on its water security. That is why the colonial treaties accorded water rights

© The Author(s), under exclusive license to Springer Nature Switzerland AG 2021
S. H. Okoth, *The MENA Powers and the Nile Basin Initiative*, https://doi.org/10.1007/978-3-030-83981-9_4

between Egypt and Sudan through the 1902, 1929, and 1959 treaties. But as we have learned from the previous chapters, Egypt is also receptive to shared water use, as evidenced by its active participation in the negotiation leading to the formation of the Nile Basin Initiative and the management of regional subsidiary programs. Cairo has equally participated in joint efforts with the rest of the basin countries to develop a new water regime to replace the colonial ones. The culmination of that effort was the 2010 Cooperative Framework Agreement (CFA). Subsequent negotiations leading to the commissioning of the International Panel of Experts to conduct initial studies on the dam and its effects, the mediation led by Sudan that produced the 2015 Agreement on the Declaration of Principles, and the mediation by the United States all demonstrate Egypt's commitment to finding a shared solution for the Nile water use issue.

Ethiopia, on the other hand, justifies its right to construct a dam on the Blue Nile on three principles. One, the principle of sovereignty entitles politically independent nations to use resources within their territories as they deem appropriate. However, international laws require the use of transboundary water systems be guided by two fundamental principles: "equitable utilization in a fair and reasonable manner" and not to impose "significant harm" on the downstream states. Significant harm can imply altering the quality of the water through pollution, but it can also reduce in amount because of waterworks upstream—such as diversion for irrigation and to some extensive damming. Opinions, however, differ on whether impounding water through huge dams can have consequential effects downstream. Although environmental impacts are known to be real, the rate by which dams can reduce the amount flowing downstream is still confounding to experts. As Tijan Sallah, a former World Bank economist who spent years on Africa's water and agricultural projects, confirms, hydroelectric power dams are inherently not consumptive projects; irrigation activities are. Such dams do not hold water indefinitely. All the water that's stored is released through the sluices which in turn, power he turbines to produce electricity (T. Sallah, Personal Communication, May 4, 2020). Therefore, following years of studies that began in 1964 to construct dams on the Blue Nile territory, Ethiopia decided to do so in 2011. It did so on the legal basis provided by the 2010 Cooperative Framework Agreement to which it is a signatory. Article 3 (6) of it states that "... each Nile Basin State has the right to use, within its territory, the waters of the Nile River System in a manner that is consistent with the other basic principles..." (CFA 2010, p. 6).

Although Ethiopia's decision was met with immediate opposition from the Cairo government for lack of consultation as specified in the 1929 colonial treaty, the 2010 treaty does not specifically address consultation but, instead, emphasizes the need for cooperative development of waterworks and other projects through which joint benefits can be derived. In an interview conducted by this author in Cairo in 2014, most of the participants believed Ethiopia was bent on strangling Egypt's economy by attempting to reinstitute themselves as the sole hydro-hegemon in the basin. In effect, the Addis Ababa government was perceived to be opposed to the resolution of the conflict. But this position can be contested because as has been observed over time, Ethiopia has committed to a peaceful resolution to the conflict. Moreover, their commitment goes back to the formation and management of the Nile Basin Initiative and their negotiation leading the Cooperative Framework Agreement. Its role can also be observed in the establishment of the International Panel of Experts, deliberations by the Tripartite National Committee and the negotiations that produced the 2015 Agreement on the Declaration of Principles. They have equally participated in the Washington mediation, albeit reservedly. What lessons are to be learned from the activities involving the three countries as discussed in Chapters 1, 2, and 3? What follows, therefore, are brief institutional, policy and diplomacy lessons learned.

STRENGTHS

Institutional

An institution is a set of rules, procedures and norms that either permits or constrains human behaviors and interactions within a social system; whether informal or formal. Formal institutions are legally created to come up with certain goals either in the present or the future. To achieve these goals, institutions formulate operational structures and processes to coordinate human and technological activities. Therefore, the one characteristic that makes institutions unique from other related concepts is their instrumental nature, which can be divided into "inducing" and "constraining" behaviors. Inducing implies the organization's capabilities (mechanisms) to steer the organization in the desired direction and to achieve goals. Constraining behavior is the direct opposite; taking actions that inhibit the achievement of desired goals.

The review of lessons learned from specific institutions starts with Chapter 2, specifically the colonial agreements. I use the following attributes to assess the strengths, and in the next section, the weakness. In both cases, I employ the attributes (or evaluative criteria) developed in Chapter 2 and expand on them by drawing on the extant literature. The criteria include ratification, inclusion (participatory/pluralistic), specificity, adaptability and resiliency, conflict resolution mechanisms and water security, and basin-wide organizations and durability.

Although the 1902, 1929, and 1959 colonial water agreements did not meet the conditions for formal ratification by the Nile riparian states because of lack of broad participation, the legal regimes found strengths in their specificity both in terms of the farming, constraints and water security for whom they were meant to benefit. Their resiliency, from 1902 to 2010, demonstrates the strength of the agreement. Although they were not adaptable to the changing times, a fact that has subjected them to criticism and complete overhaul, their durability of effective water regimes is unquestionable years after the departure of the colonial government that crafted them. Another strength is the specificity and the framing of the agreements. Consider the following two examples: the 1902 agreement between the British and Ethiopia's Emperor Menelik II that reads in part, "His Majesty the Emperor...engages himself...not to construct or allow to be constructed, any works across the Blue Nile, Lake Tsana, or the Sobat which could arrest their waters into the Nile except in Agreement with Britannic Majesty's Government and the Government of Sudan." The language and the framing of these words meet specific conditions because it identifies whom the legal agreement is meant for and constraints (what can and cannot be done). It, however, fails to state the time frame. Was the agreement in perpetuity?

Although fundamentally different from the colonial treaties, the 2010 Cooperative Framework Agreement demonstrated strengths in several areas. Foremost, its passage involved all the riparian states, including Eritrea as an observer. Second upon its signing, the ratification process has been followed by five states that have already done so. Three, the agreement is specific as to when and under what conditions a signatory in the agreement can withdraw from the compact (see Article 40). Another strength is the specification of the settlement of conflicts (Article 34) and the establishment of the River Basin Commission and regional subsidiary programs. Although borrowed from the 1966 Helsinki Rules and considered to contain vague guiding principles for international water sharing,

CFA has incorporated "equitable and reasonable utilization" (Article 4) and "obligation not to cause significant harm" (Article 5). There is no doubt that these conditions of both colonial and post-independent Nile Basin agreements are something to learn from. The colonial ones met the test of time—though they have been replaced. What is important is the specificity and flexibility of such an agreement. Arguably, it is for the same reason that the CFA is likely to be durable despite the refusal by Egypt and Sudan to append their signatures because of a provision concerning water security. Although Egypt's bid to rejoin the agreement in 2017 was rejected by the NBI Council of Ministers (APA News 2017), that attempt clearly demonstrates the flexibility and promising durability of the compact.

The formation of the Hydromet Regional project in 1967 and, subsequently, the Nile Basin Initiative is another strength that can be noted by practitioners and shared by international water experts and negotiators. Agreements are important because they not only reduce tensions over water rights, but specify actions that must be taken by the parties to either ensure access, use or manage the shared resource. More importantly, is the implementation of the agreement provisions to meet the interests of the parties involved. Hydromet was the first efficacious project because it brought, for the first time, the countries of the Nile Basin to jointly conduct hydrological studies and create databases and share information. Those exchanges were the beginning of basin-wide cooperation that facilitated and established the Nile Basin Initiative (NBI) in 1999. As already noted in the previous chapter, the NBI succeeded in setting up the operational structures to engage all the Nile Basin countries through meetings of water affairs (i.e., Council of Ministers), stakeholder engagement and confidence building and establishment of a secretariat able to coordinate resource mobilization and the management of two regional subsidiary programs (NELSAP and ENSAP). Moreover, the institutions have been able to implement various provisions set up by the CFA. Some of the tasks include fostering peace, ensuring water security for all and institutionalizing conflict resolution mechanisms for present and future conflicts.

Other institutional strengths are to be observed in the activities after Ethiopia declared and started constructing the Renaissance Dam in 2011. As can be recalled from Chapter 1, the first substantive effort by the three downstream states was the establishment of the International Panel of Experts (IPoE). With Terms of Reference on the table, the panel employed specific procedures to conduct a technical study on the project, including design, hydrology and the potential impact on downstream states. Although the latter activity was not completely to the satisfaction of Egypt and Sudan, it should be acknowledged that it set the process rolling and provided much-needed information to reduce uncertainty. But to satisfy the uneasiness in both Cairo and Khartoum that still prevailed, the three nations agreed to form yet another institution, albeit temporary. That institution, the Tripartite National Committee (TNC) consisting of water ministers, held seven meetings that culminated in the agreement of the Declaration of Principles. The Agreement was by de jure mediated by Sudan's President Al Bashir. It is important to recognize the mediator as an institution as well because they aim to achieve a specific goal and are guided by procedural rules and principles. A similar lesson can be learned in the mediation process by the United States under the Trump administration between November 6, 2019, and February 28, 2020.

Policy

Policy can be defined as an official statement meant to enable or constrain human actions on matters important to societal welfare. Policies can be viewed as mandates, examples of which include legislative enactments, judicial precedents, rules, sanctions, and the creation of government agencies. Accordingly, public policies are instrumental because they aim to bring about change or improvement, public order and tax-supported services. However, some policies have both positive and negative intentions and outcomes. Take, for example, the declaration of war that can bring about peace and cost human lives. When the Ethiopian government declared a new energy policy to be achieved by way of major dam construction, it created both winners and losers. The (potential) losers are those in the downstream whose objection to the project is the cause of the present water rights conflict discussed in this book. Except for the displaced population at the project site, the majority in Ethiopia are seen to be winners. Another way to view policies is styles employed to address a problem.

What follows, therefore, is a review of the strengths in the policy mandates by major players discussed in Chapters 2 and 3 from four perspectives developed by Weiner and Diez (2009): "policy style, problem-solving approach, the policy instruments used and policy standards set" (p. 19). It is argued that the prevailing context is equally important for assessing the strengths of any policy, hence, this is added to the fifth perspective. The policy actors (or players) to which each strength is individually or jointly analyzed include public officials of Ethiopia, Sudan, and Egypt, the Nile Basin Initiative, the United States government, Arab League (MENA Powers) and others who have policy pronouncements either to support or not support the two sides to the conflict (Egypt and Ethiopia). The colonial government based in Egypt is similarly considered by considering policy mandates affected the Nile water use. The strengths of colonial policies are reviewed not because of any positive contributions, but as a lesson to water officials faced with how to craft durable water agreements.

Evidence-Based Policy-Making
Evidence-based policy-making implies official decisions are informed by both knowledge and research. The purpose is to make policies not influenced by emotions or instincts but by sound data and information. Therefore, as can be recalled by the discussion in Chapter 2, the British commissioned official studies, before they could make a substantive policy for the establishment of a water use regime. For example, in 1904, Lord Cromer, the then Governor of Egypt, commissioned a study that was conducted by William Garstin—the Undersecretary for Public Works in Egypt. The recommendations of that study suggested the need to regulate and control the Equatorial Lakes water systems from which the Nile originates. It further suggested ways to tap into the waters of the Blue Nile tributary for irrigation purposes (in both Sudan and Egypt) and how to ensure uninterrupted water flow into Egypt. The results of that study further informed the revision to the 1902 agreement by adding a provision for consultations between Ethiopia and the British colonial government before any waterworks could be developed. Those revisions were included in the 1906 agreement. Two other related studies sponsored by Egypt were conducted by the Nile Projects Commission in 1920 and the Nile Water Commission in 1925. The aim was to determine the best approaches to utilizing the Nile waters for the benefit of Egypt. The ensuing policy was enshrined in the 1929 Exchange of Notes. These policies endured for as long as they did because they were informed with sound data.

Policy Styles and Problem-Solving Approaches

Policy styles signify the manner of design, coercive or non-coercive. Coercive policies are those instruments that employ sanctions to either punish or constrain a behavior. Those targeted by such a policy are bound by it; the only recourse is conformity. The problem-solving approach is about how decisions are made to address the issue at hand. This can either be by an elitist few or be group-based (pluralistic). Undoubtedly, the 1902 and 1906 agreements between the British colonial government and Ethiopia can be considered elitist because they were formulated and signed by the very top officials, mostly the official colonial representatives and King Menelik II. The same can be said of the 1929 (Britain, Egypt, and Sudan governments) and 1959 (Egypt and Sudan) agreements. Clearly, the approach was not pluralistic because it did not consider the interests of other riparian states in the upstream. Judging by the expected compliance of the treaties that is framed in those treaties, it can be inferred that the policy style was inherently coercive and the approach to ensuring uninterrupted water flow was elitist in style. This, however, does relegate non-coercive styles and elitist approaches to policy weaknesses. It all depends on the nature of the conflict and what is desirable for whom. It also depends on the political ideologies the actors subscribe to, either democratic or authoritarianism.

Policy Instruments

Policy instruments are how prescribed policies are executed by public officials. They can range from official sanctions, litigation, treaties, laws, allotments, commissioned studies, mediation, and agreements. Out of these, treaties and agreements are the visible policy instruments employed by the British and the Nile Basin countries to redress the imbalance of water regimes. Even as the Nile Basin countries continue to wade through alternative approaches to remedy water rights conflicts, mediation efforts all aim to arrive at agreements. The Cooperative Framework Agreement of 2010 is an example, though such international agreements have their limitations as well. The lesion from their usage is their efficacy in reducing tensions, signaling the end of feuds and their willingness to abide by laid out treaty provisions.

Another important but also relevant policy instrument employed by policy actors, which is reflected in the Nile water rights issue, is the creation of cross-national organizations, some temporary and some permanent. For example, the creation of the 1967 Hydromet Regional

Project and the Nile Basin Initiative in 1999 were both policy instruments made to purposely coordinate hydrological studies, share data and information, and jointly manage the river for the benefit of all riparian members. The setting up of these two institutions demonstrates how effectively policy networks can assert their individual interests to jointly create or shape any policy that benefits all parties (Peterson 2009).

A third policy instrument commonly reflected during the colonial era in the Nile Basin that shaped policy outcomes (e.g., Nile water regimes, treaties), is commissioned studies. Given the specificity of the treaties signed during the period and their durability, it is logical to conclude that studies (or policy analysis) typically should precede the formation of treaties. Treaties that are evidence-based consider an array of relevant elements to shape their effectiveness and durability. Although the information is not available on a specific study commissioned by the Nile Basin Initiative Secretariat to inform the Cooperative Framework Agreement, the 2015 Agreement on the Declaration of Principles was influenced by the International Panel of Experts studies and the Tripartite National Committee meeting outcomes.

Diplomatic

The term diplomacy denotes the engagement of state officials for talks with other countries on matters meant to either develop new relations, manage existing ones or to sort out sensitive differences that amount to conflict. Generally, the methods by designated officials including but are not limited to negotiation, interpersonal communication, tact, judiciousness, and prudence. Although it is impossible to find government officials who possess and exhibit most, if not all, these skills and attributes, what is important is the disposition and understanding of the issues. Once government officials are engaged in diplomacy, the outcome is the most critical.

Looking back at the events leading up to the conflict between the upstream Nile states and the downstream states, and between Ethiopia and Egypt over the Renaissance Dam, a couple of diplomatic engagements were instrumental for the final outcomes (e.g., reduction in tensions, reaching agreements and involvement external mediators). What, then, are the diplomatic lessons to be learned? To make a fair assessment, we employ three lenses developed by Brian Rathbun (2014): Coercive Diplomacy, Pragmatic Statecraft, and Reasoned Dialogue (pp. 2–4).

In Coercive Diplomacy, the other party is framed in adversarial linguistic terms such as "enemy number one," a threat to our survival or "our national security is in jeopardy." Such securitization of an issue, mostly popularized through government pronouncements and the media, can easily rally citizens behind an issue on which two countries are sparring over. Once the other nation has been successfully projected as hostile, the aggrieved state proceeds to justify its position by making threats. Thereafter, the official diplomatic engagement focuses on winning and, if possible, creating harm against the other party. To get what it wants, therefore, the officials employ pressures from wherever it is available. In the case between Egypt and Ethiopia, the former had used its power leverage and friends in the West, including the World Bank, to deny the Addis Ababa government any possible financing to dam projects. From this perspective, the art of diplomacy is viewed purely as a zero-sum activity in which the outcome results in one winning and the other losing. As can be recalled from Chapters 1, 2, and 3, Egypt resorted to this mode of diplomacy in the initial stages. However, it restrained from this approach because Ethiopia's response to the tactic was about the same. On several occasions, the government of Ethiopia reiterated their rights to sovereign rights, arguing that the dam construction was a matter of survival. Additionally, the leaders repeated their readiness for war to defend what they consider as theirs: the waters of the Blue Nile. Following the declaration to build the dam, the newly elected President Mohamed Morsi stated that "all options" were open to Ethiopia's Prime Minister at the time. Desalegn, responded that they have all the military might to defend themselves. Interestingly, both countries extended coercive diplomacy to the mediation table in Washington between November 6, 2019, and February 28, 2020, with each country sticking to their positions and appearing unwilling to budge.

The other diplomatic approach is Pragmatic Dialogue. In this type, those engaged in the process employ objectivity to understand the position and interests of the other party. Hence, the strategy is "give and take," in which both parties make concessions by trying to secure what is more at stake than trying to succeed in every avenue Give and take also means forfeiting matters considered trivial (Rathbun 2014). Although strength is based on compromise and the willingness to forgo some opportunity costs, the main strength of the approach is its focus of objective reality through the eyes of the opposite party. In fact, some of those interviewed by this author in Cairo in 2014 did acknowledge that

Ethiopia, too, deserves to use the Nile waters in a way that provides it with the necessary resources without causing unnecessary harm to Egypt. This notion seems to have been reflected in the negotiations that occurred between 2013 and 2020; Egyptian leaders seemed to accept the right of Ethiopia to construct the dam to benefit its citizens. President General el-Sisi has, over the period of his leadership, projected that same image and reiterated their willingness to find win–win solutions.

The third and final approach to diplomacy, and from which lessons can be drawn, is Reasoned Dialogue. As the name implies, both parties engaged in a logical and calculated dialogue. Each presents their case or proposition that they choose to defend. The goal is to persuade the other party to accept their point of view. Therefore, to succeed in convincing the other party, it is important to engage in a detailed synthesis of the issue to unravel possible explanations. Ideally, as Douglas Walton's typology reveals, a typical reasoned dialogue entails persuasion, inquiry, negotiation, information seeking, and deliberation (2008, p. 8). In the first one, persuasion, the participants employ probing techniques to disentangle the differences of opinion to resolve the conflict. It is believed this approach was at the core of the first mediation by Sudan and the second by the United States government. The second one is the inquiry. Here, the goal of the conversation is to prove or disprove one's position by focusing on tangible facts. Right from the start of the conversations over the Renaissance Dam, Egypt insisted on commissioned studies to prove their claims on the potential harm by the dam project. The third type is the negotiation. Generally, the goal of negotiation is to reach a settlement for the conflict considered by both parties as fair and reasonable. Although at the time of writing this section (May 2020), what was considered a reasonable resolution to the disagreement over the dam filling arrived by the Washington mediation team (Egypt and the United States) was not acceptable to Ethiopia. The emphasis here is the application of negotiation strategy as a strength. However, given that negotiations are generally interest-based (Walton 2008), ensuring a positive-sum outcome for all parties involved can be tricky.

The last approach to reasoned dialogue is the deliberation. The emphasis is to review alternative courses of action and debate on the merits of each to select the option considered most viable and acceptable to all the parties involved. This process is undoubtedly a rational model. Unfortunately, the author is not privy to this kind of information. What is known is that the officials representing the three countries,

Egypt, Sudan, and Ethiopia, successfully engaged in several deliberations, including deciding on the outcome of the 2015 Agreement on the Declaration of Principles. Although the outcome from Washington is still challenged by Ethiopia, for the team to have come up with 37 billion cubic meters as a compromise level of filling demonstrates that some deliberation did take place. Next, a discussion of lessons learned from institutional, policy and diplomatic efforts. The weaknesses are also examined.

Weaknesses

Institutional

In Chapter 2, structures, governance, processes, and outcomes were identified as pertinent evaluative criteria for institutional effectiveness. Upon review of each of the criteria, inclusive participation (particularly NGOs and relevant ordinary citizens) and enforcement mechanisms were found to be wanting. Additionally, three mediation elements were found to be weak. First is compliance. Egypt and Sudan failed to comply with Article 14 (b) of the CFA that deals with water security. Ethiopia, on the other hand, did not comply with the requirement of consultation with other riparian states as specified in the 2015 Declaration of Principles. It, however, is not logical to conclude that the refusal to comply, as each of these countries did, in fact, amount to weaknesses of the two legal frameworks. Theoretically, however, the ideal water regime is one endorsed by and complied by the parties concerned. Another related weakness with the mediation process is the choice of a mediator. As already discussed in the previous chapter, the decision to have Sudan in the first round of mediation remains questionable. Having deliberately changed its alliance from Egypt to Ethiopia, specifically to protect its national interests, it seems unnatural to expect that Sudan would remain totally neutral and not direct the outcome favor Ethiopia. The same stance by Khartoum was exhibited in the 153rd Arab League meeting in Cairo on March 4, 2020, when it failed to join the rest of the League members in support of Egypt's position on the dam. Interestingly, the mediation by the United States government was not exempt from the neutrality question either. When Egypt's President General el-Sisi approached the Trump administration to mediate the conflict, there was skepticism that the United States would unwaveringly stay neutral in the mediation process. After the final talks produced a contested agreement, Ethiopia failed to show up and alleged that the outcome of the talks was skewed towards Egypt. A related weakness of that process, which is also highlighted in Chapter 3, is the claim that the United States used duress to push the draft agreement down the throats of Ethiopian negotiators. Thus, the evidence of weaknesses in the process, and outcome of those institutional arrangements (treaties and mediation), were visible, hardly two months after the Washington talks. Egypt, who had appended their signature on the draft document, proceeded to drum up support among Arab League members—some of whom are considered MENA Powers by virtue of their military and economic prowess.

Policy

To analyze either the strengths or the weaknesses of a policy are to engage in policy analysis or program evaluation. For example, to assess the feasibility of proposed policy action, policy analysts will consider evaluative criteria such as efficiency (cost/benefit), effectiveness, political feasibility, social/cultural feasibility, administrative feasibility, and risk assessment. Instead of focusing on those stated criteria, what follows is a review of the policy styles, policy instruments, problem-solving approaches, and outcomes. The aim is to identify areas of weakness as lessons to be learned by policymakers involved in shared water rights. As in the previous section, we refer to the activities discussed in Chapters 1, 2, and 3.

First, we discuss the policy styles employed. Although still debatable, British colonial leadership undoubtedly employed coercive approaches to develop different water regimes. The 1902 agreement between Her Majesty's government and Emperor Menelik II of Ethiopia was evidently coercive, judging by the wordings of that agreement (i.e., "His Majesty the Emperor Menelik II, King of Ethiopia, engages himself…not to construct or all to be constructed, any work across the Blue Nile…"). Britain then wielded a lot of power as it controlled extensive territories from Egypt, the East African region, and Southern Africa. The same approach, involving Britain and Egypt, led to the signing of the 1929 Exchange of Notes. Its coercive nature is similarly depicted in the wordings of the agreement that inherently mandated complete compliance by the upstream states. The most important paragraph of that treaty is repeated here.

> Save with the previous agreement of the Egyptian Government, no irrigation or power works to be conducted or taken on the River Nile or its branches, or on the lakes from which it flows so far as these are in the Sudan or countries under the British administration, which would, in such a manner as to entail any prejudice to the interest of Egypt, either reduce the quantity of water arriving in Egypt, or modify the date of its arrival, or lower its level. (Howell and Allan 1994, p. 84)

Arguably, the far-reaching consequences of the 1902 and 1929 treaties triggered water rights conflict within the post-independent Nile Basin countries. Therefore, policymakers faced with similar conflicts ought to consider more inclusive and non-coercive approaches to developing agreements. The design and the wording of the agreements should not in any way sound controlling. Evidently, the subsequent treaties (the CFA and the Declaration of Principles) engaged stakeholders in the process and avoided coercive wordings in the text. However, they both failed to include water allotments for each riparian states. This is a strategy considered viable for resolving water rights conflicts in the long term. This is will be explored further in Chapter 8.

The second policy weakness is the determination of who the mediator should be. Ideally, the theory of mediation suggests that only an objective and impartial person on the issue at hand should engage in that role. It is what Marian Roberts (2007) calls a "non-aligned third person" (p. 69). It is assumed that it is through objectivity that the mediator can orchestrate and cut deals acceptable to the warring parties. In practice, the ideal mediator does not impose in any preferred direction. As already discussed in Chapter 3, the neutrality of Sudan and Washington in their respective mediation roles remain contested. Sudan's stand on the dam issue, is what Ethiopia thought they would benefit from. Although Washington's possible bias in favor of one party (Egypt) is debatable, the invitation of President Donald Trump by Egypt's President el-Sisi was viewed with suspicion by Ethiopians because Egypt and the United States have had more intimate diplomatic relations for more than 50 years. Egypt continues to be the second largest United States recipient of military assistance after Israel in the MENA Region. Hence, Ethiopia didn't expect a fair outcome after that meeting.

The third weakness is the failure to apportion the water among all the riparian states. Although this policy instrument involves a rigorous and meticulous application of hydrological data, water allocation among the basin states seems to be a viable solution to such water rights conflicts. The British were, for example, able to allocate the water, though the upstream states were excluded. The consequence of such a policy decision is the conflict we have witnessed between downstream and upstream states. Whereas this approach is the subject of detailed discussion in Chapter 8 under long-term solutions, it would suffice to suggest that this was a major weakness in the two agreements that have been reached by the Nile states: the 2010 Cooperative Framework Agreement and the 2015 Agreement on the Declaration of Principles.

Diplomacy
Of the three diplomacy approaches, coercive, pragmatic dialogue and reasoned dialogue, the weakness is in the first one. The primary interlocutors (Egypt and Ethiopia) found this approach befitting the initials stages of the conflict. It also seems natural to expect the behaviors to align with this approach when conflict begins. The aggrieved party employs coercive bargaining tactics, including the use of threats and pressure, to make the perceived aggressor give in to demands. The goal is triumph rather than loss. As can be recalled from Chapters 1 and 3, Egypt employed coercive bargaining but later changed tactics that are characteristics of reasoned dialogue and pragmatic statecraft. The former denotes the consideration of each other's perspectives to arrive at a win–win solution. The latter is slightly different because each party tries to focus on the more salient issues while sacrificing minor issues. From the description provided in Chapter 3, it seems reasonable to conclude that Egypt narrowed down its areas of concern to two elements—the speed of reservoir filling and dam operations. Before that, the Cairo government briefly insisted on no dam construction but later changed position to support a win–win approach.

COLLECTIVE ACTION PROBLEM: STRENGTH OR WEAKNESS?

The question of the Nile Basin Initiative's lack of involvement in trying to resolve the conflict is curious and deserves some explanation. It is, however, acknowledged that the NBI has appropriately cushioned itself from blame by adding a provision for conflict resolution mechanism in the Cooperative Framework Agreement. As stipulated in Article 34 (b),

> ... if the State concerned cannot reach agreement by negotiation requested by one of them, they may jointly seek good offices, or request mediation or

reconciliation by the Nile River Commission or other third part, or agree to submit the Conflict to arbitration, in accordance with procedures to be adopted by the Council [of Ministers], or to the International Court of Justice. (CFA 2010, p. 52)

Part b of the same article goes on to suggest taking the issue to a neutral fact-finding should the negotiation approaches fail after six months of attempt. The decision by the NBI to stipulate mechanisms to resolving water conflicts is clever for three reasons. First, under democratic institutional practices under pluralism and the rights of each interest group (or member of a group-based organization) are respected and typically stipulated in existing rules and procedures. Therefore, by including such provisions as in Article 34, the NBI not only demonstrates adherence to democratic practices but also gives the members the freedom to choose how they want to go about resolving conflicts and whom they want to involve. Second, by doing so, the NBI indirectly invokes the collective action problem. Originally developed by David Hume (2000) and popularized by American political economist Mancur Olson (1965), the collective action problem suggests that when a large group of people decides to pursue a goal of common interest, some will refrain from active participation. They will, therefore, "free-ride" for two reasons. One, the outcome will be achieved with or without their contribution. Two, they will assess the individual costs to be incurred against the greater good. If the cost of involvement is probative, they would rather not get involved, and vice versa.

This theory of group behavior can enhance our understanding of why collective action by the Nile Basin Initiative has been absent. Guided by this theory, it can be argued that to involve the entire NBI body politic, consisting of ten countries, is to subject the process or its outcome to the collective action problem. True or not, the upstream states in the Equatorial Lakes region have played it safe with less or no active involvement in the resolution to the conflict between Egypt and Ethiopia over the Renaissance Dam. As Olson contends in his work (1965), each group member in the group (read: upstream states) is careful not to disrupt either existing good relations with Egypt, trade arrangement or other geopolitical arrangements vital to their mutual benefits. This supports Olson's proposition that the bigger the group, the smaller benefits to be derived. Also, by being averse to related costs, the NBI seems to acknowledge the difficulty of distributing fairly the costs that might be incurred individually or as a larger group. Moreover, given the anarchic nature of international organizations such as the NBI, the use of coercion is not only difficult but unimaginable in a body that relies on goodwill cooperation. All in all, the efficacy of the NBI about the water rights conflict in the basin, collective action presents a problem in finding a resolution. But at the same, its recognition also presents Egypt, Sudan, and Ethiopia with a faster and more efficacious mechanism to the conflict resolution because the free-rider problem is greatly minimized.

The Tragedy of the Commons: Strength or Weakness?

Equally important to policymakers and other actors involved in finding solutions to international water rights conflicts, is the acknowledgment of the "tragedy of the commons" in relation to the Nile water rights. As explained by Garrett Hardin (1968), a public good (such as grazing land, air, a river or lake) is free for all to use without restrictions. This, however, acts as an incentive to maximize the access to use or even abuse. Consider Lake Victoria from which River Nile originates. If all the upstream states used it any way they want, including the dumping of municipal wastes, countries in the downstream (Sudan and Egypt) would be harmed significantly from contamination. The same would apply to the fisheries and other species. Alternatively, if every riparian state had to construct a dam along the Nile because it is free for all to use, then the consequence to those in the downstream would be significant—in terms of reduction in water flow during reservoir filling and in dry seasons. The policy lesson to be learned is that any time a public good (or "the commons") is free for all, the result is ruin for all. More importantly, it becomes extremely difficult to find common ground on how best to use the resource without damaging or denying a vulnerable member of the commons the benefits others derive. This is the situation that the Nile Basin states found themselves in. Ethiopia, like the rest of the riparian states, subscribes to the "free for all" principle in the access and use of the Nile and its tributaries. Hence, their decision to construct the Renaissance Dam, which Egypt has expressly contended, will destabilize the consistency of water flow to their territory.

Specific lessons most relevant to policy and diplomacy can be summed up as follows. One, resolving conflicts over shared water system can be complex and time-consuming. Those engaged in developing policy for use and access to such a resource must, therefore, recognize the reality of the tragedy of the commons. This means all those who own the right to use the resource ought to be educated on the necessity to regulate the use for the benefit of all. Two, those tasked with negotiating water use legal framework should ideally focus on allocating the right of access. This does not necessarily mean a fee, but an actual apportionment to each member based on internationally accepted criteria. To date, the criteria developed by the 1966 Helsinki Rules, Articles V (International Law Water Project 2020) have provided a useful guide. This will be discussed further in Chapter 7.

Chapter 5 details theoretical explanations including the Prospect Theory, Collective Action Theory, Cross-Cultural Communication, Contact Theory and Pareto-Improvement principle. The aim is to deconstruct each theory in relation to the resolution of the conflicts such as between Egypt and Ethiopia over the Renaissance Dam.

References

APA News. 2017. "Egypt's request to rejoin the CFA agreement on Nile waters rejected." *Journal du Cameroun.com* (May 17).

CFA (River Nile Basin Cooperative Framework). 2010. *Agreement on the Nile River Cooperative Framework* (Accord-cadre Sur la Cooperation dans le Bassin du Fleuve Nil).

Garrett, Hardin. 1968. The Tragedy of the Commons. *New Series* 162(3859) (December 13):1243–1248.

Howell, P. P., and J. A. Allan. 1994. *The Nile: Sharing a Scarce Resource. A Historical and Technical Review of Water Management and of Economic and Legal Issues*. Cambridge: Cambridge University Press.

Hume, David. 2000. Collective Action. Encyclopedia Britannica.

International Law Water Project, The Helsinki Rules. Last modified May 26, 2020. https://www.internationalwaterlaw.org/documents/intldocs/.

Olson, M. 1965. *The Logic of Collective Action. Public Goods and the Theory of Groups*. Cambridge: Harvard University Press.

Peterson, John. 2009. "Policy Networks." In *European Integration Theory*, edited by A. Wiener and Thomas Diez, pp. 105–123. 2nd ed. Oxford, UK: Oxford University Press.

Roberts, M. 2007. *Developing the Craft of Mediation: Reflections on Theory and Practice*. London: Jessica Kingsley Publishers, *American Journal of Clinical Hypnosis* 50(4):355–356. https://doi.org/10.1080/00029157.2008.10404305.

Rathbun, Brian C. 2014. *Diplomacy's Value: Creating Security in 1920s Europe and the Contemporary Middle East*. Ithaca and London: Cornell University Press.

Walton, Douglas. 2008. *Informal Logic: A Pragmatic Approach*. 2nd ed. Excerpt. Cambridge University Press.

Weiner, A., and T. Diez. 2009. *European Integration Theory*. 2nd ed. Oxford & New York: Oxford University Press.

PART II

Navigating Solutions Through Theoretical Lenses

CHAPTER 5

Theoretical Solutions

INTRODUCTION

Despite technological developments and integrated development approaches in the twenty-first century, the biggest challenge facing humanity is how to share the limited resources among competing claims by our rapid growth in population. What makes it even harder is the near universal allegiance to democratic ideals, the demand for equity and fairness, and the global call for shared benefits of public goods. The United Nations' Sustainable Development Goals (SDGs) is the bearer of these beacons of hope for all. Sustainable Development Goal No. 6, for example, calls for access to water and sanitation for all. Undoubtedly, water security is a human right to which all people are entitled. The challenge to policymakers, diplomats and the managers of shared water organizations is how to devise approaches that are acceptable and meet different human demands. Another challenge is developing policy approaches as well as institutions that can manage shared water resources and distribute the benefits in a way that is non-conflicting and thereby foster cooperation. Whereas these challenges are practice-oriented, theoretical approaches can be useful in conceptualizing the problem and provide solution regarding how to go about devising a solution. The theories framework bears some degree of efficacy because in their conceptualization, various elements that might directly or indirectly influence behavior, are considered. For one, or a combination of the elements, to be considered an explanatory factor that can be generalized as a theoretical explanation of a phenomenon, it must go through the rigors of scientific analysis.

The popularity of theories in academic discourse lies in their ability to explain a behavior or an occurrence. Another reason is their ability to predict what will happen when indirect influences are statistically controlled. This implies that a good theory is consistent in their explanations. The other reason why we defer to theories on substantive issues is because of their ability to inform practice; hence, the common academic strand of thinking, "from theory to practice." The only problem with this is the conceptualization in linearity terms. It gives the wrong impression that all forms of practice begin with a theory and not vice versa. As qualitative researchers will confirm, theories can emerge from practice or observed behavior; the so-called "grounded theory."

What follows is a review of four theories: Prospect Theory, Collective Action Theory, Cross-Cultural Communication Theory and Pareto Improvement Principle. Although the theories not addressed here are equally relevant, these four are more apt to the conflict between Egypt and Ethiopia. The goal is to present each as a tool for understanding the behavior of the actors within the Nile Basin Initiative and the MENA powers. The chapter ends with a table that summarizes the four theories, as well as the identification of the areas in which they can prove useful.

Prospect Theory

Originally formulated by Daniel Khaneman and Amos Tversky (1979), this theory suggests that humans frame and make decisions not based on perceived outcomes, but on potential gains and losses. Each of these values serves as a reference point for making decisions. The second premise is that humans tend to be risk averse. Therefore, they will take any action at their disposal in order to minimize losses. Implicit in value is that decision-makers treat a loss with greater attention and concern than with gains. This is because a loss of something of value threatens one's status quo. This brings us to a third premise: humans have the propensity to stick to the status quo than they do to something new, unless the gains will add to what they already have. The fourth premise is the perceived tendency to overvalue what we currently own. This is what Kahneman and Tversky term "the endowment effect" (Chung 2014, p. 3). Fifth, individual actors place more emphasis on differences rather than on similarities. Each (or a combination) of these premises is analyzed with respect to the water rights of both countries.

Losses, Gains, and Other Premises

The logic of this theory, therefore suggests that states, like individuals, will put more weight on the perceived losses than on gains. This lends credence to Egypt's behavior throughout the ten years of negotiation. Judging by the direction of their focus in the negotiations that took place for the last ten years, Egypt framed their reasoning and expected outcomes in terms of risk and loss minimization. That trajectory of the thought further confirms the inclination by states to maintain the status quo disposition (Levy 1992). As will be recalled from previous discussions, Egypt persistently maintained their preference of ten or more years in filling of the dam's reservoir. A shorter period, they argued, could impose significant harm to the Aswan High Dam's capacity by reducing the water flow into Lake Nasser reservoir, especially during droughts and dry seasons. That reduction could translate into lower power generation and less water for irrigation on which Egypt depends on its livelihoods. Another reason why Egypt (and Sudan) previously detested the construction of Ethiopia's dam is the defense of its hydro-hegemon position. The colonial government accorded Egypt and Sudan the "most-favored" status by allocating all the Nile waters to these downstream states and none to the upstream states. Hence, the two have been willing to take on preventative measures and risks to defend the status quo. For example, Egypt threatened Ethiopia with a possible military faceoff soon after Prime Minister Meles Zenawi announced his decision to construct the dam.

Ethiopia, however, took a different position. Instead of sticking to the status quo (i.e., no right to build a dam on the Blue Nile), the government decided to take actions specifically to maximize gains. This violates the core premise to the Prospect Theory in which it is assumed that individuals, or states, have the proclivity towards minimizing losses rather than maximizing gains. However, the theory gains potency on the endowment effect. Since the inception of the dam project in 2011, Ethiopia has been preoccupied with acquiring some ownership of the Blue Nile, a right hitherto denied by the colonial treaties. For example, the Washington D.C. mediation proposed the reservoir filling to be at the annual flow of 37 BCM. Egypt, however, preferred 35 BCM ostensibly to minimize losses, while Ethiopia considered 40 BCM to be acceptable. That way, Ethiopia makes substantive gains at the expense of Egypt. According to the endowment principal advanced by Levy (1992), Ethiopia will readily accept any gains it can get, while Egypt will not be as quick in accepting a loss. Consequently, Egypt will engage in risky behaviors to ensure recovery of any projected loss to maintain its present hydro-hegemon position.

Another premise to the Prospect Theory that deserves a brief comment for its relevance is deterrence. In international relations, the concept of deterrence implies the ability of one party to challenge another either by warning or a substantive threat. The goal is to deter the (potential) aggressor from taking an action that will inflict harm against the aggrieved party. In the Renaissance Dam contest, in which Ethiopia seeks to gain an equal or greater advantage over the use of the Nile for power generation, Egypt initially responded with threats to deter the actual construction. The belief in the efficacy of deterrence is rooted in the Cold War era, in which the West (mainly the United States) and the East (Soviet Union) engaged in nuclear development leading to the accumulation and eventual usage of these deadly weapons. More specifically, deterrence is an economically efficient means of preventing direct war. It is better to prevent than to prepare for and take address the impacts exacted by war. Although Egypt initially mooted the possibility of preparing its forces to attack Ethiopia, it is not certain whether it was merely a bluff or signal of retaliation. Either way, the aim was to instill fear and possibly have Ethiopia refrain from the project.

Judging by the subsequent events, Ethiopia likely construed Egypt's threats as bluff and in response, declared their readiness for war. In both cases, threats and counterthreats are manifestations of deterrence. But as Egypt later came to learn, a threat must be credible in order to be believed (De Luca and Sekeris 2013). As briefly cited in Chapter 3, Egypt made its threats credible by making a deal with South Sudan and Eritrea to set up military and airbases. Both could be used to launch attacks against Ethiopia should the conflict escalate with no recourse at hand. Evidently, the threats were deemed credible because of those activities.

A third means of deterrence is power parity. In the international relations literature, power parity denotes comparable state capabilities, along with given "soft" and "hard" power dimensions. These dimensions include the total population, urban population, energy consumption, size of military personnel, and total military expenditure to the Gross National Product (GDP) (Bremer 1992, p. 322). The assumption is that comparable power will either act as a deterrent or instigator of possible armed conflict. The literature suggests violent conflict (or even war) is likely to occur between nations that have about the same strengths—where strength is defined by the capacity along the stated dimensions. This strand of reasoning is anchored on the idea that states that have high and equal strengths tend to engage in active foreign policy matters and have the tendency to be more aggressive than those who have less power. That kind of behavior can be abrasive at times and may cause tensions with nations that have comparable behaviors and strengths. The converse of this assumption may be true as well. Nations that have dissimilar power are less likely to engage in violent conflicts because it would be irrational for the one with less power to fight the one with more power. The loss by the weaker state would be prohibitively costly. Considering the events described in Chapter 1, in which the two countries used fighting words, how then do they compare on power parity? If the assumption in the literature is something to go by, then power parity between their countries could predict the possibility of a future war. If their powers are dissimilar, then future war is unlikely. Table 3.8 provides a comparison of the countries. Sudan is added to the list because, in international conflicts, the possibility of involvement of allies is not uncommon. Either Ethiopia or Egypt could benefit from Sudan's support.

Judging by the numbers presented in Table 5.1, Egypt and Ethiopia are relatively comparable in terms of population and Gross Domestic Product (GDP). However, Egypt is relatively stronger based on the rest

Table 5.1 Relative power parity among Nile downstream states—2019

Measures (dimensions)	Egypt	Ethiopia	Sudan
Size of the military (2020 est.)	920,000	162,000	189,000
Military expenditure (% of GDP)	1.20%	0.64%	1.60%
Total population	104.1m	108.1m	45.5m
Urban population (% of total; 2020 est.)	42.8%	21.7%	35.3%
Energy consumption (Billion KWh, est.)	159.7	9.062	12.10
Gross domestic product[a] (Billion Dollars; est. 2017)	$236.5	200.6	177.4

Measures developed from Bremer (1992) with permission; Comparable data accessed from CIA Factbook (2020) and Global Fire Power www.globalfirepower.com; [a]Added by author of the dimensions. For example, Egypt's military personnel is almost six times that of Ethiopia's and five times that of Sudan's. Although the expenditures on the military are not as large as a percent of GDP compared to Ethiopia, even though Sudan leads, Egypt is a recipient of military assistance particularly from the United States, which is not reflected in the figure. For example, between 1980 and 2020, the United States provided the Cairo government with about $40 billion worth of military assistance and $30 billion in economic assistance (U.S. State Department 2020). Although similar data for Ethiopia is not available for the same period, other sources show them receiving $282 million in military and $366 million in economic assistance by 1978. This difference in external assistance does add to Egypt's relative power advantage over Ethiopia. On balance, it is difficult to infer any power parity between the two countries. Rather, what is clear from the numbers is that Ethiopia's relative weakness is larger than Egypt's. Theoretically, it is irrational for a weaker state to go to war with a stronger opponent. But it would also be irrational for Egypt to go to war based on geographical distance. The two states do not share boundaries, a factor known to create transnational rivalries. The costs of fighting a war over 2,000 miles away would be quite prohibitive to Egypt.

There is little doubt that the Prospect Theory enhances our understanding of the motivations behind state actions and behavior in relation to conflicts involving two or more countries. Each state aims to minimize losses and treats this element with greater importance than they do for expected gains.

Collective Action Theory

To understand what this theory is about, the concept of public goods must first be clarified. Public goods are goods that are jointly owned and whose consumption by one does not deny others to also consume. Examples include common pool resources such as air, water (in rivers, lakes, and oceans) and open land for grazing. Although others such as national parks and roads are public goods, their right to use vary from jurisdiction. Tolls, road licenses and fees may be required for access and use or to limit usage and, thereby, control quality. For example, a riparian environmental group agrees to clean up a polluted river from which all members are assumed to enjoy fishing, swimming, and the ambiance. Although there is a common interest in doing so, some will focus on their interests even though they support the common interest as well. Hence, they will avoid making any contributions, through money or by service, because they can still access and enjoy the public good. This behavior is called free-riding, or collective action problem.

Conceived by Mancur Olson (1965), the collective action (Problem) Theory suggests that when a group of people come together to act on a problem or to achieve a common goal, certain individuals within the group will avoid making any contributions required but still enjoy the collective good. This theoretical concept can help us better understand why river basin organizations or transnational bodies such as the Nile Basin Initiative, the African Union or the Arab League sometimes are not as effective because of the free-rider problem. At times, what is required of individual member states is a formal endorsement of planned action. However, certain member states will be reluctant to do so after assessing how their interest would be affected by doing so. For some, it is rational to refrain from such an endorsement so long as the perquisites of group membership are still available to all, regardless of the action. This is the kind of situation that the Nile Basin Initiative (NBI) may have found itself in. Undoubtedly, this free-rider behavior can weaken the synergy required to achieve the greater good for the greatest number. This presents a paradox (Olson 1965). The provision of public good declines when group size does. This implies that the larger the group, the less benefit is derived for the public good. The opposite is also true. The smaller number the group membership, the more benefits can be derived.

This paradox applies to the NBI. The River Nile is a public good for which competition exists and, therefore, presents a collective action problem. The upstream states aim to access and use the water, while those in the downstream challenge that attempt. Because of the paradox and the conflict of interest it creates the collective action (or, working in groups) is not the best tool for resolving the public good conundrum. Rather, incentives, negative or positive, could help conquer the free-rider problem. It is, therefore, hypothesized that water rights conflict exists partly because it is a public good that engenders rivalry. The best way to address it is by focusing on the size of groups such as The Nile Equatorial Lakes Subsidiary Action Program (NELSAP) and the Eastern Nile Subsidiary Action Program (ENSAP). The application of this theory to the resolution of the water rights conflict in the Nile will be revisited in Chapter 6.

Cross-Cultural Communication Theory

The theory of cross-cultural communication offers a good understanding of how different nations manage conflicts. Several studies conducted on this subject suggest that cultures differ in their preferred ways of managing conflicts (Ting-Tommy et al. 1991). It is even more interesting to know how this cultural difference plays out when a conflict negotiation involves western and Third World countries. Therefore, practitioners should understand how cultural values, norms, and practices influence the way societies interact. Geerte Hofstede, who developed the cultural dimensions theory, simplified this by dividing the world regions into six cultural dimensions: power distance, collectivist versus individualistic, masculinity vs. femininity, uncertainty avoidance, long- and short-term orientation indulgence vs. restraint. Another related dimension that has been adopted from Hofstede's work is "high versus low context" cultures (Hall 1976). Only two of these are expounded on because of their relevance to cross-cultural communication and how their cultural orientations influence negotiation process and outcomes. This stance is supported by Adair and Brett (2005) who observed that the difficulties experienced at the negotiating table and in within agreements can be attributed to cultural differences of those involved in the process. This is particularly true when the negotiation activity involves two or more countries.

According to Hofstede, Western societies tend to exhibit individualism while Asian, Latin America, and African countries Collectivism. The former denotes allegiance to the self rather than to the collective group preferences. Individualist cultures tend to rationalize and pay little to no attention to cultural nuances while Collectivist cultures place emphasis on feelings, values, flexibility, and relationships. The ability of Egypt, Sudan, and Ethiopia to strike the Agreement on the Declaration of Principles in 2015 can partly be attributed to their convergence within the Collectivist dimension. This further assumes that by being collectivists, their communication styles are somewhat similar, if not the same. One would also expect the clash between these two cultural traits (Individualism vs. Collectivism) to have played out during the mediation by the United States—in which Egypt, Sudan, and Ethiopia presented their case between November 2019 and February 2020.

A more apt cultural trait is "high Context versus low Context." The context here implies the extent to which extant norms and traditions influence the communication process (Gelfand et al. 2002). In high context cultures (Africa, Asia, and Latin America), communication styles tend to be indirect, less time conscious and sensitive of the feelings of the other party. The opposite is true of low context countries (mainly Western societies). Their communication styles are more direct, unambiguous, assertive and somewhat patronizing and insensitive of feelings (Hall 1976; Parker 2000; Gelfand et al. 2002). One can, therefore, imagine difficulties faced by the United States mediators when deciphering statements made by the African team. For example, when the Ethiopian delegation failed to show up in the final Washington D.C. meeting where the draft agreement was to be endorsed and signed, it was in defiance of the agreement even though they could not directly say so. The problem with these cultural dimensions is the fluidity and dynamic of the 21st-century cultures. There is increased convergence of cultures but, at the same time, a fundamental difference does exist between nations that are grouped. For example, Egypt and Ethiopia are considered collectivist cultures, and, yet the communication style of the former is largely influenced by Islamic traditions and the Arabic language; Ethiopia is not.

Intergroup Contact Theory (Contact Hypothesis)

Although somewhat different, Contact Theory is related to cross-cultural communication. This theory holds that contact between two separate groups (communities or nations) that are engaged in a conflict will promote tolerance and understanding, thus producing desired results involving cooperation and peace. Originally developed by Gordon Allport (1954), the theory works under specific conditions—common goals, equal status, cooperation, and support by existing social and institutional authorities. Arguably, contact works well because it reduces all extant stereotypes and prejudices that one group might hold against the other. Like friends previously unknown to each other, they develop a common ground of understanding and wade through their differences to achieve a common goal.

Thus, for nations engaged in conflicts such as the one between Egypt and Ethiopia, developing social, economic, and political contacts can have positive effects.

Pareto-Improvement Principle

The principle of Pareto Improvement is derived from the works of an Italian economist Vilfredo Pareto (1848–1923). Pareto Improvement suggests that any change or reallocation of a resource in a way that increases benefits for one person without decreasing the net benefits the other person already has. The converse, also known as Pareto Optimality, is when such reallocation makes one person (party) better off while at the same time making the other person worse off. As will be shown shortly, achieving Pareto Improvement, which is the ideal, is difficult, due to the constraints and assumptions about human interests engaged in joint negotiations.

This theory is critical in two ways. First, it can conceptually guide negotiators about whether to pursue an optimal decision outcome or not. Second, it offers a better alternative to decision-makers faced with the choice to distribute or redistribute a resource more equitably. Let us apply this to the case of the Nile water rights conflict. For almost ten years the Nile Basin Initiative sought the most optimal arrangement for utilizing the shared water system. As early as 1967, the riparian states, with Egypt and Sudan in the lead, agreed to form the Hydromet Project in 1967 to conduct joint hydrological studies, collect data and create and share databases. The rationale behind this initiative was to make more informed decisions for efficient management and water use for the benefit of all member states. Then came the Nile Basin Initiative created in 1999 made specifically to foster cooperation and formulate strategies for efficient use of the shared water system. Consequently, two regional programs were created: the Nile Equatorial Lakes Subsidiary Action Program and the Eastern Nile Subsidiary Action Program. The joint institution realized those strategies. However, the strategy for optimal use assumes that all the riparian countries have similar interests and are, therefore, sensitive to equitable use for the benefit of all. As a result, attempts at securing optimal allocation and use cannot realistically be achieved. Instead, what is achieved are sub-optimal solutions because, in the process, each party must forgo opportunity costs while others will try to maximize benefits to fulfill self-interests (Mnookin 2003). Given these limitations to achieving a more efficient outcome, negotiators tasked with resolving a conflict over shared resource should instead aim at sub-optimal solutions in which one party gains and the other doesn't lose what they already have.

As alluded to earlier, Pareto Improvement seeks to address the inadequacy of Pareto Optimal solutions. Thus, it attempts to ensure reallocation improves the welfare of one party without decreasing the net welfare of the other party. This can be applied to two scenarios in the Nile Basin. First is the Nile Cooperative Framework Agreement (CFA) of 2010. Although missing in the agreement, the reallocation of the water to all members was expected. The goal of such corrective action is not to take away the water allotment to Egypt and Sudan but to redistribute it among all riparian states. Although this will be addressed more in-depth in Chapter 8, the pareto-improvement approach enables policymakers (as in the case of Ethiopia's dam construction) to design water infrastructures that consider the gains versus losses. Though such waterworks will add value to Ethiopia, it should not concurrently reduce the net benefits to Egypt. Translating this theory into reality might appear complex and daunting but as scholars have established, good theories can be practical and, therefore, inform practice.

References

Adair, W. L., and Brett, J. M. 2005. The Negotiation Dance: Time, Culture, and Behavioral Sequences in Negotiation. *Organization Science* 16: 33–51.
Allport, Gordon W. 1954. *The Nature of Prejudice*. Reading, MA: Addison-Wesley.
Bremer, Stuart. 1992. "Dangerous Dyads: Conditions Affecting the Likelihood of Interstate War." *Journal of Conflict Resolution* 36(2):309–341.
Chung, Ozzie. 2014. Prospect Theory in International Relations. *Clocks and Clouds* 47(2). American University.
De Luca, Giacomo, and Petros G. Sekeris. 2013. Deterrence in Contests. *Economica* 80.
Gelfand, Michele J., Marianne Higgins, Lisa H. Nishii, Jana L. Raver, Dominguez Alexandria, Fumio Murakami, Susumu Yamaguchi, and Midori Toyama. 2002. "Culture and Egocentric Perceptions of Fairness in Conflict and Negotiation." *Journal of Applied Psychology* 87(5):833–845.
Hall, Edward. T. 1976. *Beyond Culture: Theory of Low/High Context Communication*. Garden City, NY: Anchor Books/Doubleday.
Khaneman, Daniel, and Amos Tversky. 1979. "Prospect Theory: An Analysis of Decision under Risk." *Econometrica* 47(2).
Levy, Jack E. 1992. Prospect Theory and International Relations: Theoretical Applications and Analytical Problems. *Political Psychology* 43(2):283–310.

Mnookin, Robert H. 2003. When Not to Negotiate: A Negotiation Imperialist Reflects on Appropriate Limits. *U. Colo. L. Rev* 74:1077 (2003).

Olson, M. 1965. *The Logic of Collective Action. Public Goods and the Theory of Groups.* Cambridge: Harvard University Press.

Parker, Donna. 2000. *Cross-Cultural Considerations in Mediation. ProQuest Dissertation Publishing.* California State University, Dominguez Hills.

Ting-Tommy et al. 1991. Culture, Face Maintenance and Styles of Handling Interpersonal Conflict: A Study in Five Cultures. *The International Journal of Conflict Management* 2–4:275–296.

U.S. Department of State. 2020. *Countries and Areas.* Available at www.state.gov.

PART III

Short-Term Solutions

CHAPTER 6

Ideal Third-Party Mediation

INTRODUCTION

Resolving international water rights conflicts is and will always be one of the most complex and daunting challenges facing humanity in this century. There are a number of reasons for this. First is the issue about deciding who has the right of control to a river, or its tributary, that flows through two or more politically independent nation-states. Presently, and based on international laws, such watercourses are jointly owned. But international laws also guarantee the right of use by individual nation-states from which the watercourse emanates or through which it flows before entering another. The question of individual or joint ownership, and by how much, is complex and presently one of the leading causes of conflicts to shared international water systems. Answering this question is daunting because the water increases or decreases in volume over the course of its journey, due to consumptive uses or changing hydrological patterns. The second challenge is devising a mechanism for upstream water use that does not affect the amount received downstream. Hence, the associated problem is how to resolve the conflict that arises out of the upstream riparian water use and for what purpose. This is tied to the riparian territorial rights when constructing waterworks or even diverting water for irrigation and other consumptive uses, even if it's at the expense of those in the downstream. A third challenge is a reliance on international water laws, rules, and conventions. The Helsinki Rules of 1966, for example, guide riparian states on how best to share international water systems. Those rules, in particular, which mention "equitable and reasonable utilization" and "no significant harm/" are invariably contradictory. The first rule defends the right of upstream states to use shared water system but in a fair and reasonable manner. This implies using due diligence to not obstruct or deny the riparian nation downstream of its share. The second, "no significant harm," is the legal defense for downstream states against waterworks upstream that might pose harm by reducing the amount received and, thus, destabilizing their historical rights.

To address continued conflicts between these two contradictory international principles, the UN General Assembly adopted what became to be known as the UN Convention on the Law of the Non-Navigable Uses of International Watercourses (UNWC) in 1997. Although it emphasizes the same principle enunciated by the Helsinki Rules, it went further to include participation along with the obligation to give prior notice for any planned waterworks. The intent of parity under the "equal utilization" principle, and the requirement to give prior notice to other riparian members before embarking on a project on a shared water system has, in some cases, been rejected by upstream states. Ethiopia in the upstream of the Nile Basin, for example, voted against the adoption of the UNWC. In fact, although the convention was adopted by the majority of member states, five out of the 35 countries needed to ratify the convention still have not done so. This is surprising, especially because the convention laid out the rights and duties of each state that share the 276 international rivers (Loures and Rieu-Clarke 2013). Whereas most of these international water laws and conventions have become the cornerstone of basin-wide agreements and shared management and institutional arrangements, the limitations are entrenched in their inflexibility as well as enforcement mechanisms they lack. A related weakness common in international water laws is the absence of, or inadequacy in, enforcement. Individual riparian states operate in an anarchic international system. The UN is not a world government endowed with the authority to enforce mandates or to use force against a sovereign state. Instead, the body and its varied organs can only provide well-conceived rules endorsed by member states to guide the peaceful sharing of transboundary resources.

A fourth challenge is the securitization of water. This is particularly true for nations in the MENA region who have no rivers of their own. Syria and Iraq, for example, rely on the Euphrates and Tigris Rivers that emanate from Turkey. The same applies to Egypt on the downstream of the Nile. With the variability of precipitation occasioned by climate change, the MENA Region and the lower basin of the Nile Basin stand to be negatively affected. This combined with the rapid population growth in the Nile Basin (Ethiopia at 108.1 million and Egypt 101.2 million in 2020), as well as the increased regional demand for economic growth, will put more pressure on the available water resources, creating tensions over use.

Fifth is the problem associated with governing shared water systems. Although the riparian states that have already signed about 400 international river basin treaties (Loures and Rieu-Clarke 2013, p. 7) are better off than those with no such arrangements, the overall management of these water regimes remains daunting, either because of lack of capacity or halfhearted political support.

The sixth and final challenge faced by states sharing international rivers is the inability to identify and implement specific and realistic guidelines. One such guideline is water allocation. This arrangement has greater potential of averting future conflicts because each riparian state knows how much they own year by year—unless, of course, that amount is threatened or reduced due to unforeseen climate changes. As I will argue in Chapter 8, the avoidance of this magical solution (i.e., water allocation) in the design of treaties, cleverly framed to accommodate changes in hydrology and socioeconomic factors, is worrisome.

Finally, given that conflicts over international water systems are, for the most part, politically generated, the solutions should, at best, be political. Therefore, the lack of political cooperation in choosing a neutral mediator who understands the history of the conflict, the cultural dynamics, and the negotiation environment and has the appropriate competencies, can be unnerving and lengthen the time it takes to reach a resolution.

Despite these challenges, humans are an ingenious and resilient lot. Even when forced to militarily confront each other, nations still have been able to strike peace deals. In fact, as shared international water expert Aaron Wolf has irrefutably claimed repeatedly, nation-states in water conflicts have, by necessity, struck cooperative arrangements to ensure win–win solutions and avoid military confrontation. Though somewhat an outlier example, the Thirty Years' War in Europe caused by the debacle within the Roman Catholic Church, resulted in the 1648 Treaty of Westphalia. Signatories in that treaty, whom themselves fought on the frontlines, came to agree and codify the principle of sovereignty. It is that same treaty that defined territorial rights over water use. That principle has since defined what water rights entail. The same treaty culminated into what is known as the Harmon Doctrine. This doctrine will be revisited later in this chapter.

After years of research about how some international water conflicts were evaded or resolved, I can claim to have found some commonalities in these approaches. These include third-party mediation, agreement (bilateral and multilateral), litigation (arbitration by the Courts), and institutional framework (river basin organizations). One approach that is efficacious, although often avoided, is water allocation. The approach is part of a solution discussed and highly recommended in part two of this work.

This chapter is the start of a conversation about possible ways to resolve international water conflicts. I must admit, it is no easy feat. This is because the solutions to water conflicts are difficult to generalize from one context to another. However, third-party mediation is discussed at a greater extent because it is more dominant. With a few exceptions, most international water conflicts that erupt are tamed by third-party mediators who either volunteer or are asked to intervene by one of the parties in the conflict. However, the success of this approach depends on the ability to understand the negotiation context and the possession of relevant competencies in order to guide the warring parties to lasting solutions. It also assumes a complete neutrality of the mediator; any express support of one party by the mediator will weaken the final outcome.

Chapter 7 explores, first, bilateral treaties and argues in favor of this approach over multilateral ones in resolving the Egypt–Ethiopia water conflict. It is suggested that bilateral agreements are, by far, one of the best approaches for obtaining lasting peace. Whereas most bilateral agreements are secured by involving a third-party mediators, I suggest that such agreements are weak and malleable because it is difficult to find neutral mediators in a world where self-interest is more common than public interest (utilitarian principle). Hence I propose that the best outcome in bilateral conflicts is achievable when the two warring parties battle it out alone until they exhaust themselves and reach a deal. The chapter then presents litigation as alternative means for arbitrating such conflicts.

Although not commonly used in resolving international water conflicts, the International Court of Justice (ICJ) has adjudicated a few of such cases. Consequently, the role that regional courts can play is discussed, along with the rationale for creating a similar legal institution to arbitrate transnational cases involving. The chapter ends with a brief discussion of relevant international experiences with bilateral water treaties and litigation. The purpose is to demonstrate the extent of their efficacy and why the Nile Basin countries, particularly Egypt and Ethiopia, should find these two approaches practical.

Chapter 8 argues that international water conflict is heavily influenced by either the failure to allocate or misuse by those in the upstream that either affects the quality or reduces the amount that flows downstream. The chapter presents water allocation as an absolute necessity for averting long-term water conflicts. This model contrasts with the benefit approach in which a basin focuses on joint projects rather than direct water allocation to each riparian state. I further contend that water allocation works even better when a multimember basin is partitioned into two sub-basin institutions for ease of interaction, coordination, conflict resolution and water development and management. I, therefore, make a strong argument in favor of semi-autonomous upper and lower basin institutions for the Nile River. Finally, international experiences are provided to corroborate the evidence-based efficacy of each of the approaches (i.e., water allocation and sub-basin institutions).

Though these approaches, discussed in this chapter and Chapter 7, I address the conflict between Egypt and Ethiopia, as they provide a valuable example for averting or resolving similar conflicts over the use of shared international waters systems. Moreover, given the spate of damming on the Nile, the basin states will find these approaches invaluable—in particular, the efficacy of bilateral agreements and water allocation.

The engagement of third-parties to mediate conflicts involving two or more parties has become a global heuristic. Mothers mediate conflicts between siblings, teachers between students and social workers, as well as judges, mediate between divorcing couples. The UN Secretary-General, Presidents, the Pope, Imams and a plethora of independent local or international organizations are often called upon to mediate social, religious, and political conflicts. Given the near allegiance to the efficacy found in third-party mediation, it has, therefore, emerged, in the twentieth and twenty-first centuries, as a serious area of study and professional practice. Despite the expansion of the field and the greater level of expertise that exists today, mediating environmental-related conflicts remains complex and daunting. In some cases, mediated settlements can take years and at times, are subject to relapse once resolved. Although the courts have had success in mediating divorce cases, this approach has not had the same effect on water conflicts. As will be discussed in the section detailing litigation as an option for resolving water conflicts the International Court of Justice in the Netherlands cannot claim nor pat themselves on the back for successfully arbitrating shared international conflicts brought before them.

Third-party mediation is, therefore, treated with greater attention in this section of the book because of its perceived efficacy when resolving conflicts. Despite its near-universal appeal, mediation is complex and requires a great deal of expertise, experience, understanding of the context (or the negotiation environment), and complete neutrality. Therefore, parties involved in a conflict should be extremely careful about their choice of a mediator. In overly complex and sensitive issues, such as environmental ones, the wrong choice of a mediator might worsen the conflict and make it intractable. As expected in all mediation, the reduction of tension or impasse is the primary goal. The mediation should further aim to restructure the relationships between the parties from rivals to allies. Only then can the mediated settlement become durable.

But the success of the mediation is generally viewed through a dyadic lens—from process to outcome. Hence, it is conceived as a straight shot activity in which the warring parties engage in resolving their differences within the shortest period possible. I argue that though this practice has brought about occasional settlements, it overlooks the in-between nuances that are key to the sustainability of the outcome. What follows is a fresh look at mediation by building a typology for an "Ideal Mediator." In this context, it is contended that the very soul of mediation lies within the *capacity* of the mediator. Hence, most of this chapter focuses on the mediator's capabilities (preparedness, knowledge, expertise, and ability to structure an outcome that lasts).

As revealed in the remainder of this chapter, the ideal mediator is self-aware of their competencies and limitations, are able to structure a process conducive for exchange of ideas, positions and interests, is knowledgeable about the issue and contextual realities and uses the process to restructure relationships beyond the mediated settlement. Table 6.1 expands on the evaluative criteria developed in Chapter 3 (Table 3.3) to identify the mediator's core competencies. The merits of each are discussed below.

Once the conditions have been determined by the warring parties for the intervention by a third-party, have decided who that mediator is, where they are from and evaluate how well they do in the process to bring

Table 6.1 Ideal mediator competencies

Criteria	Description
Origin, neutrality & affiliation	Not affiliated or allied to either of the warring parties; origin: local or regional[a]
Competencies	Knowledge of the context; expert/ability to frame and reframe the problem; successful mediation history; experience; pragmatic strategies
Process	Timing; neutral location; participation. Facilitation; generate own solutions; discuss merits and limitations; absence of duress
Outcome	Agreement reached considers relationships for stability, parties guided to exchange information, express interests
Compliance	Settlement implemented; parties comply (Ad Hoc/Permanent Institution in place)
Client satisfaction	Concerns and interests addressed fairness on both sides

[a] Mediator selected from the region in which the conflict occurs
Developed from: Sandu (2013), Hoeffler (2014); personal knowledge

about desired outcomes for each party, the mediation process can begin Although often overlooked, where the mediator comes from can either create trust or mistrust among, before or during the mediation process. This is important because cultural orientations shape the way mediators approach conflict resolutions.

As discussed in earlier sections, those from Individualist and Low Context western societies tend to be direct in their communication styles and place a high premium on formalized agreements. Everything up for discussion is rationalized, while cultural values are undervalued or even avoided. The converse is true for non-western societies that exhibit Collectivist orientations. Indirectness in communication means intended meanings are implied through verbal or non-verbal expressions. Abstention or lack of response could mean rejection. In these cultures, paying attention to values, as well as feelings, rather than facts could be key to disentangling an impasse. It, therefore, makes more sense, whenever feasible, to identify a mediator who meets specified conditions and competencies but at the same time shares the same cultural orientations as the warring parties. That choice has its advantages. One, is the ability to quickly immerse oneself and understand cultural nuances behind the positions taken by each party. Two, the ease of communication that leads to effective negotiation may be enhanced if both parties and the mediator come from Collectivist/High Context cultures. This, however, should not be taken as a rule rather than the exception; it all depends on the context, the nature of the conflict and the mediation style employed. The following example illustrates this point further.

In December 2007, ethnic conflict erupted in Kenya following presidential and legislative elections. The results of presidential elections between the incumbent Mwai Kibaki and the opposition leader Raila Odinga were disputed as each claimed victory. The incumbent went ahead with the swearing-in even before all the votes were received at the tallying station. That action triggered protests in the opposition's stronghold locations and in the capital city of Nairobi. The then UN Secretary General Koffi Anan jetted into Kenya and spent 41 days negotiating a settlement. Despite the difficulty of the process, a peaceful resolution was achieved that established a coalition government. This success can be attributed, foremost, to the Secretary General's competencies, the aspect with which he was viewed, his experience and the fact that he was an African (from Ghana) who easily understood the history of electoral politics in the continent. He was also best suited for this role because as an African, he expressed empathy for good politics, peace, and accountability. As stated earlier, sharing the same cultural orientation may help mediate a conflict when combined with other competencies. For example, the African Union Chair and Ghana's President John Kafuor had tried to do so but failed. Former presidents of Tanzania, Botswana, Mozambique, and Zambia as well as Nobel Laureate Desmond Tutu had all mediated but failed, yet they share with Kenya's cultural orientations (Collectivist and High Context) touted by Geert Hofstede (1981). Anan's success, therefore, can be attributed partly to his international stature as the UN Secretary General that accorded him respect and trust. Moreover, he had previous experiences in mediating complex conflicts across the globe during his term of office. He was also viewed to be neutral with no self-interest in the ultimate outcome.

The interplay of these three factors in the mediation process can be applied to the case between Egypt and Ethiopia. Sudan's leader Al-Bashir met the condition of "place of origin." Sudan is geographically located between Egypt and Ethiopia. That proximity meant that the three countries share some similarities either religiously, culturally or even politically. More specifically, racially, culturally, and linguistically. Both Sudanese and Egyptians are Arabs, Moslems and, linguistically, speak Arabic. Politically, the two countries belong to the 22-member Arab League. Although Ethiopia is distinctively different ethnically, the political, economic, and social interactions between Khartoum and Addis Ababa have been closer and even cordial, compared to Addis Ababa and Cairo. Therefore, Sudan was better placed to mediate, though its neutrality on the issue remains debatable. The issue was discussed in Chapter 3.

COMPETENCIES

Understanding the Context

Whenever there are flare-ups over shared international water systems, either because of pollution upstream, diversion of water into irrigation canals or development of a dam (large and small), negotiators often take up the matter with the hope of finding a peaceful resolution before it gets worse. As the case of Egypt and Ethiopia illustrates, the declaration to construct the Renaissance Dam ignited, at least initially, a diplomatic standoff between Cairo and Addis Ababa. The events that followed prove that nations caught up in a conflict will always attempt to resolve their differences either forcefully or peacefully. As discussed in Chapter 2, Egypt, the aggrieved party, immediately engaged Ethiopia in fiery exchanges, including threats of possible military attack. Experience tells us that such threats tend to be a natural reaction during the initial stages of conflicts. But once Ethiopians stood their ground, Cairo turned to diplomacy and initiated formal negotiations with them. That effort resulted in a joint technical study by the Panel of International Experts whose findings informed future discussions as well as the mediation led by Sudan's President Al-Bashir.

The first round of the mediation process took three years before the Agreement on the Declaration of Principles was reached and signed on March 23, 2015. Subsequently, tensions resurfaced leading to the second round of negotiation by the United States government between November 2019 and February 2020, which did not go well. Therefore, to strengthen this heuristics approach, this section makes a case for a greater understanding of the negotiation context. Accordingly, I define successful mediation as a process in which the contending parties strike a win–win deal that is less prone to relapse. Understanding the negotiating context is the first step in this lengthy process.

Negotiating Context

The hypothesis that links contextual realities to the mediation process and the outcome find support in the literature (Crump 2009, 2011). Crump argues that there is a reciprocal relationship between the negotiation process and its external environment. His assertion is anchored on the Linkage Theory of international relations which suggests that the behavior or action of a state is not only influenced by the internal dynamics, but by external factors. Hence, for a typical negotiation to produce desired outcomes, whoever leads the process must be cognizant of exogenous influences, direct or indirect. It in this context that Crump (2011) builds his argument by describing (issue) linkage as an event in the negotiation process that shapes the outcome. Although no studies have been conducted to date, the incidence of the COVID-19 pandemic reduced the intensity and frequency of the ongoing negotiation over the remaining Renaissance sticky issues, such as the timing for reservoir filling without a formal agreement in place, clear mechanisms and procedures for dispute resolution and what is to be done during dry seasons and droughts.

For the sake of brevity, contextual factors can be divided into internal and external. Internal factors are those attributes from which the mediator draws from to make their work possible. These include core competencies in knowledge, skills, and abilities. As discussed in Chapter 3 (Table 3.6), the mediator should be fully knowledgeable of the issue, its history and causes of the conflict, factors that have inhibited resolution and other external interests and exigencies on the matter. The requisite skills include communication, listening, and the ability to engage in intuitive observation of the undercurrents and to stay neutral. The latter can prove difficult in the 21st-century world in which power politics has increasingly become more apparent. The ubiquity of neoliberal economics and its practices has further entrenched the practice of self-interest at the nation-state level. That is why finding a neutral mediator can be daunting.

Though opinions differ depending on where one stands, Sudan, as discussed in Chapter 3, met the evaluative criteria on knowledge. Geographically nested between the two warring nations (Ethiopia and Egypt), Sudan's Al Bashir reign of 30 years (1989–2019) accorded him a reasonable amount of information and knowledge of the Nile water rights conflict. The country was party to the 1967 Hydromet Projection creation, the NBI formation, the discussion and drafting of the 2010

Cooperative Framework Agreement (though it differed from water security provision) and partially aggrieved party to Renaissance Dam conflict. Historically, therefore, Sudan's experience with the Nile is about the same as Egypt's. There could be no better country as knowledgeable as Sudan on the issues. That, however, does not fully qualify Sudan for their situations. Sudan was able to broker a deal that led to the signing of the Agreement on the Declaration of Principles on March 23, 2015.

External Factors
External factors are important for the success of any mediation, and more importantly, for their durability. It is also my contention that the inability of mediators to strike a deal that rests, not solely on their competencies but on understanding the factors in the external environment and how to integrate that feedback into the process. To neglect these extraneous factors is like entering into a cave blindfolded. All you feel and hear is a danger that never ends. But to be aware of extraneous factors is like having light to explore the inside of the cave. Examples of external factors include political stressors, social stressors and interests (direct and indirect). The linkage between each of these stressors with the process and mediation outcome is illustrated in Fig. 6.1. The arrows depict forces (or stressors) from the external environment. What those forces are, and

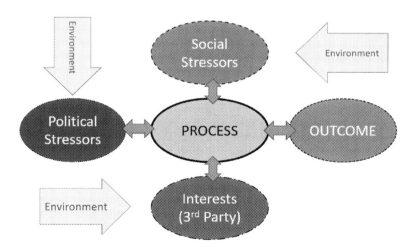

Fig. 6.1 External contextual factors

how they independently or jointly influence the mediation outcomes, are explained.

Political Stressors
Events in the political environment, such as political instability in one or more of the countries engaged in a negotiation, can influence the mediator's approach, how the process proceeds and the outcome. Let us consider the conflict between Egypt and Ethiopia. When Sudan took up the role of mediating the conflict, Egypt was amid political chaos instigated by the Arab Spring. President Hosni Mubarak was ousted, giving way to the election of Mohamed Morsi of Muslim Brotherhood. His term of office was short-lived (June 29, 2012–July 3, 2013), as a faction opposed to the Muslim Brotherhood took the protests to Tahrir Square after the military announced his ouster. The constitution was subsequently suspended, thereby creating uncertainty.

In fact, two months after Morsi got elected (August 20, 2012), Ethiopia's Prime Minister Meles Zenawi died and was succeeded by Hailemariam Desalegn (2012–2018). In April 2018, Abiy Ahmed replaced Desalegn. Political instability was even more apparent in the Republic of Sudan, headed by Omar Al-Bashir. The 21 years of civil war between the Muslim North and Christian South weakened disrupted institutions of governance and political cohesion. Moreover, by July 9, 2011, South Sudan formally seceded from the North after a referendum was held in January of the same year. Not only that, Sudan's President Al-Bashir was further frazzled by the International Criminal Court's order of his arrest in 2009 and 2010 for war crimes in Darfur. In 2019, he was toppled by the military, following protests over the spike in fuel and bread prices in 2018. Like Egypt, Sudan remains under military leadership.

An additional political dynamic that has the potential to influence the mediation process and its outcome is existing alliances. As noted in Chapter 3, Egypt and Sudan have, for a long time, been political allies. This goes back to colonial times when both countries were ruled as one polity by the British. Both were also hydro-hegemons after the 1929 and 1959 treaties accorded them monopoly rights over the Nile waters by apportionment. Both are also tied together through membership to the 22-member Arab League. But this alliance began to shift with the construction of the Renaissance Dam in 2011. Guided by national self-interest on expected gains from the project, Sudan readily announced its support in what signaled a shift in alliance to Addis Ababa. Moreover, the

Khartoum government has had an uneasy relationship with Cairo over the conflicted territory of Halayeb to the northeast of the country. Whether the newly formed alliance with Ethiopia is temporary or permanent, that shift compromises Sudan's neutrality in the mediation role.

Another related political factor is the regime type. Democratic Peace Theory, for example, suggests that democratic countries are unlikely to go to war with other countries that are also democratic. This is because of their presumed shared values, including accountability, transparency, participation, and shared protection of human rights. This theory further assumes that most democratic countries, at least in the industrialized north, are wealthy. They will, therefore, avoid violent confrontations that can lead to the destruction of capital investment, social institutions, infrastructure, and accumulated wealth. Democratic principles thus promote interactions between and among countries with the same principles. If this is true, then the opposite can also be assumed to be true: Authoritarian governments rarely fight each other because they hold the same principles; belligerency, use of force, lack of accountability and containment of citizens' participation and free speech. Therefore, Momar Gaddafi's Libya was less likely to go to war with Egypt's dictator Hosni Mubarak. This hypothesis, however, needs to be empirically studied before it can be endorsed in the discourse of international conflicts.

But the importance of regime type cannot be isolated when attempting to understand the context in which mediation takes place. Interestingly, a certain degree of congruence exists among the three countries involved in the Renaissance Dam conflict. Both Egypt and Sudan share the attributes of authoritarianism. Mubarak (1981–2011) and Al-Bashir of Sudan (1989–2019) were a mirror image of each other; and both ruled for 30 years. Although Ethiopia conducted its elections more regularly once the Marxist regime of Mengistu Haile Mariam toppled in 1991, the heavy-handedness of Prime Minister Zenawi equally passes for authoritarianism. I bring this aspect to the discourse to underscore the importance of how existing norms, rules, and behaviors of those at the top can act as stressors to the negotiation process. Therefore, a mediator must not circumvent such realities but, rather, deconstruct each side to inform the process.

Another determinant in the negotiation environment that will affect the direction of the mediation process or its outcome is the adversarial or cooperative history, between the nations in the conflict. In a situation involving historical hostilities, the mediator should expect a zero-sum outcome as one party tries to outdo the other to increase their benefits at the expense of the other. However, if the relationship between the two states has been characterized by cooperation, then the mediator should reframe the issue and its outcome in terms of a win–win situation. Accordingly, the case between Egypt and Ethiopia should be viewed in terms of the first scenario ("adversarial"), rather than the second ("cooperative"). This is strange to say because, in the recent past (1967–2010), Egypt and Ethiopia both worked in partnership with the rest of the Nile upstream states to build a living water institution, the Nile Basin Initiative. And, presently, both are members of the Eastern Nile Subsidiary Program, a regional body with the head office in Addis Ababa. However, before the formation of that body, Egypt and Sudan were part of a pact against upstream states (i.e., Ethiopia, Kenya, Uganda, Tanzania, Rwanda, Burundi, and the Democratic Republic of Congo) to protect their monopoly water rights granted by the colonial treaties. Those colonial privileges resurfaced and were reasserted by both Egypt and Sudan soon after the Cooperative Framework Agreement was signed by six out of the ten riparian states in 2010. As was expected, Egypt and Sudan reneged and did not sign the pact.

Despite these political realities, it is difficult to imagine a mediation process that is not impacted by those imperatives. For example, on the one hand, Sudan's mediation role in the conflict between 2013 and 2020 may be viewed as a goodwill attempt to bring about a peaceful resolution to the impasse. But on the other hand, the political undercurrents may have influenced the direction of the process. Although the author is not privy to the actual influences on Sudan's ability to strike the deal, which culminated the Agreement on the Declaration of Principles of 2015, an argument is made in favor of recognizing how those factors can infiltrate the process and skew the outcome in a certain direction.

Social Stressors
Another element that can either promote or impede a mediation process is social realities. These include interests, positions, perceptions, customs, values, belief systems, religious principles, and networks (Crump 2011; Kong 2015).

At the core of mediation are interests and positions. In the context of a conflict, interest is what each party wants to gain out of a settlement. Interests can be different or the same for two parties in a conflict. In the case of conflict between Egypt and Ethiopia, the latter's interest is the right is to construct a dam, while Egypt wants to maintain uninterrupted water flow. Position denotes an emotional attachment to an issue; what a party asserts and believes should be the outcome. There is a problem with this. If each party in a conflict holds on to a position without listening to reason, reaching a settlement becomes problematic. This seems to be the case in the conflict between Ethiopia and Egypt. For instance, Ethiopia holds on to the principles of territorial (or sovereignty) rights to justify the construction of the dam. Moreover, it has been unwilling to change its position over the course of the negotiation. Egypt, however, has exhibited some degree of flexibility by yielding to the construction of the dam when it signed the Agreement on the Declaration of Principles in 2015. And as the tension intensified over the ideal period for filling the dam's reservoir, Egypt again loosened its tight position on the amount of water release from 35 to 37 BCM as proposed by the United States mediators. Ethiopia still insisted on 40 BCM.

Perceptions is another stressor to the mediation process. For a long time, as defined by past historical relationships, mistrust existed between Egypt and Ethiopia. In the early 1900s, the British colonial government sought to control access to Ethiopia's Blue Nile. That led to the 1902 and 1906 treaties that denied Ethiopia the right to construct any waterworks unless given the approval of Her Majesty's government. All subsequent attempts by Ethiopia to construct dams on the tributary were further blocked by the Egyptian government. From that time on, Ethiopians developed suspicion, mistrust, and hatred for Egyptians that are difficult to eliminate. As we will shortly find out, mistrust is a static phenomenon that is difficult to erase completely. To address the relevance of the mistrust in conflict negotiations, therefore, the two concepts—trust and mistrust—must first be deconstructed.

Trust is about faith or confidence in either an action or statement expressed by someone else (outgroup). To trust someone else's words or actions is to believe in their truth-bearing characteristics. Because the test of trust is in their reality, it often takes time to verify. By implication, trust builds over time and therefore is "path dependent." This is when the growth of a phenomenon is determined by history and subsequent events. On the opposite side is mistrust. Also path dependent, mistrust contains doubt, suspicion and questionable truth-bearing characteristics. Given the ability to trust or mistrust in order to sway negotiation in a certain direction, it becomes critical to explain how each develops and is maintained over time. But, first, let us explore possible directions that each of the variables dictates.

Trust cultivates interactions among social groups which, in turn, enhance positive relations (Suleiman 2016, p. 23). It further creates an opportunity for cordial engagements for resolving existing conflicts because it naturally reduces wariness. Mistrust, on the other hand, fosters ill-feeling, skepticism and acts as a barrier for meaningful communication between parties in a conflict. The consequence of these feelings is uncertainty about the opponent's intentions. This is exactly the atmosphere that defined Egypt in the aftermath of Ethiopia's declaration to build the Renaissance Dam. Because of the uncertainty about Ethiopia's intentions and the mistrust it created, Egypt invested in risky responses and behaviors. First, it articulated response in terms of military threats backed by the securitization of national existence. Although interceded by bilateral talks, a study and formal mediation, were the second risky action and behavior the launching of military bases in Eritrea and South Sudan took place (Sudan Tribune 2017).

We can now explore how trust and mistrust develop and are sustained over time. In this regard, structural and customary belief systems are reviewed due to their explanatory abilities.

Structural factors may include political institutions that dictate or shape the behaviors of individuals living in a country, polity or any legally defined jurisdiction. Typically, such organized entities have their systems, rules, and procedures that shape how members ought to behave. What to say and how to behave or act are by and large circumscribed by norms and values. To do the opposite, even in a democracy, is to attract derision, however subtle. Examples of these structures include authoritarianism (elitist/oligarchy), democracy (pluralism), monarchism, and fascism. But some structures are social-based and, therefore, influence behaviors, both temporarily and permanently. These may include civil unrest, stereotypes, and secretive tendencies, past actions or even communication styles. (Sztompka 2016; Alon 2016).

Another important but related factor are the customary beliefs associated with ethnicity and religious practices. Some cultures are collectivists and therefore defer to group norms, values and practices. Such societies tend to have values and belief systems subscribed to by the majority. Complimentary to this cultural attribute is "high context" societies. These are countries (e.g., MENA Region, Asia, Africa, and Latin America) in which forms of communication tend to be indirect with certain meanings implied. Often non-verbal communication may portray agreement or disagreement. It is, therefore, difficult for an outsider to easily decipher what is intended. In the low context societies (e.g., Western Europe, USA), communication is more direct and the meanings of what is intended, verbal or written, can easily be understood. Distinguishing between these attributes is important to a mediator because without knowing the subtle differences, resolving a conflict might become more convoluted than it should be.

Although little work has been done to determine the differences that religious belief systems and values play in conflict negotiation, the work done by Jacob Bercovitch and Kadayifci-Orellana (2009) highlight some of the trivialities that cannot be ignored. Using a typology with which to assess the effectiveness of any conflict mediation (i.e., mediator identity, resources, motivation, and strategies), the authors suggest that being aware of either conflicting or convergence in religious texts, narratives or vocabulary, and the way they are being projected in a conflict, can facilitate or hinder the process as well as the outcome. Therefore, for a mediator to be successful, he or she must understand these religious nuances and how they play out in any negotiation.

Knowing the history of trust or mistrust and the specific structural, social, and cultural influences (e.g., regime types, cultural attributes, communication styles in "high" and "low context" societies and religious narratives) might be key to unraveling inhibitions to a mediation involving two or more countries. Egypt and Ethiopia are, for example, different in some of these dimensions including religion and to some extent, communication styles. Although not an authority on this, I would like to suggest that Egypt maintaining a predominantly Arab population, and both collectivist and "high context" culture, will exhibit indirect forms of communication and defer to higher authorities than Ethiopia.

One other attribute of comparison between the two nations is the degree of authoritarianism of either existing political regime or by extension, its entrenchment into extant political cultures of each nation. In the absence of empirical evidence, it is risky to label either country as more authoritarian than the other. However, for the most part, or in its entire political history, Egypt has exhibited militaristic and authoritarian tendencies beginning from the Ottoman Empire that reigned over the country and beyond for over 600 years. Upon independence in 1952 and thereafter, Cairo's political regimes have been led by military leaders starting with Gamal Abdel Nasser, Anwar Sadat, Hosni Mubarak, and General

Abdel Fattah el-Sisi. The only democratically elected leader, Mohamed Morsi, served for one year (2013–2013) before being ousted by General Sisi. Although those leaders have been authoritarian in their styles, it is curious as to how much that practice has infiltrated the Egyptian political culture and psyche. The same authoritarian trend can be said of Ethiopia. Between 1930 and 1974, the country was ruled as a feudal system under Emperor Haile Selassie. He was overthrown by military leader Mengistu Haile Mariam who ruled between 1974 and 1991. His successor, Meles Zenawi (1995–2012) similarly ruled with an "iron fist" until he died in 2012. His successors, Desalegn and Ahmed Abiy currently, have been more democratic in their approach to leadership and thus do not neatly fit into the category of authoritarianism.

Although not all these attributes may or may not have any significant effects in the mediation process or outcome, third-party mediators can learn from them as they work on the modality, structure, and communication with the interlocutors. This is particularly critical in politically charged conflicts. I do, however, recognize that external third-party mediators may not have the luxury of time to be apprised of all these contextual factors. But sparing a bit of time to understand them will go a long way in shaping the process as well as an informed outcome.

Framing the Problem

Much has been narrated about mediation as a process, in the earlier sections. The aim here is to underscore the importance of framing the problem more precisely and fittingly. This is because how a problem is perceived and framed tends to determine the nature and the timing of the solution (Bardwell 1991). This perspective resonates with the literature. Posner (quoted in Bardwell 1991, p. 605), for example, lends credence to this view by asserting that,

> The initial representation of a problem may be the most crucial single factor governing the likelihood of a problem solution. What may appear as a formidable problem in one representation may be solved immediately in another format. A mere change in representation may by itself provide a solution. Whether a problem is solved or not, and how long the solution will take depend a great deal upon the initial representation.

Generally, how a public problem is defined by a government or group of people reflects different values, perceptions, assumptions, and positions. These, in turn, influence the range of options available to resolve a problem and the time frame take out. For example, at the onset of the Ethiopian dam conflict, Egypt defined the problem as a threat to national security. Foreign Minister Sameh Shoukry put it more bluntly as "a threat of potentially existential proportions" (Tadros 2020). From that perspective, citizens easily rallied behind the government's position to reject the dam project because it was perceived as a threat to their survival. Therefore, the desired response was to stop Ethiopia from building the dam. Although the issue was subsequently reduced from non-construction to the filling and operating the dam, the way the problem was defined by Egypt further complicated the resolution of the conflict. Had the problem been defined differently, say "by how much would the dam reduce Egypt's consumption of water and how could the shortfall be addressed," the negotiation would have taken a different direction—with Egypt being forced to turn inwards for introspection. In that case, the government would have, first, engaged water and engineering experts to evaluate the potential impact of the dam and what they could internally do to remedy any future shortfall. This could have also necessitated the call for citizens to develop conservation approaches. With that kind of framing, the mediation would have been more participatory, thereby creating chances for a durable solution. Undoubtedly, an experienced and skilled mediator will first consider how each side defines the problem and then, lead both parties to a more consensual reframing. Otherwise, to negotiate directly how each defines their perceived problem can subject the entire process to positions rather than interests. The result of which is arguments and counterarguments.

Experience

Experience matters because whoever is charged with mediating a conflict can draw from what went right and wrong in previously mediated settlements. The UN Secretary General Koffi Anan was probably successful, particularly in the Kenyan case, where former presidents had failed, although because of his past experience in mediation. He had, for example, mediated the Syrian withdrawal from Lebanon and the conflict in Kosovo but unsuccessful in bringing about peace to the Syrian War and the persistent Israeli–Palestinian conflict. Obviously, these, and more, of his interventions served as lessons to draw from to fix Kenya's political impasse in 2008. How, then, did Sudan measure up to the experience requirement?

Sudan's President had, in mid-2018, brokered a peace deal between South Sudan's civil leader President Salva Kiir on one side and opposition leader Riek Machar on the other. Although the peace deal was breached within hours after the signing ceremony, al-Bashir had acquired experience and knew what went well, what went wrong and why. Despite the short-lived deal, al-Bashir succeeded because he had leverage as the former president of Sudan before it split into Sudan and South Sudan. Second, his success was partly due to his commitment to ensuring gains for his country. For one, peace in South Sudan promised to allow the resumption of oil production that was desperately needed to stabilize Sudan's economy. Successful mediation could also boost his self-image as a dealmaker. In fact, Sudan had been blacklisted in 1997 as a sponsor of terrorism by the United States (Al-Karib and Hassan 2019). Therefore, by taking up the mediation role Sudan stood a better chance of being removed from that list by the Trump administration.

Pragmatic Strategies

The mediator's ability to employ pragmatic, but flexible, strategies during the mediation process is critical to achieving the desired outcome. Although strategies will vary from conflict to conflict and from context to context, the following, as summarized in Table 6.2, are some that I believe are commonly applied. It ought to be noted that because conflicts vary in nature, the mediator must choose wisely when deciding which approach to implement. Though the merits of each are discussed,

Table 6.2 Pragmatic mediation strategies

Strategy	*Description*
Distributive	A rational process: parties focus on distributive self-gain, preferences; competitiveness; positioning
Elicited/integrative	Reconcile different interests. Incorporate cultural factors
Transformational	Beyond immediate outcome

Adopted from: Huang and Bedford (2009), Gelfand et al. (2002) Adair and Brett (2005), Parker (2000) and Lederach (1995); with permission an attempt is made to rationalize those specific to the Egypt–Ethiopia conflict. The limitations are explicated as well.

Distributive Strategy

Ideally, a distributive strategy is employed by mediators when a resource being claimed by parties to a conflict is fixed in amount. A good example is the waters of the Nile for which Egypt and Ethiopia are competing. The interests in the amount and value being claimed are the same, except that the interests are mutually exclusive. For example, Egypt claims a specific amount of water but rejects any action by Ethiopia that will reduce it. On the other hand, Ethiopia is trying to claim and add value to its water usage—which in the view of Egypt, will reduce the amount it has historically received. Given this rivalry in use, both parties take contradictory positions. That is why, in this type of situation, one party gains and the other loses. Hence, the ideal approach for the mediator is to focus on concessions and compromises.

Let us examine the contentious reservoir filling period as the first example. Ideally, the mediator should initially push for what each party is willing to accept (i.e., concession). For instance, in its proposed settlement to the conflict held in Washington D.C. between November 2019 and February 2020, the United States used this tactic. They first allowed the interlocutors to state what they could accept. Egypt considered a water release of 40 BCM as acceptable, while Ethiopia preferred a release of 35 BCM during the initial stages of filling. Based on this, the American mediators recommended a mid-point of 37 BCM. That meant each party had to make some concessions. At the final meeting held in the last week of February 2020, Ethiopia rejected that "zone of agreement," not because of what it deemed as duress, but rather what it considered as a zero-sum deal, with Egypt as the winner, and Ethiopia the loser.

Elicited/Integrative

In this type of approach, the aim is to solve the sticky issues so that each party meets its desired goal or outcome. Since there is no specific item to be distributed, the mediator should focus on how each interest is to be satisfied. The appropriate approach is to have in place a set of procedures that will guide the team in developing alternative options to solve the problem. This approach works best where there is an ongoing partnership (Rinehart and Page 1992). Technically, the Elicited approach developed by Lederach (1995) is no different from the Integrative approach. Like the latter, it welcomes the knowledge that the parties bring to the negotiation table. This can include cultural factors that might enhance understanding and improve the negotiation mechanics, process and outcome. It, thus, underscores the importance of appreciating cultural differences and how they can translate to opportunities. It is not clear from published literature and reports whether the United States negotiators were comprehensively apprised of Egyptian and Ethiopian cultural nuances and how those factors inform the process or even the expected outcome.

Transformational Strategy

This approach is based on the idea that humans, as social animals, interact variously. That form of interaction that individuals or groups choose can either promote peaceful coexistence or conflictual relationships. As briefly discussed in Chapter 3, understanding how people communicate across cultures can facilitate conflict resolution between the two warring nations. Also cited were rhetorical phrases by Egyptian and Ethiopian leaders, some of which were utterly provocative. To mediate that kind of relational conflict, foremost, the mediator must listen to and observe forms of communication (written and verbal) employed by the interlocutors. Second, it is critical to perform a SWOT analysis (Strengths, Weaknesses, Opportunities, and Threats). Although the analysis of all necessary attributes may not be necessary because conflicts differ in nature, dimension and context, the mediator may find it useful to have each team identify their strengths and weaknesses. This activity will help them become more realistic about what is possible and what is not. Next, the mediator should lead the negotiation team to explore what opportunities exist to improve communication that empowers each party. With that empowerment, the parties will begin to take control of the process. Any attempt at coercion should be avoided because it might degenerate into abrasive contestations. Overall, the advantage of this approach is that it focuses not only on the desired outcome, but also on improved relations, in the present and the future. Additionally, for mediators, this approach may be ideal in situations where two conflictual parties have nothing tangible to fight over except bad relations brought about by communication styles.

Duress-Free Mediation

A successful mediation that meets desired outcomes for each party is one in which the contending parties freely examine each other's positions and interests, debate alternative solutions as well their merits versus demerits and able to reach a mutually desirable agreement. But, for an agreement to last, the mediator must desist from employing duress as a tactic to reach a quick agreement. This brings into question the mediation style led by the United States government team to resolve the Egypt–Ethiopia Renaissance Dam impasse. Short of the final meeting in which the signing of an agreement was expected, Ethiopian officials accused the United States mediators of undiplomatic language (i.e., "heavy-handedness") to try to force them into signing the agreement. Assuming the accusation is true, it seems reasonable to suggest that the tendency to employ such a tactic is only common in situations when the mediator has limited time for the activity. This is a dangerous approach because it can lead to the collapse of the process as the mediation of the Renaissance Dam in Washington D.C. clearly illustrates. Mediators should also be aware that it is unrealistic to presume that a conflict that has taken close to ten years or more to grow, can be mediated in four consecutive meetings, as was the case in the United States mediation of the Renaissance Dam. Given that mediators also gain some prestige when they successfully bring about a negotiated settlement, it is worthwhile to dedicate as much time as possible to the process.

Outcomes That Last

Prospect Theory reminds us that parties enter negotiation (or decision-making) driven by the perceived outcome. As we have learned about the contest over the Renaissance Dam, Cairo focused on protecting its perceived loss, while Addis Ababa was fixated on gains as well as minimizing losses after completing the $4.6 billion infrastructure. Each party is risk-averse and, therefore, must stick to its position with an eye on the price, the outcome. The theory also reminds us that in conflict situations, each party tends to overvalue what they have, which leads them to fall into a state of inertia—which makes reaching outcomes strenuous to the mediator. Therefore, to reach an agreement, regardless of how long it takes, justifies the process.

Despite the push and pull approach, and the reluctance by each party to take a risk in order to reach a mutually beneficial agreement, by June 2020 the three countries—Egypt, Ethiopia, and Sudan—continued with virtual meetings that brought them close to an agreement. On June 26, for example, the three leaders, General Sisi of Ethiopia, Abiy Ahmed of Ethiopia, and Abdalla Hamdok of Sudan, agreed to shift the mediation from the United States government to the African Union to resolve the remaining issues (UN News 2020). Three days later (June 29), a high-ranking UN official briefed the Security Council on the need for the three countries to resolve their problems amicably. This was in response to Egypt's request for intervention because, in their view, the issue threatened regional stability and international security, if not resolved. Another expected outcome, but one which is not agreed on yet, is how to deal with the filling during future droughts. Certainly, to achieve these desired outcomes, it will require that each party accept some risks and minor gains.

COMPLIANCE

Once the parties in conflict reach an agreement, preferably, the signing of it should make it binding. The goal is to ensure that the signatories do not violate any of the legal provisions but use it as a guide to action. The challenge is compliance. In the anarchic international system, with no world government except for the United Nations, which is a voluntary organization, agreements are susceptible to violations. To avoid such breaches, it is suggested that treaties are accompanied by ad hoc or standing committees, transnational institutions, commissions or such similar institutions. The susceptibility of the Declaration of Principles to defection by Ethiopia can, to some extent, be attributed to the absence of such a body. Therefore, it is important to have one that can follow-up, monitor activities and arrange for future discussions whenever necessary.

CLIENT SATISFACTION

Reaching an outcome is one thing, while reaching an outcome that satisfies both parties is another. That is where the principle of Pareto Improvement comes into play. This principle suggests that a distributive action (or decision) should be taken if, and only if, it improves the welfare of an individual (or group) without reducing that utility being enjoyed by another group. Hence, the outcome of the Renaissance mediation should allow Ethiopia to enjoy benefits from the Blue Nile without reducing the benefits presently enjoyed by Egypt. As we have noticed in the narratives by chapter, striking a deal that meets this condition is no easy task. The idea is for Egypt to accept an action by Ethiopia that minimizes its losses, while at the same time enabling Ethiopia to acquire some gains. This is the best of possible scenarios.

Summary

The effectiveness of third-party mediation is shaped primarily by four factors: (a) the choice of the mediator (his origin, neutrality, and affiliation as a hedge against bias, (b) competencies (knowledge of the negotiating context, history of bilateral relations, actors past behaviors, and experienced negotiators) (c) personal influence and (d) the degree of commitment to the process. Personal influence should be employed with caution because it can derail the process if, for example, the mediator draws on their authority to force an outcome in a certain direction. Though duress may be necessary for certain mediation situations, it sure didn't work to resolve the Egypt-Ethiopia water conflict.

References

Adair, W. L., and J. M. Brett. 2005. "The Negotiation Dance: Time, Culture, and Behavioral Sequences in Negotiation." *Organization Science* 16:33–51.

Al-Karib, Hala, and Hassan, El-Sadig. 2019. "Sudan's New Government Can't Succeed If It Remains on the U.S. Blacklist." FP News, December 9.

Alon, Ilai. 2016. "Some Comments on Language as a Barrier for Trust in Arabic-Speaking Islam." In *The Role of Trust in Conflict Resolution*, 83–115. https://doi.org/10.1007/978-3-319-43355-4_6. January.

Bardwell, Lisa V. 1991. "Problem-Framing: A Perspective on Environmental Problem Solving." *Environmental Management* 15(September):603–612.

Bercovitch, Jacob, and S. A. Kadayifci-Orellana. 2009. "Religion and Mediation: The Role of Faith-Based Actors in International Conflict Resolution." *International Negotiations* 14(2009):175–204.

Hoeffler, Anke. 2014–03. "Can Intervention Secure the Peace?" *International Area Studies Review* 17(1):75–94.

Crump, Larry. 2009. "Linkage Theory and the Global-Multilevel System: Multilateral, Regional, and Bilateral Trade Negotiations. *SSRN Electronic Journal*. June. https://doi.org/10.2139/ssrn.1484792.

Crump, Larry. 2011. "Negotiation Process and Negotiation Context." *International Negotiation* 16(2):197–227.
Gelfand, Michele J., Marianne Higgins, Lisa H. Nishii, Jana L. Raver, Dominguez Alexandria, Fumio Murakami, Susumu Yamaguchi, and Midori Toyama. 2002. "Culture and Egocentric Perceptions of Fairness in Conflict and Negotiation." *Journal of Applied Psychology* 87(5):833–845.
Hofstede, Geert. 1981. *Culture's Consequences: International Differences in Work-Related Values*. Beverly Hills: Sage.
Huang, Yi-Hui, and Olwen Bedford. 2009. "The Role of Cross-Cultural Factors in Integrative Conflict Resolution and Crisis Communication: The Hainan Incident." *American Behavioral Scientist* 53. November 30.
Kadayifci-Orllana. 2009. *Ethno-Religious Conflicts: Exploring the Role of Religion in Conflict Resolution*. https://doi.org/10.4135/9780857024701.n14. January.
Kong, Dejun, T. 2015. "Narcissists' Negative Perception of Their Counterparts' Competence and Benevolence and Their Reduced Trust in a Negotiation." *Personality and Industrial Differences* 74:196–201.
Lederach, John Paul. 1995. *Preparing for Peace: Conflict Transformation Across Culture*. Syracuse: Syracuse University Press.
Loures, F., Rocha, and Alistair Rieu-Clarke. *The UN Watercourses Convention in Force: Strengthening International Law for Transboundary Water Management*. London and New York: Routledge.
Parker, Donna. 2000. "Cross-Cultural Considerations in Mediation." ProQuest Dissertation Publishing, 2000. California State University, Dominguez Hills.
Rinehart, Lloyd M., and Thomas J. Page. 1992. "The Development and Test of a Model of Transaction Negotiation." *Journal of Marketing* 56(4):18. October.
Sandu, Antonio. 2013. "Communicative Action and Philosophical Practice." *Romanian Journal for Multidimensional Education / Revista Romaneasca pentru Educatie Multidimensionala* 6(1):39–66, 28. June 14.
Sudan Tribune. 2017. "Egypt to establish military base in Eritrea." Retrieved from www.middleeastobserver.org/2017/04/18/egypt-to-establish-military-base-in-eritrea. February 15, 2021.
Suleiman, Ramzi. 2016. "Effects of Expectations, Type of Relationship, and Prior Injustice on Trust Honoring: A Strategic-Experimental Approach." In *Role of Trust in Conflict Resolution: The Israeli-Palestinian Case and Beyond*, edited by Ilai Alon and Daniel Bar-Tal, 23. Gewerbestrasse, Switzerland: Springer Nature.
Sztompka, P. 2016. "Two Theoretical Approaches to Trust; Their Implications for the Resolution of Intergroup Conflict." In *The Role of Trust in Conflict Resolution: The Israeli-Palestinian Case and Beyond*, edited by I. Alon and D. Bar-Tal, 15–21. Springer International Publishing AG. https://doi.org/10.1007/978-3-319-43355-4_2.

Tadros, Amjad. 2020. "Ethiopia Filling Mega-Dam that Egypt Calls an "Existential" Threat." CBS News, July 17.
UN News. 2020. "UN Officials Welcome Court's Guilty Verdict in Charles Taylor Trial." Retrieved from https://news.un.org/en/story/2012/04/409542-un-officials-welcome-courts-guilty-verdict-charles-taylor-trial.   October 30.

CHAPTER 7

Bilateral Agreements and Litigations

INTRODUCTION

Bilateral agreements (or treaties) are, by far, the most popular and resilient mechanism for resolving international water conflicts. Of the 145 water-related treaties that govern the 263 international river basins, 86% (124) are bilateral and only 14% (21) are multilateral (Abukhater and Sanders 2010). This is proof of the efficacy of bilateral agreements, which can foster peace and closer interactions between two contending co-riparian states. This, in turn, translates into the better management of shared water resources. Bilateral treaties are also preferred over multilateral compacts because the fewer the actors in a conflict, the fewer the contending interests and positions to deal with. Thus, the creation of a transboundary water agreement is not only desirable but a more practical response to the spike in international water rights conflicts due to population pressure and attendant economic growth. These factors, combined with the envisaged reduction in precipitation in the MENA region and parts of the Nile Basin due to climate change, further justify the preference for bilateral agreements. Even more compelling for bilateral agreements, is the weakness of international water laws, conventions, and protocols to address such conflicts. This, however, does not discount their importance in providing guidance to shared water use and fostering cooperation.

Despite the popularity of bilateral treaties, certain water conflicts involving two co-riparian states can prove difficult to resolve, due to

© The Author(s), under exclusive license to Springer Nature Switzerland AG 2021
S. H. Okoth, *The MENA Powers and the Nile Basin Initiative*, https://doi.org/10.1007/978-3-030-83981-9_7

the complexities surrounding sharing rights. For example, the history of hatred and mistrust, opposing political cultures, extant political regimes, the personalities of the primary actors involved in the conflict and the hydrological and geographical factors can militate against negotiated settlements. Moreover, the pressure to negotiate a quick settlement for the impasse can lead to "superficial" agreements that lack depth and attention to relevant details. Such superficial agreements mirror what Kenya's President Uhuru Kenyatta has called "ceasefire agreements" when referring to Kenya's 2010 Constitution. Broadly speaking, such agreements are created to evade conflict and potential strife, but not to eliminate the root cause. Moreover, such quick-fix approaches are not resilient and, therefore, do not prevent the conflict from reoccurring. Another problem with the rush to find negotiated settlements is the failure to appreciate the reality that a conflict that has taken years or generations to grow cannot be resolved in 4–10 days, no matter how experienced and knowledgeable the deal makers are. This suggests that any mediator who agrees to engage in the activity should set aside as much time as possible with an eye on a win–win outcome, rather than timing the process. In fact, it is presumptuous for the mediator to measure both his competency and the negotiated settlement in terms of the time spent or period taken in the process.

As will be explained shortly, striking a bilateral deal between Egypt and Ethiopia is justified because it has the potential to unleash a legal and binding framework that protects the water rights of each state. Additionally, collaboration on social, economic, and political affairs is easier to foster and implement in bilateral agreements because of the limited number of players involved.

In cases in which bilateral agreements cannot be reached, either through third-party mediation or by diplomatic efforts, the next best option is to turn to the courts for arbitration. Although a viable approach and acceptable international practice, litigating shared water conflicts should be considered only as the last resort because, based on experience, the international court system, primarily the International Court of Justice (ICJ), receives fewer such cases than those related to human rights violations. Moreover, the court as the only international arbiter can be overwhelmed, thereby lengthening the period of settling such disputes. Additional reasons why it is a viable option are discussed further in the chapter.

Bilateral Treaties

Riparian states engaged in shared international water conflicts should, at best, aim at reaching agreements that yield long-term cooperation. This is because treaties provide several benefits, including the structure to facilitate interactions, the reduction of uncertainties and tensions, the possibility to improve access to and exchange of information (Abbott and Snidal 1998) and the mechanisms to monitor and detect defectors. Violators can easily be held accountable through such legal pacts. Thus, the overall benefits of bilateral treaties and agreements include improved cooperation in the management and sharing of an international water system. Not only that, but bilateral treaties enable the ease of negotiating conflicts by reverting to the enduring legal framework to evaluate defections and addressing issues as they emerge. However, whether there is a conflict or not, co-riparian states should create a formal agreement (or treaty) to manage a shared water system and to provide something legal to fall back on should conflicts emerge or reemerge.

Although the establishment of a formal bilateral agreement is necessary, even more critical is its effectiveness. Experts concur that the effectiveness of an international water treaty is largely shaped by its design (Mitchell and Zawahri 2015). Preferably, a well-designed bilateral (water) treaty should possess the following attributes: an institution (set of rules and procedures that are binding; or an intergovernmental river basin organization), conflict resolution procedures, information exchange, monitoring, enforcement, water allocation, clarity, and flexibility. This is not to say that all these attributes have equal weight in the ability to promote cooperation and other benefits. In fact, each treaty design has different effects that also vary by degree (Mitchell and Zawahri 2015).

Although a bilateral treaty can be reached without any existing formal river basin organization, the ideal approach is to specify some of the rules and procedures based on agreed-upon international principles. When Sudan, for example, mediated the conflict between Egypt and Ethiopia, which produced the 2015 Agreement on the Declaration of Principles, specific rules and procedures were included in the document. In fact, by signing the document, it was hoped that each party would be legally bound by its contents. But, as it turned out years later, Ethiopia stood accused of flouting those rules by proceeding with its plan to fill the dam before formal studies were carried out. The perceived defection by Ethiopia can be attributed partly to the absence of a body that ensures adherence to the joint principles. It is in this light that I argue in favor of a special body or committee (permanent or *ad hoc*) to be set up, follow up, coordinate, and implement the provisions of an international water agreement. Such a body can facilitate further interaction, monitor defections, and develop activities that promote long-term cooperation. Unfortunately, the national technical or tripartite committee that was set up lacked the mandate to ensure that all the provisions of the Declaration of Principles were followed. In fact, it seems reasonable to suggest that the principles could be more effective if translated into specific rules and procedures. Otherwise, principles are merely broad propositions aimed at guiding behavior and, hence, are difficult to execute.

Although, presently, it is difficult to imagine such a permanent body in the absence of a formal agreement between the two countries, with the help of interested MENA Powers, the African Union and the Nile Basin Initiative, Egypt and Ethiopia should aim for a sub-basin formal agreement (or a reconstituted 2015 Agreement on the Declaration of Principles) and a new body to oversee its implementation. The Eastern Nile Subsidiary Program (ENSAP), as presently constituted, cannot play that role because it lacks the authority to independently make binding policy decisions about Nile water sharing mechanisms at the sub-basin level. As I hope to demonstrate in Chapter 8, long-term cooperation is only possible once the Nile Basin is formally divided into two hydro-jurisdictions, the upper Nile Basin and lower Nile Basin. Each must possess the authority to develop and implement water use and management policies that are consistent with wider basin rules and international water laws.

Another important element for a water treaty is the inclusion of conflict resolution procedures. To a large extent, a treaty's durability depends on its ability to restrain conflicts by managing issues as they appear. The Nile Basin countries, for example, enunciated specific dispute resolution procedures in the 2010 Cooperative Framework Agreement (CFA). In March 2015, Egypt, Sudan, and Ethiopia incorporated such a mechanism in the Agreement on the Declaration of Principles (DoPs) as Article X stipulates below.

> The Three countries will settle disputes, arising out of the interpretation or implementation of this agreement, amicably through consultation or negotiation in accordance with the principle of good faith. If the Parties are unable to resolve the dispute through consultation or negotiation, they

may jointly request for conciliation, mediation or refer the matter for the consideration of the Heads of State/Head of Government. (Declaration of Principles 2015, p. 5)

The 2015 Declaration stipulates three distinct mechanisms—negotiations (or consultation), mediation, and referral to the heads of state. The countries in a dispute must, first, consult with each other by negotiating the best way forward. If that does not work, then the case is open for mediation by preferably a neutral third-party. This is the process that Egypt and Ethiopia followed in their search for a resolution to the Renaissance Dam conflict. As a process, mediation can take a long period depending on the complexity of the issue and, of course, other extraneous factors, as well as competencies of the mediator. The two countries in the conflict must also be genuine and committed to the search for resolution. Only after these mechanisms have been exhausted, can the issue be referred to the heads of states.

Another attribute to a well-designed bilateral agreement is the provision for an exchange of information about hydrology, meteorology, and physical conditions that influence regular water flow or changes to the pattern. This is particularly important for the downstream states to avoid any uncertainties or even suspicion. Egypt, for example, developed suspicion towards Ethiopia's waterworks because it lacked the information with which to evaluate the potential effects of the dam. It was after the exchange of accusations and face-to-face negotiations that Ethiopia agreed to the formation of a study conducted by the International Panel of Experts between 2012 and 2013. The study heavily focused on the physical elements of the dam, hydrology and, to some extent the potential effects downstream, Egypt was able to reevaluate its position and how to proceed with the negotiation. Without the information that was gathered, it would not have been possible, for example, for Egypt to finally narrow its demand to the reservoir filling and dam operation. Hitherto, Cairo focused on the rejection of water works.

Sudan's entry into the mediation role was undoubtedly made easier with the information that came out of the study. Although Egypt's push for a more comprehensive study was never achieved by the time this book was written (2020), it seems much of the tension that remained could have been resolved had Ethiopia agreed to a formal structure for the collection and sharing of information about the dam, hydrology, and other meteorological conditions. That kind of information was essential for Egypt to be able to assess the approximate impacts of the reservoir filling and future dam operations. Hopefully, this could have changed with the signing of the Agreement on the Declaration of Principles in 2015. However, as stated in Article VII of that Agreement, the three countries (Egypt, Ethiopia, and Sudan) agreed to a limited form of information sharing as the following text illustrates: "Egypt, Ethiopia and Sudan shall provide data and information needed for the conduct of the TNC joint studies in good faith and in a timely manner" (Declaration of Principles 2015, p. 4). Note that the information was needed to enable the TNC to conduct joint studies and not as an established process for long-term data collection and dissemination.

The lack of information exchange increases tensions and, consequently, reduces the ability of the parties to successfully implement the provisions as a mandated treaty. A classic example is the difficulty experienced by Israel and Jordan when implementing the 1994 Peace Treaty, regarding Jordan's water withdrawal from the Sea of Galilea. That was because the treaty did not include provisions for water sharing (Mitchell and Zawahri 2015). In contrast, it is the Indus Water Treaty of 1960 that successfully stifled potential conflicts by way of institutionalized exchange of information between Pakistan and India. With access to that kind of information, the downstream states can hedge against potential floods or droughts. Similarly, with that kind of evidence, the downstream riparian can make informed decisions, including water conservation strategies, rather than putting the blame entirely on the upstream riparian.

Despite the differences in water policy environments, and in the way they influence information possibilities, these two international experiences suggest the indispensability of an institutionalized information and data exchange system by a water treaty. It is in the same vein that the establishment of the Hydromet Project in 1967, solely created for the exchange of information between the upper and lower Nile basin countries, can be perceived. Undoubtedly, the actual cooperation in the exchange of such information helps subdue any tensions for several years. Hence, by default, any future agreement signed between Egypt and Ethiopia, or between other riparian states, should at least include this imperative.

These advantages, however, do not discount the sensitivity with which governments guard hydrological data for the sake of state security (Tir and Stinnett 2011). To avoid this problem associated with how the information might be used by another riparian state, co-riparians should defer such a task to an existing intergovernmental organization, such as the Nile Basin Initiative or Eastern Nile Subsidiary Action Program. This is likely to elicit less or no suspicion, because its members are drawn from respective riparian states. Moreover, this approach ensures accountability and ease of violation detections.

Water agreements should also include provisions for monitoring. This activity reminds us of the famed Russian proverb: "doveryai, no proveryai"—meaning "trust but verify." By implication, a signed treaty can be trusted upon signing, but must be regularly monitored to verify compliance. As such, there are several advantages of including monitoring provisions in a treaty. First, it allows early detection of any cheating or defections by a member state. This is achieved by inspection from a designated team or by an intergovernmental institution representing all co-riparians. It also presents the opportunity to collect information to assess compliance or non-compliance. Without this approach, breaches can occur without being noticed. For example, five years after signing the Agreement on the Declaration of Principles of 2015, Ethiopia was accused by Egypt of not adhering to the Principle number five which states that the three countries, including Sudan, will have to use the outcome of joint studies to establish rules and guidelines for the first filling of the dam. Ethiopia's apparent resistance to this procedural requirement was the reason tensions spiked and, subsequently, reached the doorsteps of America's White House for mediation, though it ended in failure.

Second, monitoring not only lessens chances of violations but reassures co-riparians of the degree to which each member complies with specific treaty provisions (Tir and Stinnett 2011). The third advantage lies in the information provided to the downstream states. Such information can be used to hedge against uncertainties such as changing climatic patterns. It is, therefore, not surprising that the American mediators attempted to disentangle the measures that Ethiopia should have taken to ensure continuous water flow during future periods of drought and in dry seasons. Undoubtedly, Egypt's insistence on the latter must be viewed as rational and necessary, given its dependence on the Blue Nile waters, drains into the Ethiopian highlands.

Ethiopia, located in the northeastern corner of Africa, is subject to weather variations. For example, between 1950 and 1984, up to 12 droughts have been observed ("USAID" 2015). The two most serious droughts occurred between 1973–74 and 1984. The result was combined deaths of about 1.2 million people—though government policies bore the brunt of those deaths, especially for those that occurred in the 1970s. The fourth rationale for monitoring lies in its ability to regulate the behavior of potential violators to treaty provisions. Based on this logic, timed monitoring of Ethiopia's dam project and plans for filling the reservoir could have minimized the tensions and, at the same time, provided a timely opportunity to address the problem.

As Tir and Stinnett (2011) have noted, the challenge facing the implementation of monitoring provisions of an international water treaty is the sensitivity by which such data is held and treated by governments. At times, it seems as if data and information on international rivers are so sacrosanct that to share it with another country is tantamount to an infringement of national security apparatus. That is why Tim and Stinnett (2011) suggest giving the responsibility of monitoring treaty provisions to an intergovernmental (or international) body. For example, within the Nile Basin, that responsibility could be left to either the Nile Basin Initiative Secretariat based in Uganda or the Eastern Nile Subsidiary Program (ENSAP) based in Addis Ababa. Unfortunately, the agreement (The Declaration of Principles of 2015) signed between the two warring states, and co-signed by Sudan, failed to specify any monitoring provisions. Rather, it was implied in Principle V of the Agreement that a coordination mechanism would be formed to foster cooperation.

Despite being a necessary instrument to either deter or lessen potential breaches, enforcement remains an indispensable element to any treaty's survival. Therefore, had monitoring mechanisms and enforcement been instituted by the 2015 Declaration of Principles, Ethiopia's intentions would have become more apparent, which would thereby attract prompt attention and response. But there is another problem. Treaties or formal agreements can only have legal force once they are ratified by respective legislative bodies of signatory states. In the absence of this, enforcement, or even monitoring, mechanisms will have little meaning, respect, or adherence.

Accordingly, the only treaty to which Egypt, Sudan and Ethiopia are all signatories is the Agreement on the Declaration of Principles. Procedurally, according to internal rules, once an agreement involving multiple countries has been signed by the relevant state representatives, the next step is for each country's legislative body (e.g., Parliament or Congress), to formally debate and endorse the accord before being sent to higher authorities such prime minister or president for signing. Articles 10 and

18 of the Vienna Convention on the Law of Treaties of 1969 clarifies this process as follows:

> Ratification defines the international act whereby a state indicates its consent to be bound to a treaty if the parties intended to show their consent by such an act. In the case of bilateral treaties, ratification is usually accomplished by exchanging the requisite instruments, while in the case of multilateral treaties the usual procedure is for the depositary to collect the ratifications of all states, keeping all parties informed of the situation. The institution of ratification grants states the necessary timeframe to seek the required approval for the treaty on the domestic level and to enact the necessary legislation to give domestic effect to that treaty. (ask.un.org/faq/14594)

In view of the foregoing, the provisions of a treaty involving two or more countries are, therefore, easier to enforce upon ratification. It is also on this basis that the Declaration of Principles signed between Egypt, Ethiopia, and Sudan is to be judged. It was not a treaty, per se, but rather a set of principles that serve to guide a future treaty. Hence, the Declaration could not have been held to the same standards as a ratified treaty.

SUMMARY

A treaty that fails to specify monitoring and enforcement procedures cannot be expected to survive the test of time. In the present world in which political, economic, and social forces are constantly changing, a standing compact can easily be destabilized or even forced to reinstitute. Political and economic forces, for example, led to the dismantling and renegotiation of the 25-year-old North America Free Trade Agreement (NAFTA). Subsequently, in 2018, the compact was reinstituted into the United States–Mexico–Canada Agreement (USMCA). It is also noted that even in multilateral basin settings, bilateral treaties are preferred because they are manageable and encourage closer cooperation. In 1960, for example, five countries (Argentina, Uruguay, Paraguay, Brazil, and Bolivia) that share the La Plata River acceded to the formation of additional bilateral treaties to promote deeper cooperation and development (Zawahri and Mitchell 2011). On another end, South Africa and Botswana entered several such treaties regarding the use of the upper basin of the Limpopo River. The agreement to do so took place before the creation of the Limpopo River Commission.

It should be further noted that the existence of bilateral treaties, alongside multilateral ones, do not weaken existing cooperation among members of the larger body, but rather strengthen joint water use and management. Additionally, the reason why a bilateral treaty is more appealing is its resiliency. It is easier for two actors to regroup in order to address any emerging issues that threaten the status quo than it is for the multimember basins. Likewise, it is much simpler to coordinate or assign responsibilities over shared water management with this kind of legal arrangement. As Zawahri and Mitchell add, the most powerful members of the riparian group often will prefer bilateral agreements over multilateral ones, as the former stands a better chance of gains (2011). Although this does not holistically explain why Egypt refused to sign the 2010 Cooperative Agreement, Miriam Lowi (1993) suggests that location dictates and serves as a predictor of whether an agreement will be signed or not. When the most powerful riparian is in the downstream (as for Egypt), most likely it will refrain from signing the treaty unless it promises benefits. This is also true when the upstream state is a hegemon; it will avoid an agreement that might deny them the right of use the shared water resource. Turkey, for example, has been reluctant to enter into any such agreement with Syria and Iraq regarding the Tigris and Euphrates Rivers.

So, in essence, the only downside to bilateral treaties is how the location factor can be used by the riparian hegemon to either enter into an agreement or not.

LITIGATION

Currently, the main body through which international water conflicts are formally litigated is the International Court of Justice (ICJ). The ICJ, based in The Hague, Netherlands, was created by the United Nations in 1945 and started operations in 1946. Despite its mandate and the role, it has in resolving wide-ranging international and serious domestic conflicts, the court remains a mechanism of last resort. This is because nations prefer to negotiate directly with each other and, occasionally, choose to engage international mediators instead of the court. These direct negotiations take the form of ministerial meetings, diplomatic negotiations and engagements by the heads of state. Experience shows that only when these efforts failed, do riparian nations in conflict turn to the court. Despite this significant role, the number of international water conflicts arbitrated or adjudicated by the court is outweighed by those directly negotiated with the affected parties or with the help of independent third-party mediators. This claim is corroborated by the actual number of cases litigated by the court (see Table 7.1). Thus, the court's active role in mediating international water disputes must be judged by (a) the number of cases brought before the judges and (b) the number successfully arbitrated with little to no recurrence of the settled dispute.

With respect to the number arbitrated, the court receives several non-water-related cases, some of which are of greater urgency and importance. Like any other top judicial system anywhere in the world, the ICJ is bound to address cases prioritized by the gravity presented to the 15-judge bench. Between 1986 and 2016, for example, there were nine international water-related cases that the court produce legal opinions (International Water Law Project 2020). Table 7.1 lists those cases and identifies one (The Silala River case between Bolivia and Chile) that is

Table 7.1 International water cases adjudicated by ICJ, 1987–2016

River/basin	Countries involved	Period/judgment
Silala (*status and use*)	Chile v. Bolivia	2016–No judgment
San Juan River (*road construction*)	Nicaragua v. Costa Rica	2011–2015 (Yes)
San Juan River (*dredging/territory*)	Costa Rica v. Nicaragua	2010–2015 (Yes)
River Uruguay (*Pulp Mills/notification*)	Argentina v. Uruguay	2006–2010 (Yes)
San Juan River (*Navigation/Visas/fees*)	Costa Rica v. Nicaragua	2005–2009 (Yes)
Niger River (*Boundary/Ownership*)	Benin v. Niger	2002–2005 (Yes)
Chober River (*Kasikili/Sedudu Island border*)	Botswana v. Namibia	1996–1999 (Yes)
Danube River (*Gabcikovo-Nagymaros*)	Hungary v. Slovakia	1994–1997 (Yes)
Gulf of Fonseca (*Land, border, Island*)	Honduras v. El Salvado	1986–1990/2003 (Yes)

Developed from International Water Law Project Website
Source http://www.internationalwaterla.org/cases/icj.html; 9/12/2020

still pending. Equally, the significance is the degree of success by the court when resolving such cases. As the table illustrates, the court has successfully mediated eight of the nine cases brought before it.

Although the number presented and resolved are, by any standard, less than one would expect of the major global arbiter of disputes, its degree of success provides an alternative approach to mediating water conflicts, such as the one between Egypt and Ethiopia.

Let's consider one case arbitrated by the court, which testified to the efficacy (in terms of ability and speed) of the litigation approach, and from which Egypt and Ethiopia can learn, is that of the Gabcikovo-Nagymaros project involving Hungary and Slovakia. The two countries were embroiled in a dispute over the Gabcikovo power project, after Hungary quit a formal partnership established through a 1977 treaty. Under that treaty, the two countries were to construct joint hydroelectric power dams, enhance navigation and control floods. Unfortunately, after the initiatives began, the Nagymaros Dam project, located in the south, had to be abandoned by Hungary in 1989 due to pressure by environmental groups, primarily The Danube Circle (Furst, n.d.). In 1992, Slovakia continued with the construction of the Gabcikovo Dam by diverting and extracting water from the riverbed. Hungary later accused Slovakia's continuation of the project as harmful to its water needs. Although the nature of potential harm varied by successive political regimes and positions taken by interest groups, Slovakia believed the dam helped reduce the devastating annual floods in Hungary. They further demanded compensation by Hungary for the expenses already incurred in the Nagymaros project. Unable to strike a bilateral agreement, the two countries agreed to take the case to the International Court of Justice. In presenting the case, Hungary claimed that the dam had enabled Slovakia to apportion between 80 and 90% of the water to themselves, an action it asked the court to stop (International Water Law Project 2020). After lengthy deliberations, the court ruled in favor of Slovakia's dam's completion and ordered the two nations reestablish cooperation on the remaining portion of the project. In 2017, the case came to an end after the two countries formalized the closure, which the court affirmed in writing ("Overview of the Case" 2020).

Although some outlier disputes still linger between the two nations, the involvement by the court helped minimize what would have proven intractable or possibly even an instigator for greater tensions or violent conflicts in the future.

Another case presented to the court, and from which the rationale for litigating international water conflicts can be justified, is that of the Silala River. Although the Court's opinion has not yet been rendered, it is of relevance primarily because it demonstrates at what point an international water rights conflict should be directed to the global judicial arbiter. It also shows that the degree of complexity of the shared water issue merits the opinions of legal experts such as the ICJ. Moreover, Chile and Bolivia water tussles mirror that of Egypt and Ethiopia. Egypt is a desert land as is Chile, that is largely occupied by the Atacama Desert, the second hottest in the world. Both, therefore, rely on the customary international water law that protects downstream riparian rights via the "no significant harm principle." Moreover, both share a history of water treaties and territorial claims. Egypt and Bolivia also claim "historic rights" or "prior appropriation" rights. The only difference is that the Nile is indisputably an international watercourse while that of the Silala's is contended.

The Silala River originates in Bolivia, South America, where it is apparently fed by a ground spring that overlaps the border with Chile. Although it does not directly flow into Chile, some claim that it once did, although what is presently evident is that it connects to another river, the San Pedro that flows through Chile and empties into the Pacific. History also suggests that through a 1908 colonial agreement, Chile was granted, by Bolivia, the right to build canals from the Silala across from the border before it joins the Pedro. During that period, Chile needed water for the copper mines and steam-engine trains. However, in 1977, that right of access and use was withdrawn by Bolivia on the premise that Chile had diversified the use of the water, using it for activities not specified in the 1908 agreement. Unable to solve the dispute through bilateral negotiations, Chile took the case to the ICJ in June of 2016 arguing that the Silala is an international watercourse that rightfully is to be shared by the two countries. Second, they have historically used the water as specified in the 1908 agreement. Bolivia objects to the notion that Silala is an international watercourse and, therefore, has the exclusive sovereign right not to share with Chile. Moreover, they demand compensation for water used by Chile for non-specified activities contrary to the 1908 agreement. The court, therefore, is expected to decide whether the river is an international watercourse or not. Second, in passing judgment, it must apply the principles of equitable utilization and reasonable use and the no-significant harm principle.

It must be acknowledged, even as the court gathers evidence of how to resolve the dispute that both the Silala and the Ethiopian dam tussles call for a synthesis of historical, economic, and political nuances that define water rights for each claimant. This, as well as the interpretation of the previous treaty, along with what constitutes an international watercourse and prior use, are activities that legal and neutral experts can better handle. As the attempts by Bolivia and Chile illustrate, bilateral negotiations occasionally fail because of the inherent historical mistrust and political differences. Although the political nature of some of these shared water conflicts can be overwhelming and can call for independent mediators, an independent judicial system can help reduce the degree of tensions by applying customary international laws most nations subscribe to. Therefore, Egypt must have acknowledged the degree of complexity of the dam issue by suggesting that the case be taken to the ICJ. The court substantially reduced the tensions between Hungary and Slovakia and offered recommendations based on facts and internationally accepted legal guidelines, without taking sides.

Litigation Limitations

Despite being neutral and competent in the law, the International Court System is not the favorite for nations in conflicts over water or shared water use. This reluctance comes from the court's decisions that are not legally binding, as they serve as legal advice anchored on international water laws. This view applies to all UN agencies, given that the international body is not a sovereign state with the authority to enforce compliance. Another reason is that the ever-changing political and social dynamics within the nations concerned can complicate the opportunity for a compromise. Additionally, as the only international judicial system, the court is swamped with other exigent and more serious cases, such as those involving human rights violations, genocides, and civil conflicts in which lives are lost. That kind of trajectory obliges the bench to prioritize the cases by their degree of gravity. Luckily, most conflicts over shared water systems are hardly violent, though some have raised tensions between and among the nations involved. For example, River Jordan (Israel, Syria, and Jordan), Tigris, and Euphrates (Turkey, Syria, and Iraq), Indus (India and Pakistan) and Ganges-Brahmaputra (India and Pakistan). Although the Indus River was appealed to ICJ's arbitration wing for consideration, it was never adjudicated by the court.

The Ganges–Brahmaputra conflict made it to the UN General Assembly, which advised on further goodwill negotiation and cooperation but never made it to the court.

Summary

The ICJ is the single most important judicial system through which the riparian nations in conflict can have their cases arbitrated. Although the next best alternative to third-party mediation, the court is not frequently used. In fact, between 1987 and 2016, the court adjudicated only eight disputes involving rivers shared by two or more nations; one is currently pending. This low number is, in part, due to the reluctance of the nations in conflict to take such cases to the court because of (a) preference for third-party mediation, (b) the time it takes to render opinions can be long, at least a minimum of three years and, (c) the fact that the decisions rendered by the court serve only as advice and are not legally binding. All the UN agencies operate in an anarchic environment because they lack the power of enforcement or compliance. Moreover, the cases can prove difficult to arbitrate because of the reliance on international principles, many of which are deliberately framed in vague and conflictual language to give interpretations with more flexibility. This limitation constrains the court's ability to make precise interpretations to avoid bias in judgment. Given that the ICJ and its arbitration body are the only available arbiter for nations in dispute, it is difficult to imagine the possibility for quick and informed judgments. Therefore, nations with high tension, have the option of looking for third-party mediations. Though recommendations are reserved for the last chapter of this book, it is noted that the ICJ's centralized position in The Hague constrains its ability to address numerous deserving cases and, probably, its ability to successfully adjudicate cases. Presently, the court serves over 190 countries. With the possibility of increased conflicts over shared resources, due to the effects of climate change, it seems appropriate for the judicial body to spread out branches in different regions of the work, particularly in Asia, Africa, and Latin America. That way, the few cases that arise within each region can be adjudicated more promptly than they are presently. Moreover, such diffused structures will enable the judges to better acquaint themselves with contextual matters and cultural nuances than they are able to while at The Hague. Although the limitations to the litigations approach may appear obvious, they, however, offer the next best alternative to resolving international water conflicts.

References

"USAID." Climate Variability and Change in Ethiopia: Summary of Findings, December 2015. USAID Technical Report.

Abbott, Kenneth W., and Snidel, Duncan. 1998. "Why States Act through Formal International Organizations." *Journal of Conflict Resolution* 42(1): 3–32.

Abukhater, Maher., and Sanders, 2010. Edmund. *Palestinian Leaders threaten to quit peace negotiations. The Baltimore Sun, 2010–10–03.* Baltimore, MD. Tribune Publishing Company, LLC.

Declaration of Principles. 2015. *Agreement on the Declaration of Principles Between the Arab Republic of Egypt, the Federal Republic of Ethiopia and the Republic of the Sudan on the Grand Ethiopian Renaissance Dam Project (GERDP).* Khartoum: State Information Service.

Furst, Heiko. n.d. *The Hungarian-Slovakian Conflict over the Gabcikovo-Nagymaros Dams: An Analysis.* Retrieved from http://www.columbia.edu/cu/ece/research/intermarium/vol6no2/furst3.pdf. October 30, 2020.

International Water Law Project, The Helsinki Rules. Last modified May 26, 2020. Retrieved from: https://www.internationalwaterlaw.org/documents/intldocs/.

Lowi, Miriam R. 1993. Bridging the Divide: Transboundary Resource Disputes and the Case of West Bank Water. *International Security* 18(1) (Summer): 113–138.

Mitchell, S. M., and Zawahri, Nade A. 2015. "The effectiveness of treaty design in addressing water disputes." *Journal of Peace Research* 52(2): 187–200.

Overview of the Case: Gabcikovo-Nagymaros Project (Hungary/Slovakia). Retrieved from www.icj-cij.org/en/case/92.

Tir, Jaroslav, and Stinnett, Douglas M. 2011. The Institutional Design of Riparian Treaties: The Role of River Issues. *Journal of Conflict Resolution* 55(4): 606–631.

Zawahri, Neda A., and Mitchell, Sara M. 2011. "Fragmented Governance of International Rivers: Negotiating Bilateral Versus Multilateral Treaties. *International Studies Quarterly* 55: 835–858.

PART IV

Long-Term Solutions

CHAPTER 8

Renegotiate, Partition, Apportion the Waters, and Contextualize Negotiation

INTRODUCTION

This chapter is divided into three sections. The first details what I believe to be the most important action for Egypt to take in order to secure its water security: renegotiate the Cooperative Framework Agreement (CFA) of 2010. The second section conveys the need for the countries of the Nile Basin to formally partition the basin into two parts, the upper Nile Basin (consisting of Kenya, Uganda, Tanzania, Rwanda, Burundi, and the Democratic Republic of Congo) and the lower Nile basin (Ethiopia, South Sudan, Sudan, and Egypt). This means that both the current NELSAP (the Nile Equatorial Lakes Subsidiary Action Program) and the ENSAP (Eastern Nile Subsidiary Action Program) must be reconstituted and structured to give each sub-basin the necessary autonomy in order to have a voice in the shared water affairs of which they are a part. The third section addresses what I believe to be the ultimate solution for reducing tensions for an extended period of time: apportionment of water to each riparian state. This last solution described in depth in this last section has been deliberately avoided by the Nile Basin countries, more so by their international technical advisers who continuously emphasize the efficacy of the benefits approach for when riparian states engage in joint projects. However, the efficacy of the joint benefits approach in reducing tensions, as displayed in the conflict between Egypt and Ethiopia, remains questionable. If it is designed well and addresses all necessary factors,

© The Author(s), under exclusive license to Springer Nature Switzerland AG 2021
S. H. Okoth, *The MENA Powers and the Nile Basin Initiative*, https://doi.org/10.1007/978-3-030-83981-9_8

the apportionment of the Nile waters to each sub-basin riparian state can bring lasting peace. However, adjustments to such allotments may be necessary every so often, as water levels are affected by utilization and climatic conditions over time. The chapter ends by introducing a new model to negotiating international water rights, "Contextualized Negotiation."

Renegotiate the CFA

As much as nations attempt to sign agreements/treaties to come up with lasting solutions for disputes, the reality is that these agreements are never permanent even after being adopted and ratified by national governments. It is this reality that has promoted Stephen McCaffrey (2003), a famed international water scholar, to suggest that treaties ought to be designed to allow for flexibility in the future. This is because changes in the domestic and external environment occur throughout the entire life of an international treaty. Therefore, it is only through this flexibility in treaty design that nations in a compact can adapt to unpredictable changes, such as ones in climate and demands that originate from increases in population and economic growth.

Whether a treaty is flexible or not, various conditions justify the need to renegotiate. Specifically, these conditions can attempt to address ongoing and unstable issues (legal and anticipated benefits), uncertain and emergent issues (environmental, social, and economic), legal requirements (e.g., clause to either terminate or renegotiate), regional peace and stability, various externalities, improved communication, and the need to strengthen co-riparian pledges to reach win-win solutions.

Conditions to Renegotiate

The first condition to renegotiate an existing treaty is to ensure one party or more choose to revisit unsettled issues or ones in which the compact has failed. In doing so, this would guarantee the achievement of anticipated benefits for the complainant(s). The Nile Cooperative Framework Agreement (CFA) of 2010 for example, was signed by all ten riparian states but not ratified by the two downstream states—Egypt and Sudan. The two nations based their stand on the controversial language reflected in Article 14 (b) that requires member states "not to significantly affect the water security of any other Nile Basin States" (CFA 2010, p. 20).

Egypt and Sudan rephrased the text to read, "Not to adversely affect the water security and current uses and rights of any other Nile Basin State" (ibid.). With the majority of upstream states unable to agree on the revised text, Egypt and Sudan immediately suspended their participation in the NBI meetings. However, in 2012, Sudan returned to the pact because it recognized the potential benefits it could receive from Ethiopia's Grand Renaissance project. Feeling isolated and left behind in terms of the future of its water security, Egypt rejoined the NBI in 2017. In fact, its seven years' of absence did exactly what they had feared it would: increased mistrust, worsened relations with the upstream states and gave Ethiopia the opportunity to begin its construction of the Renaissance Dam. As a former Sudanese minister for water resources, Seifedin Hamad observed that when group membership is seized, states lose the opportunity to be heard. However, when one is part of the group, his concerns are brought to the table and the chance of finding a group solution are much higher (Alabass 2017). Quintessentially, by not including the interests of both countries, the CFA failed to ensure the future water security for both Egypt and Sudan. Moreover, the agreement had failed in its quest to get all the ten member states to ratify the agreement—though technically, only two-thirds (six out of the ten) is required to formalize the treaty and to give way for reinstituting the NBI into The Nile Basin Commission.

The second condition for renegotiating is the opportunity to address the uncertain and emergent issues that might come up (Krantzberg 2009). Although it is often difficult to anticipate future consequences and their potential effects on the provisions of a bilateral or multilateral treaty, it is necessary to include some degree of flexibility into the language and treaty design. Therefore, it can become possible for water institutions (rules, procedures, and organizations) to readily tackle issues as they emerge. This is particularly relevant in the twenty-first century, as the behaviors and threats posed by climate change have become increasingly more unpredictable. Within the Nile basin, challenges originating from environmental governance (Cohen and Norman, n.d.) and the struggle over diminishing freshwater resources downstream are two related issues that are, for example, new to the Cooperative Framework Agreement of 2010 that were not factored in its original framework.

A third condition that necessitates a treaty's renegotiation (read: CFA of 2010) is legal requirement. An example is the clause in the Columbia River Treaty that details the choice to either "terminate or renegotiate"

(Cohen and Norman, n.d.). The treaty, adopted in 1961 and ratified in 1964, specified the life of the treaty to be 50 years, after which the parties (Canada and the United States) had to review the terms and decide to either terminate or renegotiate the provisions put forth in the treaty. The caveat to this clause was a ten-year notice before such actions were taken. This meant that by 2014, the treaty was due for review. As of October 2020, a published article called for former President Donald Trump to renegotiate the treaty because it was deemed unfair to Americans. This alleged unfairness pertains to the deal that required the United States government to pay Canadians to construct three dams in order to supply Americans with cheap power and ensure floods were controlled. The annual payments to Canada averaged between $150 and 350 million. By 2020, the United States had settled its bill for the hydropower projects. Though the Canadian– the United States deal does not exactly mirror that of the Nile's CFA, Egypt saw the 2010 agreement as a vehicle for imposing negative externalities, including the reduction of water flow and effects to its farm and electricity production. This claim is based on the CFA's failure to protect its historic water rights. On the flip side, the CFA's failure opened a window for Ethiopia to begin its construction of the Grand Renaissance Dam, which is at the center of the present Egypt–Ethiopia conflict. It should also be noted that that window of opportunity was widened by CFA's article that states, "Each Basin State is entitled to an equitable and reasonable share in the beneficial uses of the water resources of the Nile River System" (CFA 2010, p. 12). Undeniably, that provision legitimized the construction of waterworks, including dams, as long as the interests of those in the downstream are factored into such decisions. These examples, therefore, suggest that unless treaties are adjudicated in a way that is consistent with the specified clauses, any lack of compliance should necessitate renegotiation.

A fourth condition for renegotiating a treaty is the need to reconceptualize the provisions that might be open for defection and could reignite past conflicts. One provision that might be overlooked or difficult to craft is conflict resolution mechanism. In fact, the crafting or ability to easily agree on such mechanism eluded the team negotiating the Renaissance Dam that met in Washington D.C. between November 2019 and February 2020. Instead, they focused on the more urgent and sticky issues, including the plan for filling the reservoir and the dam's operations. Based on these priorities, it can be inferred that the design and agreement of the conflict resolution mechanisms are often considered secondary to the stated sticky issues. Although the tendency to defer this important mechanism to later stages of negotiation seems to be the general practice (e.g., Article 34 of the CFA that addresses settlement of disputes is treated under Part V titled Miscellaneous Provisions), it seems reasonable to suggest that all treaties should prioritize this legal provision. Without it, the possibility for conflict resurgence will necessitate renegotiation. This caveat, however, does not justify the need for Egypt to renegotiate.

The unintended consequences of a treaty for members, both in terms of transactional costs and risks, is another condition that dictates the renegotiation of a treaty. At times, the terms of the treaty or its general vagueness can lead a member to flout the rules. This can ether reduce the benefits to other parties while at the same time increase its own well-being. Such opportunistic tendencies, including abrupt undertakings that redistribute a shared resource can, in the long term, cause frictions among members to the treaty. Moreover, partners in a treaty will likely object to the sharing in those opportunistic risks (or negative externalities). These circumstances have the potential to convince the affected parties to renegotiate.

Although the poor flow of information is not a major reason to renegotiate an existing treaty, it is an important factor that might push a riparian state to push for renegotiation. For one, when the previously agreed exchange of data and hydrological information is no longer followed by states, especially by an upstream one, the downstream state, which considers data key when monitoring its water security, will propose a renegotiation. Additionally, the inability to monitor hydrological events in the upstream will further constrain the downstream state's ability to prepare and react appropriately (Sergio and Zlatkovic 2015). Even when the upstream renege on supplying the information due to national security concerns, such an action will either create or worsen the existing mistrust between the treaty partners. Regardless of the rationale not to further provide this vital data and information, the aggrieved party should seek to renegotiate.

The seventh rationale for the renegotiation of a treaty is to strengthen co-riparian pledge for a win-win solution for all parties. Although a desirable outcome, the promise of a win-win solution for all is not practical, although it may be easy to justify. Under the win-win model, nation-states that share an international watercourse are expected to walk away satisfied upon signing an agreement. This also assumes that a treaty provides for an equitable framework in which every riparian state is allowed equal and reasonable utilization of the shared water or the use of water by one riparian will not diminish the amount already used by the other in the downstream. Under the international watercourses law, this is governed by the principle of "no significant harm." In economics, the latter mirrors "pareto improvement," in which a resource is allocated in a way that makes state A better off without making state B worse off. Egypt, for example, in the Renaissance Dam conflict, evoked this principle to demand fixing the technical aspects of the dam (including the filling, operations and the amount of water release during filling). As noted in that conflict, neither the "no significant harm" nor Pareto improvement provided a win-win solution.

The only condition in which a win-win approach presumably works is through joint project arrangements, as currently designed in the Nile Basin. The two sub-basin arrangements, the Nile Equatorial Lakes Subsidiary Action Program (NELSAP) and the Eastern Nile Subsidiary Action Program (ENSAP), were meant to enable members of each sub-basin to engage in joint projects such as power projects from they could benefit from. As it was envisioned by the designers, such arrangement would prevent future disputes. However, this win-win approach did not prevent defection by Ethiopia that has caused the longest water conflict ever experienced in Africa. Obviously, even when win-win approach is conceptually touted to be a better avenue to avoiding future conflicts and renegotiation, it is, in fact, a recipe for renegotiation as the case of the Nile joint projects have demonstrated. Based on the evidence, the joint benefits approach did not prevent the eruption and current stalemate between Egypt and Ethiopia over the Grand Renaissance Dam. When, for example, Egypt proposed to invest in the dam, the proposal was rejected by Ethiopia. This comes as no surprise, given the inclination by states to pursue national self-interests. It is this limitation of a win-win approach that calls for renegotiation of the existing treaty. The Egypt–Ethiopia saga falls into this flux and therefore justifies, the need for Cairo to renegotiate the CFA.

But before renegotiating the CFA, Egypt ought to consider some of the costs that are often associated with this kind of effort. By comparing the conditions reviewed above with these costs, Egypt can, then, be in a position to either proceed or not proceed with the renegotiation. But as the reader will notice regardless of the cost–benefit analysis presented here, the goal is to encourage Egypt that it is in its interest to actively reengage in the Nile Basin Initiative and renegotiate the CFA. Cooperation matters for Egypt's future security and, therefore, that must play a leading role. It is beneficial to be a member of a team whose concerns can be taken into account.

Renegotiation Costs: Constraints and Solutions

There are multiple costs associated with the renegotiation process. Foremost is the cost of designing and bargaining in order to reach an agreement acceptable to all parties (Sergio and Zlatkovic 2015). Additional costs are linked to monitoring and ensuring compliance as officials commit funds and time to these activities (Arino and Reuer 1993). These activities can take a minimum of one year to complete, though the length of time for the process can be longer depending on the number of nations involved. Consider the renegotiation of the North America Free Trade Agreement (NAFTA) involving Mexico, United States, and Canada as an example. The process took almost two years from the reconceptualization, preparation, negotiation to the signing and eventual ratification by Congress.

The reconceptualization stage entails research and information collection to help with the reframing and renegotiating the existing treaty. Once the reframed document is prepared (by either one or all the parties) and agreed upon, the next stage is to prepare for the meetings. This includes identifying official representatives for each nation and organizing the desired timeline for meeting. At this point in the process, changes are expected due to prior commitments and/or prevailing and anticipated circumstances. Such circumstances may include events that are unique to a particular country that are difficult to circumvent—such as national elections, outbreak of diseases, protests, and even natural disasters. Briefings for representatives are complete and this, too, can take time. In the United States, the designated representative may have to be endorsed by a Congressional Committee. For example, after the signing of the Executive Order to mandate and to kick off the process in January 2017, the Senate confirmed the designated official on May 15th (Lopez 2018). In other countries, this may not be necessary once an appointment has been made. Congressional approval gave way for comments from interest groups, including business associations and influential corporations. Those comments helped shaped areas of concern. It was not until August 16, 2017 that the negotiation officially started.

Round one of the meetings focused on the identification of and agreeing on the goals, timeline and meeting locations. As would be expected when sovereign states participate in such forums, expression of varied national interests and disagreements were voiced. This was the case in rounds two and three. But it also presented the opportunity for each side to iron out any conceptual gaps and adjust positions. That was not easy, as was exhibited in rounds five and six when the talks almost stalled completely; it was, thus a situation, of "Now or Never." In situations such as this, it is the political will that keeps the negotiation going. That commitment by elected officials led to an agreement-in-principle for a renegotiated treaty in round eight. Because of to the process, on August 27, 2018, the renegotiated accord took its new formal standing as the "United States–Mexico–Canada Agreement."

To legalize the treaty, the officials informed Congress of the intention to sign the new pact within three months after the meeting. But it was not until September the same year that the document reached Congress just for ratification (Lopez 2018). It is evident from this account that took one year and nine months from the reconceptualization, preparation, negotiation, signing, and ratification by Congress that it cannot be a lengthy and frustrating ordeal. Although the process will not be the same for every group of nations attempting to renegotiate a treaty, it does illustrate the stages and the time it can take from start to end. Second, two hypotheses can be derived from this reality: the fewer the countries (e.g., two to five) involved in the process, the shorter the period (one to two years) it will take to reach an agreement. The opposite is also true. The more countries involved (e.g., five to ten or greater), the longer the period (two to four years) it will take to renegotiate elements of a treaty that has existed for a long time. This hypothesis is subject for future research.

Lessons for Egypt

As stated at the onset of this chapter, it is in the interest of Egypt to renegotiate the Cooperative Framework Agreement (CFA) of 2010 to ensure its present and future water security. To resolve the differences over the wordings embedded in Article 14 (b) on water security, Egypt must re-engage all upstream states in the conversation rather than expecting it will be resolved in their absence. It is only by having a seat at the table that one's voice can be heard, and their interests considered. Put differently, it is better to be part of the solution rather than a critic, especially when your own interest is at stake. In fact, by distancing itself from the Nile Basin Initiative for seven years, although it later rejoined, Egypt missed the window of opportunity to renegotiate the contentious wordings of Article 14 (b) over water security. Secondly, during that absence, the six upstream states proceeded to ratify the agreement without Egypt's viewpoint.

With a two-thirds majority ratifying the agreement, Ethiopia found the legal ground to launch its construction of the Grand Renaissance Dam in 2011. That legal ground embedded in Article 4 (1) reads in part, that the "Nile Basin States shall, in their respective territories, utilize the water resources of the Nile Basin System in an equitable and reasonable manner..." (CFA 2010, p. 12) This statement also finds the legal backing in territorial (sovereign) rights to which all politically independent states are granted.

Another basis for Egypt to take a leading role, rather than vindictively distancing itself, rests on the political theory of realism. The theory suggests that in the world of international politics, states compete for power and possible hegemonic superiority to ensure their own security. Therefore, to survive, states aggressively pursue their self-interests, whether economic, social, and/or political. This same concept can be applied to the willingness to negotiate a shared water regime. Studies have, for example, shown that if the most powerful state is located in the upstream (such as the United States versus Mexico over the Colorado River dispute, and the Mekong with China in the upstream), it is less motivated to negotiate shared water agreement (Rieu-Clarke and Lopez 2012). However, when the most powerful state is in the downstream, then it is motivated to take the lead in championing desirable framework for shared water use (p. 37). The latter points to Egypt's situation and, therefore, guides it regarding what action it should carry out: take the lead and renegotiate the contentious CFA Article on water security.

Although the renegotiation process can be daunting because of different perspectives and changes in the internal and external environments, it should not be the same for Egypt. Compared to the numerous rounds of talks for NAFTA, renegotiating the CFA should, ideally, involve fewer steps. This is because it involves only the reconciliation of the two opposed phrases pertaining to water security for all co-riparian states.

The first step, therefore, is preparation. To this end, Egypt is already ahead by having rejoined the Nile Basin Initiative in 2017. As an insider, Egypt can readily embark on buy-in by marshaling alliances, gathering information, conceptualizing, and reframing—if necessary—what it will put on the table.

In the second step, Egypt could explore and formalize renegotiation protocol by calling for a special meeting that involves foreign ministers, water affairs ministers and/or heads of state. Such high-level meetings, especially involving the heads of the Nile Basin countries, has, by and large, been extremely rare. Egypt could use the forum to present its proposal for a renegotiated settlement. Appealing to the political will of the Nile Basin's heads of state is key to untangling the existing differences.

The third step entails the negotiation over the wordings of Article 14 (b), as phrased by the upstream states and in another version presented by Egypt and Sudan. Each proposed statement is broadly informed by Article 14 of the CFA which reads as follows:

> Having due regard to the provisions of Articles 4 and 5, Nile Basin States recognize the vital importance of water security to each of them. The States also recognize that the cooperation management and development of waters of the Nile River System will facilitate achievement of water security and other benefits. Nile Basin States therefore agree, in a spirit of cooperation (CFA 2010, p. 24).

a. To work together to ensure that all states achieve and sustain water security
b. As proposed by Upstream States (Burundi, DR Congo, Ethiopia, Kenya, Rwanda, Tanzania, and Uganda) (p. 70):

- Not to significantly affect the water security of any other Nile BasinStates.

As proposed by the Downstream States (Egypt and Sudan):

- *Not to affect the water security and current uses and rights of any other Nile Basin State.*

The stance by the upstream states is influenced by Article 7 of The UN Watercourses Convention (UNWC) that requires a co-riparian in the upstream of shared water system to "take all appropriate measures to prevent the causing of significant harm to other watercourse states." (UNWC, n.d.) The Convention was adopted in 1997 by the UN General Assembly but to-date, only 30 out of the required 35 have submitted the instrument for ratification. This implies that the Convention cannot enter into force (Rieu-Clarke and Loures 2013). Part of III of the Convention, which is tied to Article 7 on "no significant harm" principle, further states that

> Each riparian state to an international watercourse is entitled to prior notification, consultation and (in some cases) negotiation where the proposed use by a co-riparian may cause serious harm to its rights or interest. (UNWC Online User's Guide, n.d.)

Ethiopia, as well as Rwanda in the upstream of the Nile Basin, opposed the provision. Since then, the refusal by Ethiopia to endorse Part III of the Convention can be interpreted to signal its fears of Egypt not approving its planned waterworks even after formal consultations. The refusal could have also signaled Addis Ababa's determination to move on with its planned waterworks, the Grand Renaissance Dam. Additionally, Ethiopia may have felt sheltered by the proposed Article 14 (b), which requires states "not to significantly affect the water security of any other Nile basin States." But that provision is open to interpretation.

For one, it does not specify what constitutes "significant harm" or by how much. Ethiopia could still argue, and as it did on numerous periods of the conflict, that the dam would not impose any significant harm. Two, the phrase "will not impose significant harm" could also imply that the proposed waterworks has the potential to cause harm, although not at the pre-determined significant levels if they even exist. Another challenge to the phase is Egypt's inability to prove, by any degree of certainty, the level of significant harm expected from Ethiopia's waterworks. Some estimates published in *Africanews* (2020) suggests that the dam will reduce the water flow to Egypt with the potential to reduce jobs by one million, with annual economic output by $1.8 billion, and reduction in annual electricity at $300 million.

According to the CFA, Egypt's preference for a reworded provision to read, "not to adversely affect the water security and current uses and rights of any other Nile Basin states" suggests two things. One, that the agreement considers and, in effect, allows the two downstream states to maintain their colonial privilege codified under the principle of historic rights (or "prior-in-use"). Two, the word "adversely affect" has more weight in its legal implication than "to significantly harm." To further disentangle these seemingly convoluted phrases, I deferred to the Online Dictionary. The former ("adversely") implies the ability of a phenomenon to negatively affect, while the latter ("significantly") denotes the ability to substantially or appreciably affect. Accordingly, to "adversely affect" suggests a verifiable bigger threat to the status quo, while to "significantly affect" entails an unsubstantiated degree of harm. It is, thus, easier to prove the former than the latter, with respect to shared water use. To the masters of the language, Egypt seems to have a point when they insist that the contentious wordings be changed. This statement, however, does not imply agreement or taking sides.

The final step of the renegotiation process is for the legislative bodies of the Nile Basin countries, including Egypt and Sudan, to ratify the CFA with a reworded Article 14 (b). The process should take shorter time, given that the upstream state had already completed all the steps except for the rewording.

Partitioning the Nile Basin

The need to partition a shared international river basin rests on the principle of collective action discussed in Chapter 5. At the core of this theory, advanced by Mancur Olson (1965), is the idea that it is in the best interest of the beneficiaries of a collective good (such as an international river basin) to cooperate because failure to do so can lead to sub-optimal outcomes. One problem with cooperating for the public interest is the aversion by some members even when they acknowledge the potential benefit for everyone involved. Therefore, cooperation should not be assumed to be spontaneous.

This aversive behavior can be reflected in two ways. One, some group members may decide to defect by violating the collective arrangement for selfish gains; a premise emphasized by the Prospect Theory (see Chapter 5). Two, some members may prefer to "free-ride" to avoid any costs associated with the collective action arrangement. Also inherent to this theory is the possibility of reduced benefits by each member from the arrangement, especially when the membership is large. That is, the share in a collective good diminishes with increased size of the group.

Hence, the most optimal solution is to design the sharing of such a good based on the size of the membership. Consequently, the smaller or the less diverse the group sharing a collective good, the greater the benefits and the rarer the conflict. The opposite is also true: the bigger the size of the group sharing a collective good, the greater the potential for conflict or its frequency. It is on these premises, free-rider problem, the potential to defect and the link between the benefits to the group size that the partitioning of the Nile Basin into two, the upper Nile Basin and the lower Nile Basin, is considered to be desirable.

Free-Rider

Within the Nile Basin (Initiative) as presently constituted, the "free-rider" problem is rooted in the win–win benefits approach that has promoted shared projects since 1999. The shared projects are institutionalized through the Nile Equatorial Lakes Subsidiary Action Program (NELSAP) and the Eastern Nile Subsidiary Action Program (ENSAP). The former consists of the riparian states in the upstream located within the Equatorial Lakes region. These states include Kenya, Uganda, Tanzania, Rwanda, Burundi, and DR Congo. The ENSAP riparian states include Sudan, Ethiopia, Egypt and more recently South Sudan, after it became politically independent in 2011. Although joint benefits are a well-conceived approach and an avenue to reducing conflicts, because it ensures that each riparian share in the joint projects such as power trade, not all members have been financially responsive to it. Some of the members free ride by delaying the required contributions for the joint activities. In the 2018–2019 financial year, for example, all the riparian states except Ethiopia and Rwanda had overdue payments to the Nile Basin Initiative (NBI Corporate Report 2019). Although this does not imply, they won't pay the balance but, rather, the incentive to do so is reduced, as these debtors still expect to benefit from the payments from other states. The situation in the ENSAP group of nations (Ethiopia, Sudan, South Sudan, and Egypt) further demonstrate this free-rider problem. For example, by the end of the same financial year on June 30, 2019, out of the four riparian states, only Ethiopia had met its full financial obligations to the regional program.

Defection and Group Size

The Collective Action Theory, as conceived by Olson, submits that members in a group do not spontaneously cooperate, even when the expected outcomes will benefit all members. In fact, the likelihood of defection by a member is much greater when the size of the group is bigger. The incentive to do so is more attractive when the size of the membership is larger because the chance of detection is minimized. A good example is when Ethiopia decided to build the controversial dam in contravention to the Cooperative Framework Agreement of 2010. A provision of that agreement requires that a co-riparian with the intention to build waterworks on the Nile must, first, converse with the members and not embark on such projects unilaterally. That agreement, though not signed by Egypt and Sudan, consists of ten riparian states. These are too many states to be able to effectively monitor their individual actions or intentions and to quickly reprimand or punish those who break the rules. Moreover, such sanctions are particularly difficult where the actors are individual sovereign states that share a river basin (as in the Nile). As sovereign states, there are multiple interests involved and protocols that need to be followed. Therefore, the ability of a basin-wide organization to either reprimand or punish depends on the domestic political and socioeconomic climate at the time.

The large size of the group not only incentivizes a collective action problem, such as the reluctance to meet shared costs and opportunity for defection, but also reduces the ability of the broader membership to understand the persona of respective state actors. Ideally, the expectation of any collective action (read: basin-wide organization or joint agreement) is to transform the behavior of each riparian state actor so that all decisions are consensual, in order to optimize the greater good. Obviously, as the Renaissance Dam conflict illustrates from its inception to the present, the large numbers of the basin actors have militated against the appreciation of the needs of certain members and, to some extent, their trust. Without these two forces, it is unrealistic to expect a signed agreement to modify the behaviors of the basin actors. Therefore, as a remedy to these collective action problems, I recommend partitioning of the Nile Basin into sub-basins. The following hypotheses merit this proposal.

1. *The larger and more diverse the members to a basin organization, the greater the collective problem.*

As political economist Mancur Olson has argued, and as presented in the above discussion, the collective action problem is more prominent when numerous groups come together to address a common problem. Unfortunately, this large membership works against the group's interests because some members free ride. Additionally, the diversity of the group also implies different and conflicting values. Thus, the coming together by the members does little to suppress those national self-interests. Because of this, arriving at a consensus of which action to be taken can be challenging. This is true even when all the members agree that something should be done to address a common problem.

2. *The fewer the riparian members to a basin organization, the lesser the number of conflicts.*

This premise is borrowed from the initial work by David Hume in his book titled *A Treatise of Nature* (Norton and Norton 2000). Recognizing the problem associated with group work, Hume stated that it is easier to cooperate with fewer states when addressing a public problem (such as draining a common meadow) but much harder with a larger group. He further observed that it is easier to bring these groups together, albeit much harder to have them agree on the modalities and work together. As already discussed above, this complexity is due to the fact that coming together to address a common problem does rid each member from its idiosyncrasies and personal interests. Hume's thinking birthed what we now know today as the collective action problem. Zawahri and Neda (2008) have convincingly debated this issue and acknowledged, albeit indirectly, the rationale presented here; that is, a sub-basin with fewer members is much more likely to experience less conflicts. Hence, the proposal for two sub-basins in the Nile meets Hume and Zawahiri's, et al. thinking.

3. *The fewer the riparian members in a basin (or sub-basin), the lesser opportunity for defection.*

The partitioning of a river basin reduces the number of actors involved in the overall management of the shared resources. This has the potential to reduce the chances for defection by a member because of improved ease of communication as a consequence of limited values and interests. Other factors that explain the reduced incentive to defect due to fewer members in the sub-basin include:

- Enhanced relationships and camaraderie
- Reduced impediments to organizing regular meetings
- Improved coordination in the management of shared water resource (through sharing of information and monitoring)
- Enhanced benefits by acting collectively for the benefits of all (synergy)
- Improved abilities to reduce and resolve any emerging conflicts as well as defection.

Consequently, two sub-basins are recommended for the Nile Basin: The upper Nile Basin (UNB) and the lower Nile Basin (LNB). Although the principles behind collective action are critical to the partitioning, proximity by geography (through the sharing of borders) is equally important. Additionally, common characteristics such as the availability of rainfall (either more or less) and political and sociopolitical dynamics are somewhat distinctive to each region (upper and lower Nile basins).

Although the process of restructuring can be politically daunting, for the Nile basin, this should be less of a problem given that such sub-divisions already exist— the NELSAP and the ENSAP. Each of the proposed sub-basins is briefly discussed.

The Upper Nile Basin (UNB)

This sub-basin will comprise the upstream states (Kenya, Uganda, Tanzania, Rwanda, Burundi, and Democratic Republic of Congo). The goals of formalizing the partition as separate water management entity are to:

1. Improve and efficiently manage the shared resource and
2. Enhance the economic conditions of member states.

The UNB states have unique and common characteristics that make this separation viable, including that they,

- Are members of the East African Community
- Want rich water to reach upstream

- Have geographic proximity (shared borders)
- Most, if not all, are predominantly Christian
- All signed the 2010 Cooperative Framework Agreement.

THE LOWER NILE BASIN (LNB)

Comprising this sub-basin are Egypt, Sudan, South Sudan, and Ethiopia. Having this as a separate entity rests on the following common factors:

1. Geographically, all these countries are downstream from the Nile Basin. Within this sub-basin, however, Ethiopia is in the upstream and is the source of most of the water (86%) received by Egypt at the end of the pipe.
2. Member states, except for Ethiopia, are water starved. Egypt, for example, is 90% desert while Sudan is slightly over 50% desert. South Sudan and Ethiopia are endowed with plenty seasonal rainfall.
3. All the four countries are largely Muslim (Egypt—90%; Sudan—97%; South Sudan—20%; Ethiopia—31.3%) (CIA Factbook 2020).
4. Have divided stands on the Cooperative Framework Agreement of 2010. Both Egypt and Sudan did not sign the agreement, while Ethiopia and South Sudan have bought into the compact.
5. Standardization of an irrigation system. Both Egypt and Sudan were the first in the Nile basin to use and develop complex irrigations systems by building large dams.
6. Political regimes and leadership have somewhat been less democratic. Although for the most part this authoritarian leaning of the political leadership has weakened Egypt, Ethiopia, and Sudan's ability to cooperate and resolve the conflict over the Renaissance Dam, this near-similar approach to leadership can work as an incentive to work as a co-riparian team.

Fortunately, the Nile Basin Initiative is already familiar with the process of institutionalizing and operationalizing the proposed the two sub-basins. Giving each sub-basin some degree of autonomy will foster long-term benefits such as improved management of the shared water system, the exchange of information, the close monitoring of defections, and the ability to respond to issues that emerge and to resolve any conflicts. The geographical proximity through shared borders, as well as the attributes identified above, suggest it is justified to group these downstream states in order to independently manage their shared interests.

An additional aspect to keep in mind is that splitting the basin into two does not absolve the Nile Basin Initiative Secretariat in Uganda from coordinating. If anything, its role will be similar to the federal governments, with two separate states running their own affairs. The federal headquarters (NBI) acts as arbiter and, when necessary, it determines states' needs and distributes shared resources. This is the subject of the next section.

Apportioning the Nile Waters

Although this issue is fundamentally different from the sharing of milk from one cup during my early childhood, the main lesson is still applicable. Similar to the reprimands of a father who quickly quelled the squabble among three siblings, the sharing of the waters of an international river is feasible, but daunting.

Water allotment to all members' part of an international river basin is a viable option for resolving present and future water rights disputes. However, due to the complexity of allotting quotas to each riparian state, this approach has been avoided by some of the major river basins. Such rivers include the Danube, the Mekong, the Ganges, the Columbia, the Colorado, and the Senegal.

The fear of engaging in this complex process is based on the following questions: How is it to be done? What metrics are to be used? Should the allotment be based on historical rights, population size, existing economic growth levels, and activities and/or geographic factors such as degree of water availability? Recognizing the logic of apportioning shared international waters, so that each riparian nation has right of access and use, the United Nations Watercourses Convention (UNWC) developed the following metrics as a guide (Onencan and de Walle 2018).

- "Geographic, hydrological, climatic, ecological, and other factors of a natural character.
- The social and economic needs of the watercourse States concerned.
- The population dependent on the watercourse in each State.
- The effects of the use or uses of the watercourses in one watercourse State on another watercourse States.

- Existing and potential uses of the watercourse.
- Conservation, protection, development, and economy of use of the water resources of the watercourse and the costs of measures taken to that effect.
- The availability of alternatives, of comparable value, to a particular planned or existing use" (p. 707).

Although, technically, each of these metrics merit consideration when allotting water to meet the principle of equitable and reasonable utilization, it is quite difficult to do even for the most qualified water engineers. But it has been successfully done in some places for some bodies of water, one of them being the Nile. The British colonial government was, for example, able to apportion the Nile waters, albeit in a prejudiced way, in 1929 and again in 1959. In the 1929 Anglo-Egypt Treaty, Egypt was allotted 48 BCM while Sudan was only given 4 BCM. The upstream states, including Ethiopia, were left out of that arrangement entirely. Obviously, the skewed nature of that apportionment is one of the causes of the present conflict. When the upper riparian states discovered what this treaty had done and realized that they were not entitled to the Nile water, they collectively demanded a change in the water regime. The question that must be asked, therefore, is had the water been shared, however inequitable it might have been, with the other riparian states in the upstream, would the present conflict take on a different dimension? Quintessentially, it would have only required the riparian states to negotiate adjustments to their allotments, either upwards or downwards.

Despite these universally accepted criteria for allotting shared international waters, in order to apply any of them to ensure reasonable and equal utilization, there must be sensitivity for political dynamics. To omit this important variable is to set the members for a long duel and make the looming conflict even more to solve. Because of the unique circumstances (i.e., the history and nature of the conflict) within the Nile Basin countries, geographical factors, availability of alternatives of comparable size and population size are the three most relevant criteria that factor into water apportionment for all members. There is also a fourth criterion: existence of a previously signed treaty.

The first three factors are feasible because, politically, they are less contentious due to their natural attributes that do not give humans a lot of control. The requirement of an existing treaty, however, acts as enabler because instead of starting from the beginning, the states can use existing

Table 8.1 Feasibility criteria

Criteria	Political feasibility	Economic feasibility	Administrative feasibility
Geography (climate, hydrology)	Y	Y	Y
Availability of alternatives of comparable value	Y/N	Y/N	Y
Population size	Y/N	Y/N	Y
Existence of signed treaty	Y	Y	Y

Y = Yes feasible; N = Not feasible; Y/N = Split between feasible and Not Feasible

treaty provisions to negotiate adjustments and adapt to changing circumstances. The other UNWC criteria are less feasible due to the degree of contention they are likely to create as members push for higher quantities. Even more so, they are men's creations and are, therefore, amenable to different interests and values. Table 8.1 illustrates feasibility assessment for these selected criteria.

The argument for geography, climate, and hydrology is a basis that all members are likely to agree upon, given its observable reality. Not much data is required to prove the absence of rainfall or water flow in a given riparian territory, therefore, making it difficult for states to debate. It is also easier for the members to discern how the geographic location of a state benefits it, specifically with respect to climate and hydrology. Therefore, in the table above, positive scores (Y = Yes) are analyzed based on political, economic, and administrative feasibility. It is a criterion that ought to be considered when deciding how much each riparian state should get.

Availability of an alternative source of comparable value is likely to cause political disputes because, for some, it is not about having alternatives such as additional natural springs, freshwater lakes or rivers; it's about how to get what they want from a jointly shared resource. There is little doubt that those with alternative sources might be willing to concede to lesser amounts if needed. However, all states deserve a negotiated fair share regardless. This option would be both economically and administratively feasible because each nation stands to derive economic benefits and less administrative costs during the apportionment process.

Population size is one of the most significant variables to bargain for when debating the apportionment of a collective resource. Riparian states with high populations require water-fed farms, industries that produce goods and water for domestic use. Therefore, the larger the population, the greater the demand for water. This is a compelling criterion judging by the history of the Nile and its ongoing water conflict. In the 1980s, when the upstream states began to witness an upsurge in population numbers, national governments joined hands to demand the review of the colonial treaties which gave monopoly water rights to only Egypt and Sudan. That has become a consistent rallying point when countries demand equal amounts, if not more, of the Nile waters. In fact, the signing of the Cooperative Framework Agreement in 2010 was the tipping point in that argument, and, of course, a justification based on the rising populations.

Although it is easier to employ this criterion when determining how much each state should be given, it is also much more difficult to achieve a political consensus. For some states, such as Egypt and Ethiopia which have higher populations, the application of this criteria is difficult to negotiate and agree upon. Presently, Ethiopia has a higher population (110 million) along with Egypt (106 million) (CIA Factbook 2021). To use this as a criterion for water sharing implies that Ethiopia would be apportioned more water than Egypt. But the other variables (geography, climate, hydrology and availability of alternative sources based on comparable value) will ultimately strengthen Egypt's argument. For one, geographically Egypt is a desert and has very limited precipitation annually. Two, the country does not have any viable alternatives. The oases in the northeast of the country do not have enough water because most is lost through evaporation. Other than population size, Ethiopia will not be able to use these two other variables when competing with Egypt for more water rights. Population is its only defense.

The fourth and last criteria, the existence of a signed treaty, is considered a viable and practical mean that can be used to move on to the next step and determine how much each state should be allocated. A previously signed treaty means that the signatory states already have protocols in place and don't have to start from scratch. They also make the negotiation over water sharing simply much easier. Consequently, it is politically, economically and administratively feasible. The question that remains is how should the water be apportioned equitably so that each riparian receives its share?

Allocating Water Quotas

Admittedly, this is a very complex process. That is why we study how the Colorado River, the Jordan and Yarmouk Rivers and the Ganges River were apportioned. The goal is identify the rationales, procedures, the experienced difficulties and the solutions. As will be discovered shortly, two policy actions are common in all circumstances. First, in each river basin, the riparian states signed a treaty that specified water allocation. The treaties were thus designed with flexible provisions to allow for future adjustments to anticipate changes in climatic/hydrologic conditions. The second action is to create a special body, management authority or commission in order to manage water distribution.

1. Colorado River

    In order to meet the necessary equitable sharing standards implemented for the Colorado River debate between the United States and Mexico, the two countries first entered into an agreement in 1906. Through that pact, the United States agreed to allocate 60,000 acre-feet per year (Thomas 1970). Because that agreement contained the provision for future adjustments, a joint International Water Commission, signed in 1927 and ratified by Congress in 1945, upped Mexico's share to 1,500,000 acre-feet. The United States, however, did not specify their own desired amount. Instead, the rest was distributed to each of the seven upstream states. In the earlier years, most of the river's waters were used for irrigating crops and fruits in the Imperial Valley. However, due to the overutilization of the water and the evaporation in the deserts, the Colorado water has never been adequate enough for fair allocation.

    It should be mentioned that the United States initially found it difficult to accede to Mexico's demand for equitable water sharing at all. First, as the then United States Attorney General Judson Harmon asserted, no existing international law deterred the nation from using the waters of Colorado as it pleased. This assertion was based on what is presently known as "absolute territorial integrity." Second, as it was an upstream hegemon, Mexico found it difficult to push for an equal share, due to the absence of international guidelines. In fact, it was not until 1966 that the Helsinki Rules were ratified by the community of nations in order to act as a formal guide for "equitable and reasonable use" of shared international waters. This was followed by the 1997 United Nations Watercourses Convention, and then by the Berlin Rules in 2004 (Rieu-Clarke and Loures 2013).

To address equitable sharing water rights, the two countries created the International Boundary and Water Commission specifically to properly distribute the Colorado River waters (Talozi et al. 2019). According to this commission, in 1906, Mexico was apportioned 60,000 acre-feet per year. That figure, however, was changed to 1,500,000 acre-feet in 1927 when the International Water Commission went into effect (Thoms 1970; Talozi et al. 2019). Although the agreement did not specify how much was to be allocated to the United States, it can be assumed that, as an upstream hegemon, it was given a large allocation of the overall water amount—specifically by the seven states in the upstream. But, whether that allotment framework was perfect or imperfect, the commitment demonstrated by all states involved showed great dedication towards equal water sharing rights. This solution resulted from their ability to a) design a treaty containing flexible provisions to allow water allocation adjustments and b) create a special body to administer the process. Together, those initiatives have reduced the possibility of future conflicts between the two nations over water sharing. An equally important aspect in the suppression of future conflicts is the presence of a hydro-hegemon in the upstream, like the United States in this case. As will be recalled from the earlier discussion in this book, it is hypothesized that violent conflict over water access is less likely when one of the parties is a hegemon located in the upstream. The case of China in the Mekong River dispute and Turkey's control over the Euphrates and Tigris are good examples of this.

2. The Jordan and Yarmouk Rivers

Another example is the dispute over the Jordan and Yarmouk Rivers. It is a relevant because, like the Nile, it involves multiple countries (Israel, Syria, and the Kingdom of Jordan). Both Israel and Jordan, although in active competition with each other, unilaterally launched water diversion projects to create utilization guidelines. The first attempt to finding a solution was through the signing of the 1994 Peace Treaty between Israel and Jordan. Article 6, specifically, of that treaty addresses the Yarmouk and Jordan Rivers water allocation between Israel and the Kingdom of Jordan (U.S. State

Department 1994). Enshrined in Annex II and signed in October of that year, the two nations agreed on a formula for apportioning the waters and jointly managing it. Under the treaty, the water was to be apportioned as follows.

First, Israel was to draw 12 million cubic meters (MCM) in the summer and 13 MCM in the winter annually (Talozi et al. 2019). The remainder was given directly to Jordan. Under the accord, the Jordanian government allowed Israel to tap an extra 20 MCM annually in exchange for Jordan to receive a 20 BCM in the summer. Although the plan seemed a bit complex when factors such as the erratic climatic conditions were factored in, the effort to directly apportion the water has helped reduce direct conflicts over water rights between the two countries. The success of this type of water allotment depends not only on a flexible water agreement but on the exchange of information, hydrological data, and prior notification about planned projects.

3. The Ganges River

The third example is that of the Ganges River, shared between India and Bangladesh. Although it is shared with two other countries to the upstream (China and Nepal), the upstream tributaries bring most of water downstream to Bangladesh before draining into the India Ocean through the Bay of Bengal. The conflict over water sharing started when India decided to construct, in 1975, the Farrakka Barrage close to its border with Bangladesh. The goal was to divert approximately 1,133 billion cubic meters (BCM) of water into the Hooghly River in order to boost navigation in the Port of Kolkata (Rahman et al. 2019). To counter the dispute between the two riparian nations, several steps were taken to address the shortage caused by factors such as dry seasons.

The first step was the adoption of a water allocation formula that detailed the following: (1) a 5-year agreement (1977) signed; (2) a schedule of dry seasons given; (3) water delivery divided into 10-day cycles and 4) 80% of the water given to Bangladesh based on the flow schedule (Rahman et al. 2019). In 1983, a 5-year memorandum of understanding was signed which included modifications and removal of certain provisions, such as total share and guarantee of supply. In the 1996 treaty which included a 30 years expiration timeline, the two nations agreed to the following guidelines. Bangladesh's needs had to be addressed during the dry season. More specifically, the 10-day cycle for water delivery needed to continue. Also, India and Bangladesh needed to receive an equal allocation of 991 BCM, albeit in alternate 10 day periods. According to Annex II of that treaty, the actual water allocation was based on the average flow between 1949 and 1988. In the month of January, for example, the flows detailed were as follows: "Jan. 1–10 (India—40,000 Cusecs; Bangladesh—67,516 Cusecs); Jan. 11–20 (India—40,000 cusecs; Bangladesh—57,673); Jan. 21–31 (India—40,000 cusecs, Bangladesh—50,154 cusecs)" (Rahman et al. 2019).

The ability the determination by these two riparian states to work out a formula for water apportionment has, undoubtedly, fostered cooperation and reduced the possibility of future conflicts. Like the other riparian states discussed above, India and Bangladesh relied on formal treaties, including the establishment of a joint committee made to implement and facilitate the exchange of information. Moreover, a provision was added to the 1996 agreement that required co-riparians to swiftly consult with each other to address any precipitous decline in Farrakka's water levels.

In summary, water apportionment is considered a viable solution for resolving international water conflicts. Although all metrics discussed above, as well those recommended by the UN Watercourses Convention, should be considered when allocating water among competing national claims, geography, climate, and hydrology and the existence of a previously signed treaty are more compelling. However, the metrics by themselves are not enough to yield a universal solution. Appropriate formulas must be developed by the riparian states themselves on a case-by-case basis, in order to address the states' concerns. For example, the formula used by Jordan and Israel are distinctively different from the ones applied by India and Bangladesh. Additionally, we have noted that the success of any water allocations requires a formal agreement and establishment of a special body to implement the distribution. A possible requirement might also be to monitor and institute sanctions on defectors. As the Ganges Treaty provisions suggest, it might be beneficial to include treaty timelines or expiration dates, so riparian actors can revisit and make adjustments if needed. Therefore, international water treaties should, ideally, be designed to allow some degree of flexibility. In fact, the Ganges model provides a relevant model for Nile Basin states when they are deciding how to settle this conflict.

Lastly, it is critical for the riparian states to involve hydrologists, water engineers, and policy experts to ensure that the necessary water allotment guidelines are put in place and implemented. As is expected, buy-in by political decision-makers, including heads of states, is indispensable for the success of the process and its sustenance.

Contextualized Negotiation Model (CNM)

In this section, I propose a "contextualized negotiation" model as a better alternative to existing approaches including the popular, yet one-dimensional, third-party mediation. The mediation heuristic is favored because of its assumed neutrality of the mediator, as they often come from a geographically distant country. I suggest that the overreliance on the outside third-party mediators only offer temporary solutions. Instead, the Contextualized Negotiation Model (CNM) offers a more compartmentalized and controlled approach in which the process starts within and is predominantly informed by internal dynamics, included control by the actors within (i.e., those with interest and are affected by the issue being mediated). Although the outcome of a contextualized mediation is for the benefit of those affected by the conflict, the lessons learned can benefit can external parties with similar water rights issues.

Another way to picture this model is by imagining a household in which a family is experiencing a water shortage. The head of the household agrees that there is enough water for drinking and cooking, but the amount left for bathing, laundry and washing cars must be controlled. A college-bound son insists he must wash his car at least twice per week, otherwise he will miss out on dating. A high school teenager insists on bathing each morning and evening for at least 20 minutes. The mother of the house insists on doing laundry three times a week. The father, on the other hand, is adamant about watering the lawn at least three times a week. Regardless of the disparate idiosyncrasies and how amicable the solution is likely to be, the emphasis is on the domesticated nature of the problem. More specifically, this situation concerns only the household members, not neighbors or family friends, meaning only the family members can decide what is the best for all of them.

If a neighbor were to be brought in to help resolve the conflict over water rights in the household, that too might evince bias—thought not overtly. The man could be a drinking buddy to the head of the household, or the neighbor's spouse could be a close friend to the mother of the household in conflict. Thus, in settling the dispute without any form of bias it is not advisable to rely on the neighbors, no matter how close they are to the family, to mediate. Therefore, the best and most sustainable solution in such cases is one devised by the members of the household themselves. Although this hypothetical case does not exactly mirror that of that of the Nile dispute, it serves as a conceptual template to approach the Ethiopian–Egyptian–Sudan water saga.

Despite the merits of this model, one question must be asked: Can this conception of the compartmentalized mediation be considered somewhat parochial? Sure, it is. However, the approach serves as an incentive for improved deconstruction and synthesis of the problem from all angles (relationships, uses, wastage, competing claims, and population). Additionally, the compartmentalization of the conflict resolution to the household does not prevent each member from using external knowledge and information.

In practice, what makes Contextualized Mediation parochial is allocating the responsibility of resolving the conflict over shared resource to only riparian members. Like the household example, states have much more knowledge of each other and their situation than an outsider who relies solely on limited briefings, memos, and reports. As most hermeneutic scholars would agree, reports and published material do not highlight the moods or bitter reactions, nor do they reveal degree of mistrust held by all parties involved in a conflict. Here is the rationale of why Contextual Negotiation approach is more appealing.

First, in this type of negotiation, context serves as the center from which ideas originate and factors such as economic, social, and political knowledge are synthesized. In the second stage, alternative solutions are developed and weighed against one another by the affected actors. The third stage involves review by each party and reaching an agreement.

This linkage between contextual factors and negotiation outcomes has been recognized in various literature (Crump 2009). It is for example anchored on the Linkage Theory (Deluga 1998), which suggests that actions and/or conditions in both internal and external environments affect (whether positively or negatively) the negotiation process and the outcome. Further studies by Hernandez (2014) and Crump (2009) acknowledge the importance of context in a negotiation process, as it enables a detailed understanding and appreciation of the underlying forces in a conflict. These include but are not limited to: historical, political, social, and economic factors. Knowledge of the past events (history), relationships between the warring nations or groups, cultural differences and religious belief systems, history of interactions and degree of trust, economic conditions, geopolitics, ideologies, and types of regime are critical components of contextual analysis. Contextual negotiation places the entire process of deciding on a negotiated agreement, assembling local knowledge and information, developing and weighing alternative solutions and agreeing on the most viable option on these factors.

Uniqueness

Factors that set Contextual Negotiation apart from other forms of negotiation, such as third-party mediation or arbitration, are as follows:

a. All actors (both aggrieved parties and interested groups) originate from the sub-basin or the river basin.
b. Development of ideas are initiated by actors and auxiliary staffers, although they may consult outside experts. These outside actors can acquire knowledge, learn experiences, and apply them to the problem.
c. Outsiders may serve only as observers to help shape the process, although they must desist from influencing the outcome.
d. Focus on local solutions for the local problems and the ability to tailor external and internal knowledge to the problem.
e. The negotiators are often sensitive to the cultural nuances and feelings of the other party. This is solved by an outside third-party mediator who steps in to apply a rational approach by simply looking at the facts and aiming to resolve the conflict as soon as possible. This is regardless of the less obvious subtleties that might be considered "honorable" acts in certain cultures. For example, in the Islamic culture of which Egypt is part, water is a gift from Allah whose distribution must be done equitably among all species. Egyptian society has, for generations, considered the Nile water holy and ordered it only be used for rituals or purification. But, the river is the only source of life-giving water because the country is large a desert. In Ethiopia, the Abbey (or the Blue Nile) has, for a long time, viewed it as the source of spiritual life and, therefore, pilgrimages were sent to the Lake Tana region in the Ethiopian highlands. In both countries, therefore, one can see why the level of dedication conveyed by each state is so intense.

In summary, the efficacy of this model, therefore, lies in its homegrown solutions developed by the affected parties themselves. It is hypothesized that the inability of Egypt and Ethiopia to strike a deal rests not only on the reliance on external mediators to propose a solution in the shortest time, but also on the shallow synthesis of the contextual factors and the eagerness to simply resolve the problem and move on. Rather, the success of this model lies mostly on the length of time dedicated to the process and the outcome itself. Obviously, the process requires more time for knowledge generation and assemblage of relevant information than generally spent by third-party mediators in the beginning. However, whether it takes six months, one year or one decade, once the background information has been assembled and an agreement is reached, the negotiation process should not take as long as the Egypt–Ethiopia one has. This is true considering that this dispute has been a problem since the 1920s and has taken over twenty years to negotiate (1999–2021). It should also be observed that the efficacy and sustainability of a solution lies on the involvement of those affected by the conflict and inclusion of all political, social, and cultural nuances. These are steps that third-party mediators generally avoid because they take more time than thy wish to be the case. The fast pace with which the United States for example, tried to resolve the conflict is an example. Outsiders, unless they are do it for money, do not have the time or the luxury to delve into detailed contextual analysis. Often they must rely on brief summaries presented to them but which hide factors such as feelings of mistrust, hatred, or similar subtleties.

REFERENCES

Alabass, Bassem Abo. 2017. "Egypt's Thawing Relations with the Nile Basin Initiative: What You Need to Know." ahramonline (English: ahram.org), January 24. Retrieved November 4, 2020.

Arino, Africa, and Jeffrey J. Reuer. 1993. "Designing and Renegotiating Strategic Alliance Contracts." *The Academy of Management Executive*, 2004-08-01, 18(3):37–48.

Cohen, Alice, and Emma S. Norman. (n.d.). Renegotiating the Columbia River Treaty: Transboundary Governance and Indigenous Rights. Research Articles. web.ebscohost.com.

Cooperative Framework Agreement. 2010. Nile Basin Initiative. http://www.nilebasin.org/index.php/nbi/cooperative-framework-agreement.

Crump, Larry. 2009. "Linkage Theory and the Global-Multilevel System: Multilateral, Regional, and Bilateral Trade Negotiations. *SSRN Electronic Journal*. June. https://doi.org/10.2139/ssrn.1484792.

Crump, Larry. 2011. Negotiation Process and Negotiation Context. *International Negotiation* 16(2):197–227.

Deluga, Ronald J. 1998. *Leader-Member Exchange Quality and Effectiveness Ratings: The Role of Subordinate-Supervisor Conscientiousness Similarit* 23(2):189–216. Thousand Oaks, CA: Sage (1998-06).

Hernandez, Ariel M. 2014. *Strategic Facilitation of Complex Decision-Making: How Process and Context Matter in Global Climate Change Negotiations*. Springer. New York, London: Cham Heideberg.

Krantzberg, Gail. 2009. "Renegotiating the Great Lakes Water Quality Agreement: The Process for a Sustainable Outcome." *Sustainability*, 1. https://doi.org/10.3390/su1020254.

Lopez, Edwin. 2018. "Timeline: How a New North American Trade Deal Happened." *Supply Chain Dive* (October 2). Retrieved from https://www.supplychaindive.com/news/NAFTA-timeline-how-USMCA-happened/538663/; November 5, 2020.

McCaffrey, Stephen C. 2003. "The Need for Flexibility in Freshwater Treaty Regimes." *Natural Resources Forum* 27(2) (May):156–162.

McCaffrey, Stephen C. 2013. "The Progressive Development of International Water Law." In *The UN Watercourses Convention in Force: Strengthening International Law for Transboundary Water Management*, edited by Flavia Rocha Loures and Alistar Rieu-Clarke, pp. 10–19. London and New York: Routledge, Taylor & Francis Group.

Olson, Mancur. 1965. *The Logic of Collective Action. Public Goods and the Theory of Groups*. Cambridge: Harvard University Press.

Onencan, Abby Muricho, and Bartell van de Walle. 2018. "Reasonable Utilization: Reconstructing the Nile Basin Water Allocation Dialog." *Water* 10(6):707.

Rahman, Kazi, S., Zahidul Islam, Umme, Navera, K., and Fulco Ludwig. 2019. "A Critical Review of the Ganges Water Sharing Arrangement." *Water Policy*, 21(2) (April 1).

Rieu-Clarke, Alistair, and Alexander Lopez. 2012. "Why Have States Joined the UN Watercourses Convention?" In *The UN Watercourses Convention in Force: Strengthening International Law for Transboundary Water Management*, edited by Flavia Rocha Loures and Alistair Rieu-Clarke, pp. 36–45. London and New York: Routledge.

Rieu-Clarke, Alistair, and Flavia R. Loures. 2013. An Institutional Structure to Support the Implementation Process. In *The UN Watercourses Convention Force*, edited by Flavia Rocha Loures & Alistair Rieu-Clarke, pp. 263–269. London and New York: Routledge.

Sergio, Domingues, and Dejan Zlatkovic. 2015. "Renegotiating PPP Contracts: Reinforcing the 'P' in Partnerships." *Transport Reviews* 35(2) (March):204–225.

Talozi, S., A. Altz-Stamm, H. Hussein, and P. Reich. 2019. "What Constitutes An Equitable Water Share? A Reassessment of Equitable Apportionment in the Jordan–Israel Water Agreement 25 Years Later." *Water Policy* 21(5):911–933.

UNWC (UN Watercourses Convention). n.d. User's Guide Fact Sheet Series: Number 5 No Significant Harm Rule. Retrieved from https://www.unwatercoursesconvention.org/documents/UNWC-Fact-Sheet-5-No-Significant-Harm-Rule.pdf. November 7, 2020.

U.S. State Department. 1994. "Text of Jordan-Israel Treaty of Peace. U.S. State Department, Nov. 94." *Supplement Middle East,* 5(44):6, 9. Signed October 26.

Zawahri, Neda A. 2008. "Designing River Commissions to Implement Treaties and Manage Water Disputes: The Story of the Joint Water Committee and Permanent Indus Commission. *Water International* 33(4):464–474.

PART V

Policy Recommendations and Conclusions

CHAPTER 9

Policy Recommendations and Conclusions

Egypt's geographic location, which is downstream of the Nile, makes its water security subject to the whims of those who control the tap upstream. Rationality, therefore, dictates that Egypt should recognize its disadvantaged position and try to reconcile with the upstream states and recognize the vantage point that the upstream states have. There are several options Egypt can use to ensure that the tap remains open and the quantity of water that reaches them is not diverted for consumptive uses thereby reducing the amount received. With these options, conflicts can be avoided, minimized, or resolved without subject riparian states engaging in either costly war or lengthened hostility.

Conflicts, violent or not, can be emotionally and economically draining. Moreover, disagreements fuel political feuds when, in fact, such differences could be avoided if states listened and acknowledged each other's positions and interests. As discussed in Part II of this book, resolving such conflicts is formidable. This is due to the fact that any position a riparian state takes is shaped by its unique political interests and values. Sometimes state action is influenced by the broader geopolitical exigencies. This chapter recommends policy actions that negotiators, as well as state officials, can apply to achieve the desired outcomes for riparian states in conflict.

The first set of policy recommendations is for the benefit of Egypt and Ethiopia, which were embroiled in the Nile water rights conflict for over ten years (2011–2021). When Ethiopia started the construction of the Grand Ethiopian Renaissance Dam (GERD) in April 2011, the Addis Ababa government must have anticipated a hostile reaction from Egypt in the downstream, given past opposition by Egypt towards any dam being constructed on Ethiopia's Blue Nile. But, as discussed in the last eight chapters of this book, it is evident that there is no silver bullet to resolving such a complex problem. What makes this process more daunting is the multiple memberships within the basin, with each riparian state focused on its own selfish gains. This stance is supported by the fact that nation-states, as formally constituted, serve and protect the interests of their citizens. The second problem is the transient nature of water. The amount of water flow in a river varies from season to season as dictated by the changing climatic conditions. Equally significant is the degree of use by different members as the river snakes its way downstream. These two problems make any policy meant to distribute the resource conflictual. Additionally, the provisions set by an existing treaty, which either grants or recognizes "prior-in-use" or "historic rights" to a particular riparian member (mainly located in the downstream), can complicate the ability of the negotiators to find an agreeable solution.

What follows is a set of policy recommendations and their implications for Egypt and Ethiopia. This is followed by recommendations specific to the Nile Basin Initiative. These options should also be viewed as action plans that public officials, experts, or appointed negotiators can use to bring about the peaceful resolution to water rights conflicts. The recommendations are thus divided into three categories: "Going to War," "Mitigating Water Rights Conflicts," and "Resolving Water Rights Conflicts."

Policy Recommendations: Implications for Egypt and Ethiopia

Going to War (Deploy "Hard Power")

It is of course tempting, based on the present asymmetric power relations between Cairo and Addis Ababa, for Egypt to apply threats of war against Ethiopia when its vantage point at the headwaters cannot be altered. Even if Egypt was pushed to the extreme and decided to engage Ethiopia on the battlefield and bomb the Renaissance Dam, such an action might only have short-term fulfillment. The long-term effect means the control of the tap itself cannot shift. Evidence shows that such an option would be too costly for Cairo, given the long distance between the two nations. Although to military strategists, the option is politically and technically feasible, the economic implications and administrative logistics would impose a huge burden on a country that was brought almost to its knees by the Arab Spring. Besides, the chances of such a faceoff escalating to a regional war are highly probable. This is because Egypt could easily draw its strength from the support of alliances in the twenty-two-member Arab League and, most likely, Western allies as well. Ethiopia, on the other hand, could find support from selected basin members in the upstream of the Nile, judging by hydro-alliances established during and after the 2010 Cooperative Framework Agreement. Moreover, countries such as Israel, Turkey, or Qatar, all of whom were alleged to support Ethiopia's Dam, could also declare their support to Addis Ababa.

Though not easy to assess, Sudan could go either way. Prior to the removal of President Al-Bashir, the Khartoum government had shifted her historical alliance with Egypt over water sharing to Ethiopia because of the perceived benefits from the power trade once the Renaissance Dam is complete. Moreover, Sudan and Egypt have had a sticky on-and-off relationship over a contested territory, the Halayeb Triangle. Upon the removal of former President Al-Bashir by a military coup, the political dynamics of the country vis-a-vis her neighbors changed. For example, its brief but warm relation with the Ethiopian government changed to a frosty one once the new regime took over in 2019. Between 2020 and 2021, Sudan accused Ethiopia of illegal occupation of the Al-Fashqa territory located between their two borders. In an attempt to outwit Sudan over its own dispute over the Halayeb Triangle, Egypt quickly declared its support to the Sudanese government to reclaim the Al-Fashqa territory from Ethiopia. According to a newspaper report, on March 2, 2021, a military pact was signed between Egyptian and Sudanese officials in Khartoum (Hendawi 2021). One of the provisions of that agreement was that Egypt would provide military support to Sudan at any time should they require it. Another is the provision for joint military training and exercises purposely to secure its border with Ethiopia. It was further reported that the Egyptian government had been securing, during the last six years, military hardware that has the capability to fight distant wars.

It should be recalled that, though the Egyptian head of State, El-Sisi, consistently called for a peaceful approach to the conflict, he never renounced the possibility of a war. In fact, at the onset of the conflict in 2011, a military face-off was on the table, albeit temporarily. Though Egypt later opted for a peaceful negotiation as the next best alternative to minimize damages associated with violent conflict, it is my contention that Egypt will not abandon these military maneuvers, at least during the foreseeable future. Note that in the earlier discussions, Cairo was reported to have stationed some of its military forces and hardware in Eritrea and South Sudan. Both countries share borders with Ethiopia; Eritrea to the northern border and South Sudan to the southwest. And, with the recent military pact between Egypt and Sudan, any predictions of a future war cannot be dismissed. Sudan serves as a buffer between the two potentially warring nations, Egypt and Ethiopia.

It is also the opinion of this author that there is nothing wrong, from the realist perspective, with the presence of such "hard power" or to conduct military exercises in the neighborhood of an enemy country as a show of strength. Such threats evinced themselves in 2020. For example, Ethiopian newspapers reported attempts by Egypt to hack into Ethiopian government computers. There was, in fact, evidence of intimidating messages and graffiti posted via social media by unidentified Egyptians. They sued the forum to warn of possible consequences should the dam construction continue.

From the perspective of Ethiopia, whose right to build the Renaissance Dam on the Blue Nile tributary is grounded on the principle of absolute territorial sovereignty, the probability of using military force to defend the dam is difficult to challenge. In fact, in an October 2020 news article, it was reported that the Ethiopian Air Force engaged in 24-hours surveillance over its air space to secure the dam (Tekle 2020). The Air Force Commander, Brigadier Yilma Merdasa, cautioned interested parties that his country was ready to deter an enemy that might plan on attacking the dam. Despite their persistent expression of readiness to defend the dam and territory, the Addis Ababa government, too, acknowledged the high costs as well as collateral damage it could suffer. Consequently, both Egypt and Ethiopia opted for negotiation as the most sensible and less costly method.

Given the above positions and actions by the warring nations, the following policy actions are suggested.

    a. *Threats or the show of military strength at the beginning of this kind of conflict is necessary but should be avoided.*

The costs of such threats can be astronomically high because they can escalate the dispute to an intense conflict. Although those threats can be used as a form of deterrence (Ref.: "Authoritarian Conflict Deterrence Theory"), such actions tend to work best when an enemy state plans to either annex or invade a territory. However, when it is about shared water resources, the threats can easily create a tit-for-tat situation in which the upstream states refuse to change their position.

b. *The decision to go to war over water rights when the nation in the downstream is a hegemon demonstrates a short-sighted policy focus on the means rather than the desired outcome.*

Being the dominant power located in the downstream can give the false impression of an ability to alter geographically granted water power belonging to upstream states. In fact, this relative power dynamic works best when the hegemon is in the upstream. Consider the cases of China in the Mekong River Basin, the United States in the Colorado River Basin, Turkey in the Euphrates and Tigris River Basins and India in the Ganges River Basin. In all of these, the downstream riparian states are the weaker ones—but their vantage point as controllers of the tap wield them with greater powers than the downstream hegemon.

c. *Military standoff complicates and lengthens the period of striking a deal; the best policy is to contain and reduce tension by focusing on immediate negotiations.*

Threats of a possible war generally attract outside interests and actors. Although outside intervention can help reduce the tensions or even solve them, the danger lies in the ability to delay the process of negotiating an agreement. It could also lengthen the time within which a settlement can be reached. Hence, the best policy approach is to contain the dispute by immediately engaging all the actors in diplomatic talks and negotiations.

The alternatives to belligerency or military options are numerous, though their degree of efficacy differ. Next is a discussion of the recommendations to mitigate potential water disputes.

Table 9.1 Sample international water agreements

Agreements/River	River basin	Year(s)
The Mekong River agreement	Mekong	1995
River Niger commission	Niger	1885, 1921, 1963, 1964, 1980, 1987, 1988, 1988
The boundary water treaty	Columbia	1909
The Ganges treaty	Ganges	1996
The danube river protection convention	Danube	1994

Developed from Loures and Rieu-Clarke (2013) with permission

Mitigating Water Rights Conflicts

As the saying goes, theory informs praxis. The opposite is also true; praxis can inform theory (grounded theory). In this section, I examine how past policies can be tailored to mitigate water conflicts. First, we must understand how it all began in the Nile Basin countries.

The problem over Nile water use was triggered by the British policy that apportioned the water between two of its colonies, Egypt and Sudan, and neglected the eight upstream states. That exclusionary policy did not only exhibit realist and rational thinking, in which a state seeks to fulfill its self-interest (both economic and political) but ensured that the other members remained disadvantaged in water use decision-making. The danger to this short-sighted policy approach lies in its failure to consider the long-term consequences to all riparian actors. Generally, policy decisions over the use of collective (public) goods such as water systems, should be guided by the utilitarian principle. This principle emphasizes that the goodness of a decision rests on its ability to provide greater utility for the greatest number. Quintessentially, the 1929 and 1959 colonial agreements, which allocated the waters to Egypt and Sudan, should have equitably distributed to all the members, even if they were skewed. It thus failed to meet the utilitarian requirement. It is also apparent that the British moved on with the decision under the premise that it was impossible to satisfy one's need without reducing the benefits that the other persons would typically derive from a good (or service). These are the "pareto-optimal" decisions. What, then, are the appropriate policies to mitigate water rights conflicts?

a. ***Agreements are necessary to mitigate water conflicts.***

Once the riparian states recognize the reality that they share the waters of an international river basin, it is critical for them to sit at the table to discuss and formalize the sharing of the resource. The discussion should preferably aim at developing a legal framework (or agreement) that is binding on all the riparian states. As this work has shown, the sharing of international watercourses is marked by numerous treaties. According to the most recent estimates, globally there are 145 treaties that govern shared international water systems. The majority of these treaties are bilateral (86%), while only 14% are multilateral. This proves the necessity to enter bilateral treaties even when the watercourse contains multiple members. This further lends credence that to the suggestion that members of a basin, preferably those that share borders, should consider bilateral agreements. Additionally, the collective action problem dictates that the fewer the number of actors, the greater the chances of cooperation. Table 9.1 provides sample water treaties that have restrained further conflicts.

To enter into treaties and agreements, the negotiators must consider the history of mistrust, the opposing political cultures, geographical imperatives, and the subtleties of the past and present political regimes. The latter can undoubtedly shape the process of negotiating a treaty and its outcome. When the states in conflict are democratic, the likelihood of an intense conflict or war is minimized. This is the premise of the Democratic Peace Theory. Although it is argued in this book that the opposite can also be true (i.e., "authoritarian peace theory"—authoritarian states are unlikely to go to war with one another because they share common traits and values). Opinions suggest that authoritarian regimes are characterized by erratic behavior and as such, they are averse to compromise. The case of Egypt and Ethiopia illustrates this stance. Egypt, in its political history, with the exception of 2012 and 2013, has been led by authoritarian regimes. The same applies to Ethiopia although the present leader and Nobel Peace Prize winner, Abiy Ahmed, is considered more democratic than his predecessors. Although, that depends on who is making the assessment.

While striking a water agreement is both desirable and necessary, it is recommended that the policy actors and selected negotiators desist from quick fixes, or what has been referred to in this text as "ceasefire agreements." To aim for signed agreements that quickly reduce the tensions may initially appear a success but, in reality, suppresses the undercurrents that might erupt later. Overall, agreements act as mitigating forces because they share the following critical attributes: (1) recognizing the opposing water rights claims, (2) reducing defections, and (3) increasing cooperation through regular meetings and exchange of hydrological information/data. However, for the agreements to be effectual, they must be signed and ratified by respective legislative bodies of each nation, bear conflict resolution mechanisms, be adaptable, and be characterized by inclusive participatory process.

Although for Egypt and Ethiopia, the three colonial agreements over the Nile water use existed (i.e., the 1902 agreements between Ethiopia and Britain, the 1929 Agreement between Egypt and Britain and the 1959 Agreement between Egypt and Sudan), their exclusionary nature of other upstream states failed to deter future conflicts among the riparian states. This does not undercut the importance of treaties in mitigating future conflicts but points to the necessity of equity and of fairness in any signed treaty. It is these limitations in the earlier Nile treaties that led to the eruption of conflicts among the ten riparian states in the 1990s. However, to not have any agreement is even worse. Consider the case of Turkey, Syria and Iraq that all share the Euphrates and the Tigris Rivers and have no formal treaty about water sharing. Tensions persist but the chances of war are limited because Turkey, which controls the tap is a hegemon, while Syria and Iraq and the underdogs. The political imperatives in Syria and Iraq (ravaged by persistent war and instability) make it difficult to coordinate a treaty in their favor.

b. *River Basin Organizations promote collaboration and can mitigate conflicts.*

Another mechanism instituted by nations that share river basins is a river organization. Presently, there are 61 river basin organizations that manage some of the world's 276 international river basins. Examples include the Israeli-Palestinian Joint Water Committee, the Mekong River Commission (China, Laos, Vietnam, Cambodia, and Thailand), the International Boundary and Water Commission (U.S. and Mexico), the Permanent Okavango River Basin Commission (South Africa), the International Commission for the Protection of the Danube River (14 West and East European nations), the Permanent Indus Commission (India and Pakistan), Lake Chad

Basin Commission (Chad, Cameroon, Niger, and Nigeria), Uruguay River Management Commission (Argentina, Uruguay), Orange-Senqu River Commission (Botswana, Lesotho, Namibia, and South Africa), and the International Commission for the Protection of the Rhine (Germany, France, Luxembourg, the Netherlands, and Switzerland) (International Water Law Project 2021).

These organizations are preferred because they promote cooperation, manage shared water resources, and suppress potential disputes. In addition to these functions, river basin organizations, as currently designed, fulfill the following strategic objectives: water security, energy security, food security, environmental sustainability, and adaptation to climate change and transboundary governance. To achieve these strategic objectives, river basin organizations coordinate joint activities including meetings, shared projects, water management, and the exchange of information to ensure the members' interests are addressed and their voices heard. For these reasons, the Nile Basin Initiative (NBI) was created in 1999. The structure of the organization should preferably include a Secretariat, a Council representing each riparian state and the means to fund the activities.

Even though the NBI has regional programs (NELSAP and ENSAP) from which the members are expected to derive benefits (e.g., hydroelectric power generation and attendant power trade), these sub-basin programs are part of the broader goal of enhancing cooperation. Unfortunately, the presence of these regional programs, as in the ENSAP headquartered in Addis Ababa, did not deter the eruption of an intense conflict between Egypt and Ethiopia. It is therefore recommended that the Nile Basin countries reconstitute these two regional programs into independent sub-basin organizations—the upper Nile Basin and the lower Nile Basin. By making them autonomous entities with each having the authority to make bilateral agreements if and when required, the Nile Basin will succeed in reducing the eruptions of conflicts involving all ten riparian states. This has the potential to reduce the collective action problem and at the same time enhance cooperation.

Resolving Water Rights Conflicts

a. ***Diplomacy is, and will always be, the primary instrument available to policymakers when reducing tensions and promoting peaceful coexistence.***

The art of diplomacy has been used for generations between officials of sovereign states to either negotiate a ceasefire, strike agreements over contentious claims (e.g., borders, transboundary resources) or promote cooperation in trade. Consequently, many sovereign states around the world have established diplomatic relations by opening embassies in other countries. The exchange of diplomats has, therefore, become a practice in vogue. Moreover, as an instrument of "soft power," diplomacy works. The proximate reasons for its success in most, if not all, cases include the use of tact, interpersonal communication, prudence, and patience. Negotiators who deploy the attributes of calmness, judiciousness, patience, teamwork, and, most importantly, appropriate skills, knowledge, and experience will most likely succeed in striking deals.

Three specific approaches discussed in this book are "coercive diplomacy," "pragmatic diplomacy," and "reasoned dialogue." (Walton, 2008) Coercive diplomacy involves the use of threats upon labeling the other party (nation) as an enemy that aims to destroy "us." With this kind of framing, the goal of the diplomatic team is to win or create harm. One way to exact harm is through the use of threats. This is the approach initially applied by Egypt. The problem with threats is that they work in certain situations but not all. Moreover, they are temporary and therefore suppress tensions for a short time.

The second approach is "pragmatic diplomacy." This approach is highly recommended because it is a rational process in which each party listens to the other party's positions and interests. That way, an actor is able to evaluate the issues through the eyes of the opponent. For example, in an interview conducted in Egypt in 2014 by this author, some participants admitted that Ethiopia, too, deserved to use their water. The only limitation of this approach is that it does not automatically translate into the incorporation of the opponent's perspective into the negotiation process. Despite this shortcoming, a pragmatic dialogue approach is recommended for the Egyptian and

Ethiopian negotiators to better understand each other's interests and positions and to reach an agreement.

Reasoned diplomacy is also recommended because it entails listening to each other's position and then proceeds, after assessing the information, to utilize persuasion. The opportunity to deliberate each other's position and interests makes this approach desirable and, hence, could help Ethiopia and Egypt reach a deal. The problem, however, was Ethiopia's reluctance to share information that Egypt needed to understand Addis Ababa's position and interest. Ethiopia, on the other hand, was hesitant to share information with Egypt because they considered certain hydrological and climatic material security-sensitive.

b. *Ideal Third-Party Mediation—a proven approach to resolving water conflicts no matter how daunting they are.*

To be successful, this approach requires the engagement of independent and neutral expert(s) with the appropriate skill sets and competencies. With these, the mediators can assess disparate interests and positions before they bring all warring parties to the table. Specific competencies and requirements associated with successful mediation include, but are not limited to, being a national country or member of an independent body that has no formal or close political ties with either warring party. It is also recommended that the lead mediator is from the same region where the conflict is centered. Although the latter is assumed to be ideal, it is a credible choice because by being a "local," the mediator is better exposed to the cultural nuances, history, and issues on the ground than an outside expert who must rely on briefings and published reports to deconstruct the conflict. The second, and most significant, is the ability to apply a deliberative approach rather than duress as the means to get the actors to reach and sign an agreement. The mediation by the Trump administration between November 2019 and February 2021, for example, was accused by Ethiopia of applying this tactic. Ethiopia felt offended and absconded from the last meeting in Washington D.C. That marked the end of the United States' involvement in the process.

c. *Renegotiation—provides the means for the aggrieved party to revisit the pending and contentious provisions of a signed treaty purposely to reach an agreement. It is in the best interest of Egypt to renegotiate the Cooperative Framework Agreement of 2010.*

The decision to renegotiate the Cooperative Framework Agreement (CFA) would not only be the smartest thing to do but would be the most strategic. To not do so has consequences. One, it might denote concession of defeat as well as negative consequences. Two, it might indicate the lack of vision on the part of Egyptian policymakers. In fact, the stalemate over the CFA's Article 14 (b) on water security can only be resolved by Egypt gaining a seat at the table, not by staying away from it. Moreover, the upstream states have nothing to lose from the CFA framework as presently constituted. It is, therefore, in the best interest of Egypt to take the lead in renegotiating the agreement in order to secure its future water security.

d. *Partitioning of the Nile Basin into two autonomous sub-basin organizations will increase member benefits and lower the chances of conflicts.*

The Collective Action Theory suggests that the share in a collective (public) good diminishes with the increase in group membership. The opposite is also true. The smaller (or less varied) the group members that share a public good, the greater the benefits derived by each member. Therefore, it is for the benefit of the Nile members to divide the basin into two autonomous sub-basins (i.e., the upper Nile Basin and the lower Nile Basin) because it makes coordinating shared water management and responding to emergent disputes much easier.

e. *Apportioning the water to each member will reduce or even eliminate future intense conflicts.*

To achieve peaceful cooperation in the use of a shared water system, the Nile Basin countries must not only partition the basin into sub-basins but also allocate the water to each member based on appropriate and accepted international principles and formulas. As discussed in the book, three out of the eleven existing international metrics that are most appropriate to the Nile water sharing are: geography (climatic and hydrological conditions), availability of alternatives of equivalent value, the size of the population, and the existence of a signed treaty. The latter has been added by the author because it sets the basis from which to negotiate any water allocation. In this regard, the Nile countries have the advantage due to the presence of the Cooperative Framework Agreement signed by majority states in 2010 and the Declaration of Principles in 2015 signed by Egypt, Ethiopia, and Sudan.

Although water allocation has been avoided by the Nile Basin countries in the two negotiated agreements, most likely because of its technical and complex process, it is recommended as the single most effective policy approach to settling the conflict between Egypt, Ethiopia, and Sudan. It is also a secure approach to ensuring that the upstream states can validate their right of ownership to the resource. The sense of ownership is critical to each state even when they do not actually put the water to use. Moreover, it enhances national pride when, after years of battling for water rights, the Nile basin should learn from Israel and Jordan, as both employed the allocation formula enshrined in Article V of the 1966 Helsinki Rules on the Uses of the Waters of International Rivers. The set of 11 metrics acts as a guide to allocating international waters in a reasonable and equitable manner. The choice of relevant criteria by the two countries has reduced, if not eliminated, the tensions since the 1994 Peace Agreement was formalized.

f. *Bilateral Agreements are by far the most popular form of the agreement because they have greater potential in reducing future water rights conflicts.*

Given its proven efficacy in reducing conflicts and enhancing greater cooperation among the signatories, working towards a bilateral treaty between Egypt and Ethiopia is highly recommended. This policy option is supported by the principle of collective action; that is, the fewer the number of nations involved in an agreement, the greater the share in benefits for each member. And the larger the members in collective action, the lesser the share in benefits for each member. Therefore, a smaller group size in any agreement provides a greater opportunity for close interactions, improved working relations, ease in the exchange of information and enhanced ability to quickly respond to any emerging disputes. Although the Declaration of Principle of 2015 involved fewer actors—Egypt, Ethiopia, and Sudan, the exact role of the latter—whether as a mediator or as one of the parties to the conflict—remains unclear. Instead, it is suggested that even as Egypt and Ethiopia continue to search for a final resolution to the impasse, that they seek a bilateral agreement. Sudan's position must continue to remain as that of arbiter, not one of the sparring parties.

g. *Litigation, though not relied upon as much by the nations in conflict over shared international water rights, is the next best alternative when all other options prove difficult.*

Litigation is recommended as the next best alternative to resolving shared international water disputes for several reasons. One, the international arbiters (e.g., the International Court of Justice) are, by all standards, neutral professionals who apply the logic of common law to arbitrate contentious claims presented to the bench. Two, the jurors employ international practices and standards pertinent to each case. For example, in arbitrating shared water conflicts, the ICJ has deferred to the international water laws as recommended by the International Law Commission and the UN Watercourses Convention. Most recently, for example, these two institutions have advised that the traditional application of the "absolute territorial sovereignty should not be applied in determining the right of use to shared international waters." Instead, the principles of interdependence and cooperation are more rational and appropriate (Dellapenna et al. 2013).

Given the cooperation agreement signed between the Hague-based Permanent Court of Arbitration (PCA) and the African Union in July 2015, the African states should not only take advantage of the PCA expertise to strengthen their own national arbitral tribunals but also form a similar regional or continental-wide body. The advantage of such a body is the opportunity to access a more specialized team of arbitrators. This will become increasingly critical as problems associated with the consequences of climate change promise to destabilize, cause, or even intensify conflicts over the use of resources. In fact, the demands for economic growth and consumptive uses of water systems in selected areas of Africa, as a result of the burgeoning population, are already causing tensions. The Nile basin, with an estimated population of 542.3 million, is a good example of this (Merem et al. 2020). One problem with an independent arbitral body, however, is the tendency to not consider the underlying political forces, including expressed values and positions that are unique to either the leadership of a particular state or the broad political culture of the countries involved. Thus, while litigation and arbitration are excellent means to resolving such disputes, battles over international water rights are predominantly political and must be treated as such. Its solution must always involve and/or include political nuances.

h. *Contextualized Negotiation Model (CNM) encapsulates all of the above conflict resolution strategies by a biased focus on the inside rather than outside to develop lasting solutions to water rights conflicts.*

Though this approach might be confused with indigenous conflict resolution mechanisms, CNM is different in fundamental ways. First, it is a transboundary method that puts emphasis on the internal (social, economic, and political) factors of each country engaged in a conflict. Second, it allocates the mediation role to the local actors selected from within the region but not from the states in conflict. The inward focus is based on the fair assumption that the "locals" are better poised to appreciate the social and political nuances associated with the causes and escalation of the conflict than outsiders. Moreover, because of their assumed shared norms and cultures (e.g., collectivist and high-context cultures), they can easily incorporate these subtleties into the negotiation process. This model is also a preferred choice because it sets the premise in which diplomacy, third-party mediation, bilateral agreements, litigation, and water apportionment negotiation can better work, be levied and defended by the local actors, interest groups and citizens. Though not evidently clear if this is the rationale behind Ethiopia's insistence on the African (Union) solution, it merits attention.

A summary of these policy recommendations, along with their positive and negative implications is provided in Table 9.2.

Policy Recommendations: Implications for the Nile Basin

a. *A "Seat at the Table" provides the opportunity for cooperative arrangements in which each riparian is heard and a legal water framework established.*

The history of the Nile water conflict, including the one between Egypt and Ethiopia over the latter's Renaissance Dam, provides three critical lessons. The first is that cooperation can bring multiple members of a shared water resource to the negotiation table. This

Table 9.2 Summary policy recommendations—Egypt and Ethiopia

Policy recommendations	Implications
Going to war (deploying "hard power")	
War	• The costs are prohibitive, and the collateral damage potential is high
	• Does not solve the problem permanently
	• Threats and not actual war work as deterrence; controls behavior but increases hostility
	• Military installations near the enemy are strategic but do not resolve or alter who controls the tap
Mitigating water conflicts	
Diplomacy	• Diplomacy acts as a primary tool to immediately address the conflict upon its eruption
	• Diplomats, usually foreign ministers and heads of states, engage in talks to reduce tensions and to determine the best way forward—whether to engage independent technical experts, council of ministers from each state, or an ad hoc committee
Renegotiate Existing Agreement (CFA)	• The success of the first and the only signed treaty is rare. Revision of existing treaties is necessary to remedy the weaknesses and to address internal and external changes and stressors
	• Better means to secure future water security; keeping away does not resolve pending issues
Resolving conflicts	
Third-Party Mediation	• Almost all of the conflicts involving two states are resolved by independent third-party mediators. The mediators can be individuals, selected government representatives, regional, or international organizations
Partition Basin into autonomous sub-basins	• The fewer the members to a shared water resource, the greater the benefits and the fewer the conflicts

(continued)

Table 9.2 (continued)

Policy recommendations	Implications
Bilateral agreements	• By far the most popular and lasting form of agreement. The best way forward for Egypt and Ethiopia
Litigation	• The alternative when all other avenues to mediation fail. Problem: Not possible to enforce in the anarchic international system
Apportion the water to the riparian states	• Complex process but offers a lasting solution although require adjustments as dictated by the changes in the environment
Contextualized negotiation	• Owning and localizing the process offers a genuine and lasting solution. External ideas and experiences can be incorporated for guidance

alters the dynamics of an interaction. It gives each member the ability to express their interests and position in the sharing of jointly owned resources. History shows that sharing a seat at the table has enabled several, if not all, riparian states around the world with shared international water systems to work out legal frameworks that improve how the water is managed and shared. The products are the Cooperative Framework Agreement of 2010 (though not signed by Egypt and Sudan) and the Declaration of Principles of 2015 between Egypt, Ethiopia, and Sudan.

b. *As the only legal and mandated water regime that coordinates the activities of the Basin (NELSAP and ENSAP), the Nile Basin Initiative (NBI) must desist from the "free rider" tactics but instead directly engage in the affairs affecting members.*

By not getting involved in the Egypt–Ethiopia Renaissance Dam conflict, the NBI hopes to reduce any related transactions (direct and indirect) costs. In essence, it is hoping to reap the benefits of peace once this is all over. Although, politically, that choice is intuitively clever because it keeps the organization neutral, the danger is even greater. One, the consequences of that neutrality can weaken its ability to mediate future conflicts affecting its coordination efforts. Two, it can lose trust from its members. Three, the decision to keep away also had a lethargic effect on the upstream states located in the

Equatorial Lakes region. None of them made a deliberate effort to mediate instead were reached out to by either Egypt or Ethiopia for support. This free riding strategy reminds me of a popular saying in western countries: "What goes around comes around." That is the position that Egypt and Ethiopia will most likely take when any of the upstream states face complicated problems or conflicts: Where were you when we needed you?

Article 34 Section (a) of the Cooperation Framework Agreement, however, shields the NBI from blame. It states that "If the States concerned cannot reach an agreement by negotiation requested by one of them, they may jointly seek good offices, or request mediation or conciliation by, the Nile River Commission or another third-party, or agree to submit the dispute to arbitration, in accordance with procedures to be adopted by the Council, or to the International Court of Justice." Based on the above provisions, the NBI is safe from the blame. First, Egypt and Ethiopia were required to "jointly" forward their case for intervention to the Nile River Basin Commission—which to-date has not been formalized through CFA entered into force when the sixth member (out of the 10 nations), Burundi, signed the agreement. Given the nature and the intensity of the conflict between the two countries, one or both of them did not approach the NBI Secretariat for intervention. Whether it is an intuitive or logical step, it seems rational, given the persistence of the conflict, for the NBI leadership to have called a joint session for all members to help deescalate the issue or to appoint a team of diplomats from selected member countries to negotiate.

c. *River Basin Organizations (e.g., the NBI or the NileCommission) are a necessary structural governance instrument that must continually be strengthened to enhance cooperation.*

River Basin organizations are a dominant future of shared basins. They provide the structure for governance. They also provide the means for member states to cooperate on how best to share in the benefits from a river basin. Ideally, these organizations should include their governance processes mechanisms and enforcement. Presently, there is no clearly stated approach to enforce the NBI rules requirements for conflict resolution needs to be changed to allow the body to intervene instead of waiting to be consulted by parties to the conflict (Table 9.3).

Table 9.3 Summary policy recommendations—The Nile Basin initiative

Policy recommendations	Implications
A seat-at-the-table	• NBI to maintain participatory mechanisms that give voice to all interested parties, including NGOs, citizens
Direct involvement by NBI Secretariat policymakers	• The costs associated with keeping away from the issues affecting some members might pose unintended long-term consequences to NBI, including confidence in its leadership or even a show of bias • To "free ride" or sitting on the fence can weaken the organization to mediate conflicts
Regional basin organization (NBI)	• River Organization is a prerequisite to cooperative water governance, especially when the Basin involves two or more riparian states • Collective Action makes it easier for group members to express their positions and interests

References

Dellapenna, Joseph., Allistair Rieu-Clarke, and F. Rocha Loures. 2013. "Possible Reasons Slowing Down the Ratification process." In *The UN Watercourse Convention in Force: Strengthening International Law for Transboundary Water Management*, edited by F. Rocha Loures and Alistair Rieu-Clarke. London and New York: Routledge.

Hendawi, Hamza. 2021. "Egypt and Sudan Sign Defence Pact and Blame Ethiopia for Stalled Dam Talks". *The National News*, March 2. https://www.thenationalnews.com/mena/egypt/egypt-and-sudan-sign-defence-pact-and-blame-ethiopia-for-stalled-dam-talks-1.1176240.

International Water Law Project. 2021. "Addressing the Future of Water Law and Policy in the 21st Century." *International Documents*. https://www.internationalwaterlaw.org/documents/intldocs/.

Loures, F. Rocha, and Alistair Rieu-Clarke. *The UN Watercourses Convention in Force: Strengthening International Law for Transboundary Water Management*. London and New York: Routledge.

Merem, E. C. et al. 2020. Issues in Transboundary Water Use in the River Nile Basin Area of Africa. *World Environment* 10(2):27–44.

Tekle, Tesfa-Alem. 2013. "Egypt to Establish Military Base in Eritrea." Sudan Tribune, April 18.

Conclusions

After 20-plus tumultuous years of negotiation, and as the manuscript went off to the publisher, the filling and operations of Ethiopia's Renaissance Dam conflict was far from over. That is a strange way to end a book, when in fact the issue being explored continues to evolve. However, the lessons learned over the course of the conflict and approaches discussed to resolve the impasse should inform what can be expected in this and similar water rights issues. The recommendations and evidence-based predictions made can help the riparian states, as well as the negotiators, make informed decisions and how to go about the process. This final section answers three important questions: With the failure to strike an agreement over the staged filling and operations of the dam, what does this mean for Egypt, Ethiopia, and Sudan? What alternatives does Egypt, at the end of the pipe, have? And, what are the implications for the MENA Powers and the Nile Basin Initiative in the future?

What Lack of Agreement Means for the Actors

The inability of Egypt, Ethiopia, and Sudan to strike an agreement over the filling and operations of the dam illustrates three things. First, it proves that when it comes to a shared resource that is dynamic as the waters of a river, a "win–win" strategy neither fulfills nor satisfy the needs of at least one party. In fact, as argued in this book, the sharing of a watercourse or the solution to a conflict over its use is generally a zero-sum game; the upstream riparian wins and the downstream riparian loses. This is true in two situations: when the upstream state is a political and economic hegemon (e.g., Turkey that controls the Euphrates and Tigris; China—the Mekong; the United States—the Colorado; India—the Ganges). In theory however, the win–win approach is aimed at assuaging the parties in a conflict to believe that each has something to gain. The problem with this model is that it falls short from identifying by how much each riparian state is to win. Ideally, however, a win–win solution does not mean each gets an equal share, but that X and Y gets what each deserve, or a gain rather than a loss. Another situation occurs when the upstream riparian, by virtue of its geographical location, derives more benefits from the river—a situation that is impossible to alter. Hence the best approach is for the mediators to desist from the false promise of a win–win deal—right from the beginning of the process. Instead, the ideal strategy is the minimization of losses on the part of Egypt and maximization of benefits on the part of Ethiopia.

The failure to reach an agreement further proves that despite being a non-political and economic hegemon, Ethiopia's hydro-hegemon position accords her the right to utilize the waters within its territory. Just as Turkey, China, India, and the United States have dominated in the use of the rivers that emanate from within their boundaries, so has Ethiopia followed suit. These hydro-hegemons have, for the most part, deferred to the international principle of "absolute territorial sovereignty" to justify the construction of waterworks upstream, including huge dams for hydropower generation. It is therefore my conclusion that Ethiopia's unwavering position to proceed with the dam regardless of Egypt's plea for change in the filling procedures, is influenced by how other global hydro-hegemons have handled similar disputes. Why should they be different, Ethiopia might ask? Although the "territorial sovereignty" (or the Harmon Doctrine) is not presently accepted by the international community as guide to sharing transboundary watercourses, the requirement that the members to the watercourse consult with each other before developing a waterworks failed to work in the Nile Basin. Ethiopia, a member of the basin, saw no need to do so when Egypt failed to sign the 2010 Cooperative Framework Agreement that has such a provision. This leads to the conclusion that when a state, by works of nature, is in the downstream as Egypt is, the best strategy to ensure water security is to take the lead in striking an agreement but not to keep away from the process. Ethiopia, on the other hand, should be guided by the principle of good neighborliness. Thus, both countries try to balance the tradeoffs as well as the potential benefits of their actions, in the short and long term.

Third, as argued in the book, Sudan's position as the arbiter has been both ideal and awkward. Ideal, because Sudan is geographically located between Egypt and Ethiopia. The Blue Nile from Ethiopia drains into Sudanese territory where it merges in Khartoum with the White Nile from Equatorial Lakes region upstream—before snaking northwards into Egypt. Naturally, Sudan is best placed to mediate the conflict as it understands more than any other country the history to the conflict and the political, economic, and social imperatives of both Egypt and Ethiopia. Moreover, Sudan will be directly and indirectly affected by the outcome; peace or war. For example, it will import cheap power from Ethiopia. Additionally, the dam will regulate floods and therefore reduce the destruction of crops experienced annually by Sudan.

But Sudan's role as the mediator has also been an awkward one. First, prior to the current regime that took power in April 2019, President Al-Bashir moved away from their age-old alliance with Egypt, a fellow member to the Arab League, to Ethiopia. The move was a strategic one because of Sudan's expressed interest in cheap power. Moreover, it had an ongoing dispute with Egypt over the Halayeb territory. The latter is not resolved to-date. However, since the takeover by the new military government, Sudan's leaders have changed tact by re-establishing its alliance with Egypt. This time focusing not on Halayeb but on Al-Fashqa, a disputed territory to its eastern border with Ethiopia. When that conflict re-emerged, Egypt was quick to offer its support to Sudan and even signing a military pact—which the officials acknowledged was a signal to Ethiopia that both countries would join forces should it be necessary. This shifting of alliance, and mainly to protect her interests, begs the question why the Khartoum government should be involved as the mediator. My inference is that Sudan's role has somewhat acted in reducing the chances of finding a lasting solution to the conflict. In fact, Sudan's replacement by the African Union, I believe, portends well for both parties and hopefully a lasting solution will be found.

For Ethiopia, and in as much as failing to sign the agreement denotes a win, power, pride, and achievement of its generation-long goal for the dam to boost its economy and change livelihoods, it will not be business as usual in the next 5–10 years. In my opinion, the bickering between the governments in Cairo and Addis Ababa will persist and potentially affect bilateral activities in important areas, including trade and tourism. It is therefore in the best interest of Ethiopia, as member of the Nile Basin countries, the Horn of Africa, and international community to play with the modern rules of international co-existence. In international relations, we learn that the behavior of one actor has the potential to cascade to other regions and in turn, affect the benefits that actor can derive from other nations.

Alternatives for Egypt

Striking a deal with Ethiopia is critical to Egypt. Although, in the absence of a detailed study that shows the effects of the rapid filling of the reservoir, Egypt still fears the possibility of a water loss or reduction, its government must be visionary and strategic in action. In terms of strategy, Egypt is left with four options: (1) sustained threats against Ethiopia, (2) go to war, (3) keep on track with the negotiations, and (4) refocus on harvesting underground aquifers and increased desalination of sea water.

1. Sustained threats against Ethiopia

    With less than a week before this book manuscript went to the Press, on March 30, 2021, the media reported a strong warning to Ethiopia by Egypt's President General Sisi. Speaking from the city of Ismailia, Sisi reiterated that their share of the water is "untouchable" and cautioned of "instability that no one can imagine" in the lower Nile basin and the adjoining areas if Ethiopia proceeds to fill the Dam in the absence of a mutually binding agreement (Magdy 2021). In effect, Egypt is applying these sustained warnings as a strategy to compel Ethiopia to come to an agreement. Admittedly, it is these threats that brought Ethiopia to a "Seat-at-the-Table." Additionally, these threats can be viewed as a strategy to soliciting support from the MENA Powers and beyond. When Egypt, for example, hosted the Arab League Summit in 2020, all except Sudan declared their support to Egypt's position on Ethiopia's Dam. Also, the Trump administration, in 2019, bought into the cry for support to his "favorite dictator" by suggesting a possible military attack on Ethiopia by Egypt. The Trump administration later cut funding earmarked for the Addis Ababa government. In effect, these sustained threats can have desired outcomes, but will Ethiopia cave in?

2. Go to War

The possibility of a military combat, despite the most recent warnings by Egypt, is unlikely. War between nations in the twenty-first century are rare. But, as argued in this book, such possibilities cannot be ruled out. Judging by Egypt's security activities, including the reported positioning of its military bases in South Sudan, Eritrea, and the recent military pact with Sudan, it is hard to deny the likelihood of military encounters. But, to engage in such a battle would be prohibitively costly to Egypt. For one, the distance between Cairo and Addis Ababa, which is between 1325 and 1331 nautical miles, can be a challenge. Also, the collateral damage associated with such an attack would be huge given that Ethiopia also possesses one of the largest military personnel and hardware on the continent. If the allies of each country had to be involved, then the conflict could escalate by involving Eritrea, Sudan or even Somalia.

But here is another scenario: War is no longer about physical combat; it involves cyber-attacks and proxy wars. In terms of proxy wars, it all starts with creating instability in an enemy country. In fact, the Ethiopian government pointed to "foreign hands" in the civil war in its northern Tigray region that erupted in November 2020 and continued in early 2021. Those foreign hands were alleged to be that of Egypt, though the claims were unsubstantiated.

3. Keep on track with the negotiations

We can conclude that both Egypt and Ethiopia are committed to an ongoing negotiation. The problem is Ethiopia's trust in the ability of the African Union to resolve the stalemate while Egypt is somewhat leery, relying totally on the continental body. Instead, in February 2021, Cairo called for the intervention of an international "quartet" involving the U.N. Security Council, the United States, the European Union, and the African Union. This lack of agreement as to who should mediate complicates matters and lengthens the crisis into the unknown future. As I pointed out in Chapter 6, Ideal Third-Party Mediation, the danger of "mediation-hopping" is that each set of new mediators will require time to learn about the history and related nuances to the conflict. That is why it was recommended that home-grown mediators are best suited to this role. Though Sudan's involvement was appropriate, it was compromised because of vested interests, and history of alliance with Egypt; both

are Islamic states and members of the Arab League. That relationship skewed her approach to the issue, which in turn forced Ethiopia to be suspicious. It is for these reasons that the African Union, as a neutral body, is the next best alternative to arbitrating the impasse.
4. Alternative sources of water

The effects of Climate Change do not portend well for Egypt. The erratic pattern of precipitation means some years will be worse, with droughts in the upstream, thereby reducing the amount of water feeding into the Nile. Egyptians would die of thirst and hunger, and hence forced to import food products. Although I believe in the Gaia Hypothesis that the earth has the capacity to self-generate, meaning, in this context, that heavy rains will follow droughts and vice versa, Egypt must engage in strategies for the future. Therefore, it must explore tapping into the underground aquifers and in the desalinization of sea water, however costly.

Implications for the MENA Powers and the Nile Basin Initiative

Regional Security

The failure to resolve the Ethiopia's Renaissance Dam impasse is a large threat to the regional security of the eastern Horn of Africa and beyond. It is an issue that calls for urgent international community intervention. As the event unfolds, the prediction is that direct or proxy war between Egypt and Ethiopia cannot be entirely ruled out. If that happens, it will have cascading effects in the region. Sudan would undoubtedly be involved on the side of Egypt judging by the military pact signed early 2021. Eritrea, though a small country to the north of Ethiopia, can go either way. Its forces supported Ethiopia's military in the Tigray crisis. But it could also support Egypt logistically. For example, it provided Egypt with a military base by the Red Sea. Although unpredictable, Israel could be drawn into the conflict as well given its historical or even biblical relations with Ethiopia. The Europeans to the North would also step in purposely to secure the Red Sea/Suez Canal passage. Saudi Arabia, a close ally to Egypt, and also a member to the Arab League, would probably provide support that Egypt requires in the event of a military face off.

Given the gravity of this potential (or even hypothesized) regional conflict scenario, could Egypt win? My prediction is yes, but at a prohibitive cost. The cost could include a cutback in funding particularly by the United States and its close allies. In an April 2, 2021 article in

The Washington Post, the new Biden administration signaled to Egypt that there will not be any "blank checks for Trump's favorite dictator" (Torbati and Hudson 2021). Though the administration released $197 million to Cairo for sale of missiles and other military hardware to strengthen its capability to secure its Red Sea water passages, Congress is demanding accountability on the part of General Sisi on Human Rights related issues. Moreover, things are changing and the United States may not need Egypt as much as it did in the days following the 1979 Agreement with Israel. If anything, other players in the Middle East such as Saudi Arabia and the United Arab Emirates have emerged. These Lower Gulf States are rich in oil needed by the United States but also strategically located to fend off Iran, the new enemy on the block.

To the Nile Basin Initiative, the crisis points to the need for greater involvement in the affairs of its members. The dam conflict intensified on the NBI's watch and yet failed to intervene. The rise in population, the effects of climate change and interstate competition for freshwater resources will necessitate the installation of additional water works, which will spark further conflicts in the future. Therefore, it is in the best interest of the NBI to engage all its members to do two things: One, apportion the waters of the Nile to each of its members. It is a complex undertaking but is a sure way to mitigate water rights conflicts, as it gives each member a sense of ownership even if they do not use it. Two, without a formal water rights arbitration body, which could be a group of selected experts from the riparian states, water conflicts in the Nile Basin will intensify in 10 to 20 years from now. I also conclude that by dividing the basin into two, Upper and Lower, and giving each some degree of autonomy, will substantially reduce the burden of resolving any future conflicts in the Nile Basin Initiative. Undoubtedly, this sequel obliterates my father's approach to resolving the conflicts over the sharing of milk among the three siblings; talking it over and offering options rather than reprimands.

References

Torbati, Yeganeh and Hudson, John. 2021. "U.S. Policy Toward Egypt Sparks Conflict between Congressional Democrats and Biden." *Washington Post*, April 2.

Magdy, Samy. 2021. "In Stark warning, Egypt leader Says Nile water "Untouchable." AP News, apnews.com, March 30.

Appendix 1A

Timeline of Events—GERD Project

Date	Event
October 2009	Ethiopia's survey of the dam construction begins
May 1, 2010	Ethiopia officially announces its intention to construct the dam
May 14, 2010	Five Nile basin states (Kenya, Uganda, Tanzania, Rwanda, and Ethiopia) sign the Cooperative Framework Agreement (CFA)
May 21, 2010	Egypt's minister of water and environmental affairs (Mahmoud Nasser al-Din Allam) confirms a deal with Sudan to preserve "the historical rights of both countries to the Nile's water."
May 23, 2010	President Hosni Mubarak requests Congo DR and Kenya to support and Egypt and Sudan's initiative in the basin
June 2010	Egypt expresses its official grievances to the United Nations and the African Union, and demands that the dam's funding be cut. Ethiopia, in turn, asks Egypt to participate in discussions about cooperation between the two nations
November 2010	Ethiopia announces the completion of plans for the dam. International backers require an agreement between Nile basin countries before agreeing to fund the project
March 31, 2011	Contract awarded to an Italian company for $4.8 billion without competitive bidding
April 2, 2011	Prime Minister Meles Zenawi (of Ethiopia) lays the foundation stone for the dam and establishes an airstrip for the rapid transport of aircrafts
May 2011	Ethiopia announces it will share plans for the dam with Egypt so the latter can study the impact, if any, it will have on its share of the Nile

(continued)

(continued)

Date	Event
Sept. 19, 2011	Ethiopia suggests a partnership to Sudan wherein Ethiopia would provide Sudan with electricity, probably at a cheaper rate, as a provision of their agreement
July 14, 2012	Former President Mohamed Morsi visits Ethiopia, the first time an Egyptian president makes the trip since a failed assassination of Mubarak seventeen years prior. The negations between the two countries stop a few months later
April 6, 2013	Morsi visits Sudanese president Bashir; both confirm cooperation with other Nile countries
May 28, 2013	Construction work of the dam begins by Ethiopia
June 3, 2013	Egypt broadcasts a "secret" meeting between Morsi and political forces in which they ask the president to circulate a rumor that Egypt will launch a military attack on the dam
November 4, 2003	Negotiations resume in Khartoum after Morsi's ouster

Source Mars, M. (2015, March 23). Retrieved from http://www.madamasr.com/en/2015/03/23/news/u/egypts-battle-over-the-renaissance-dam-a-timeline/

Appendix 1B

Timeline of Events—Negotiations

March 15, 2014	Declaration of Principles signed in Khartoum by Egypt, Ethiopia, and Sudan. Sudan served as the mediator
2016–2019	Series of meetings held by three nations; no deal is reached
November 6, 2019	Foreign Ministers meet with the American mediators in Washington D.C. to break the impasse
January 13–15, 2020	The three countries meet in Washington
January 31, 2020	The United States Treasury Secretary Steve Mnuchin announces that an agreement has been reached between the foreign and water ministers. Agreement to be signed in February, 2020 Issues addressed: Staggered reservoir filing; mitigation mechanism during droughts; and procedures for long-term dam operations Pending Issues: coordination mechanism, dispute resolution, information sharing, and water safety
February 12–13, 20,202	Third talks held in Washington D.C.—Chaired by Treasury Secretary Mnuchin; World Bank President David Malpass attends as observer
February 26, 2020	Ethiopian Ambassador to the United States Fitsum Arega states on Twitter that "Ethiopia will never sign on an agreement that will surrender its rights to use the Nile River

(continued)

(continued)

March 4, 2020	The Arab League meets in Cairo and declares support against Ethiopia's dam. Dam viewed as water security threat to Egypt Sudan, a member of the League, abstains

REFERENCES

"Aswan High Dam." Encyclopedia Britannica. http://www.britannica.com/.
Cooperative Framework Agreement. 2010. Nile Basin Initiative. http://www.nilebasin.org/index.php/nbi/cooperative-framework-agreement.
"Egyptian Warning over Ethiopia Nile Dam." BBC News. Last modified June 10, 2013. http://www.bbc.com/news/world-africa-22850124.
"Rwanda." Worldometer. Last modified 2016. http://worldometer.info.
"Sudan." World Bank. Last modified 2016. http://www.databank.worldbank.org.
"TeachMideast" "A Review of Relations Between Israel and Egypt." TeachMideast: An Educational Institute of the Middle East Policy Council. Retrieved from https://teachmideast.org/articles/review-relations-israel-egypt/.
"The Helsinki Rules." International Law Project. http://www.internationalwaterlaw.org/documents/intldocs/Helsinki_Rules_with_comments.pdf.
"The Helsinki Rules." International Water Law Project. Last modified 1966. http://www.waterlaw.org.
"Transboundary Freshwater Conflict Database." Oregon State University. Last modified 2016. http://www.transboundarywaters.orst.edu/database/DatabaseIntro.html.
"UN Data Country Profile." UN Data. Last modified 2017. http://data.un.org.
UNDP. 2013. Human Development Report 2013. Retrieved from https://www.undp.org/publications/human-development-report-2013. April 13, 2021.
"United Nations Development Programme, Human Development Reports." UNDP. Last modified 2015. http://hdr.undp.org/en/countries/profiles/ETH.

© The Editor(s) (if applicable) and The Author(s), under exclusive license to Springer Nature Switzerland AG 2021
S. H. Okoth, *The MENA Powers and the Nile Basin Initiative*, https://doi.org/10.1007/978-3-030-83981-9

"USAID." Climate Variability and Change in Ethiopia: Summary of Findings, December 2015. USAID Technical Report.

"World Bank- Burundi." World Bank. Last modified 2016. http://www.worldbank.org/en/country/burundi. 171–189.

Abbott, Kenneth W., and Duncan Snidal. 1998. "Why States Act through Formal International Organizations." *Journal of Conflict Resolution* 42(1): 3–32.

Abebe, Daniel. 2014. "Egypt, Ethiopia and the Nile: The Economics of International Water Law." *Chicago Journal of International Law* 15(1) (Summer):27–46.

Abukhater, Maher., and Sanders, 2010. Edmund. *Palestinian Leaders threaten to quit peace negotiations. The Baltimore Sun, 2010–10–03*. Baltimore, MD. Tribune Publishing Company, LLC.

Acemoglu, Daron, and James A. Robinson. 2012. *Why Nations Fail: The Origins of Power, Prosperity, and Poverty*. New York, NY: Crown Publishing Group.

Adair, W. L., and Brett, J. M. 2005. The Negotiation Dance: Time, Culture, and Behavioral Sequences in Negotiation. *Organization Science* 16: 33–51.

Ademola, Abbas. 2012. *International Law: Text, Cases, Materials*. Oxford: Oxford University Press.

Africanews. 2019. "Ethiopia Rejects Egypt's Proposal to Manage Nile Dam." September 19.

Al-Karib, Hala, and Hassan, El-Sadig. 2019. "Sudan's New Government Can't Succeed If It Remains on the U.S. Blacklist." FP News, December 9.

Allan, J. A. 1990. "The Nile Basin: Evolving approaches to Nile waters management." Occasional Paper 20, June. *SOAS Water Issues Group*. University of London.

Allport, Gordon W. 1954. *The Nature of Prejudice*. Reading, MA: Addison-Wesley.

Alon, Ilai. 2016. "Some Comments on Language as a Barrier for Trust in Arabic-Speaking Islam." In *The Role of Trust in Conflict Resolution*, 83–115. https://doi.org/10.1007/978-3-319-43355-4_6. January.

Anand, P. B. 2007. "Capability, Sustainability, and Collective Action: An Examination of a River Water Conflict." *Journal of Human Development* 8(1) (March):109–132.

Anna, Cara. 2020. "Satellite Images Show Ethiopia Dam Reservoir Swelling." *The Washington Post*, July 14.

AP (Associated Press). 2020. "Egypt Supports Sudan's International Arbitration Proposal in Dam Dispute with Ethiopia." TheNationalNews.com.

APA News. 2017. "Egypt's request to rejoin the CFA agreement on Nile waters rejected." *Journal du Cameroun.com* (May 17).

Arino, Africa, and Jeffrey J. Reuer. 1993. "Designing and Renegotiating Strategic Alliance Contracts." *The Academy of Management Executive*, 2004–08–01, 18(3):37–48.

REFERENCES 245

Atlas of International Freshwaters Agreements. 2002. United Nations Environment Programme. Retrieved from https://transboundarywaters.science.oregonstate.edu/sites/transboundarywaters.science.oregonstate.edu/files/Database/ResearchProjects/AtlasFreshwaterAgreements.pdf; September 22, 2021.

Arwamba Times (Addis Ababa). 2016. "Grand Renaissance Dam Lottery Winning Numbers Announced." June 27.

Associated Press. "Egypt Supports Sudan's International Arbitration Proposal in Dam Dispute with Ethiopia." https://www.thenationalnews.com/mena/egypt-supports-sudan-s-international-arbitration-proposal-in-dam-dispute-with-ethiopia-1.1172813.

Awojobi, Omotola, and Glenn P. Jenkins. 2015. "Were the Hydro Dams Financed by the World Bank from 1976 to 2005 Worthwhile?" *Energy Policy* 86:222–232.

Baligira, Robert. 2010. "Rwanda and the Nile: Water Plans and Their Implementation." In *The River Nile in the Post-Colonial Age: Conflicts and Cooperation among the Nile Basin Countries*, edited by Terje Tvedt, 13–30. Cairo: American University Press.

Bardwell, Lisa V. 1991. "Problem-Framing: A Perspective on Environmental Problem Solving." *Environmental Management* 15(September):603–612.

Barrett, S. 1994. "Self-enforcing International Environmental Agreements." *Oxford Economic Papers* 46: 878–894.

Barnard, Evan, and S. Wahab. 2018. "Aaron Wolf in Transboundary Water Conflict and Cooperation." *NewSecurityBeat*, The blog of the Environmental Change and Security Program, November 30.

Bates, A., Tuncok, K., Barbour, T., & Klimpt, J. -É. 2013. First joint multipurpose program identification: Strategic perspectives and options assessment on the Blue Nile multipurpose development—Working Paper 2. Addis Ababa.

Bercovitch, Jacob, and S. A. Kadayifci-Orellana. 2009. "Religion and Mediation: The Role of Faith-Based Actors in International Conflict Resolution." *International Negotiations* 14(2009):175–204.

Berhane, Daniel. 2012. "Nile: The Int'l Panel of Experts on Renaissance dam officially launched." Hornaffairs.com, May 22. Retrieved from https://hornaffairs.com/2012/05/22/nile-the-intl-panel-of-experts-on-renaissance-dam-officially-launched/.

Bezabih, Mitwab., and Tesfa, Belachew. 2019. "Grand Ethiopian Renaissance Dam (GERD) Filling Scenarios: Analysis of Energy and Revenue losses." *International Journal of Nile Basin (UNB)- Energy, Water, Environment & Economic* 3(5), 1–11. December.

Biniam, Iyob. 2010. "Resilience and Adaptability of Transboundary Rivers: The Principle of Equitable Distribution of Benefits and the Institutional

Capacity of the Nile Basin." Oregon State University, ProQuest Dissertations Publishing. 3425578.
Bohmelt, Tobias, Thomas Bernauer, Halvard Buhuag, Nils Peter Gleditsch, Theresa Tribaldos, and Gerdis Wischnath. 2014. "Demand, Supply, and Restraint: Determinants of Domestic Water Conflict and Cooperation." *Global Environmental Change* 29(November):337–348.
Brams, Steven J. 1993. "Theory of Move." *American Scientist* 81(November/December):562–570.
Bremer, Stuart. 1992. "Dangerous Dyads: Conditions Affecting the Likelihood of Interstate War." *Journal of Conflict Resolution* 36(2):309–341.
Brittanica. 2020. *Dams and Reservoirs*. Retrieved from https://www.britannica.com/place/Nile-River/Dams-and-reservoirs.
Broachman, Marit. 2012. "Signing River Treaties—Does It Improve River Cooperation?" *International Interactions* 38:141–163.
Burra, Elisa, Xavier Font, and Janet Cochrane. 2014. "Destination Stakeholders' Perceptions of Volunteer Tourism: An Equity Approach." *International Journal of Tourism Research* 17(5) (June):451–459.
Calabresi, G., and D. Melamed. 1972. "Property Rules, Liability Rules and Inalienability: One View of the Cathedral." *Harvard Law Review* 85:1089, 1092–1093.
Caruthers, Osgood. 1958. "Haile Selassie Mediating Sudan Dispute with Egypt." New York Times, February 22.
Cernea, Michael, M. 1997. "Hydropower Dams and Social Impacts: A Sociological Perspective." Social Development Papers, Paper No. 16, January. *Social Assessment Series*. The World Bank.
CFA (River Nile Basin Cooperative Framework). 2010. *Agreement on the Nile River Cooperative Framework* (Accord-cadre Sur la Cooperation dans le Bassin du Fleuve Nil).
Chung, Ozzie. 2014. Prospect Theory in International Relations. *Clocks and Clouds* 47(2). American University.
CIA. 2020. *The CIA Factbook*. www.cia.gov.
Cohen, Alice, and Emma S. Norman. (n.d.). Renegotiating the Columbia River Treaty: Transboundary Governance and Indigenous Rights. Research Articles. web.ebscohost.com.
Crump, Larry. 2009. "Linkage Theory and the Global-Multilevel System: Multilateral, Regional, and Bilateral Trade Negotiations. *SSRN Electronic Journal*. June. https://doi.org/10.2139/ssrn.1484792.
Crump, Larry. 2011. "Negotiation Process and Negotiation Context." *International Negotiation* 16(2):197–227.
Czech, Slawomir. 2016. "Mancur Olson's Collective Action Theory 50 Years Later: A Review from the Institutionalist Perspective." *Journal of International Studies* 9(1) (November 1):114–123.

Declaration of Principles. 2015. *Agreement on the Declaration of Principles Between the Arab Republic of Egypt, the Federal Republic of Ethiopia and the Republic of the Sudan on the Grand Ethiopian Renaissance Dam Project (GERDP)*. Khartoum: State Information Service.

Degfu, D. M. He, Weijun and Liang Yuan. 2017. "Monotonic Bargaining Solution for Allocating Critically Scarce Transboundary Water." *Water Resources Management* 31:2627–2644.

Dellapenna, Joseph, Rieu-Clarke Allistair, and F. Rocha Loures. 2013. "Possible Reasons Slowing Down the Ratification Process." In *The UN Watercourse Convention in Force: Strengthening International Law for Transboundary Water Management*, edited by F. Rocha Loures and Alistair Rieu-Clarke. London and New York: Routledge.

Delli Priscoli, J., and A. T. Wolf. 2009. *Managing and Transforming Water Conflicts*. New York: Cambridge University Press.

DeLuca, Giacomo, and Petros G. Sekeris. 2013. Deterrence in Contests. *Economica* 80.

Deluga, Ronald J. 1998. *Leader-Member Exchange Quality and Effectiveness Ratings: The Role of Subordinate-Supervisor Conscientiousness Similarit* 23(2):189–216. Thousand Oaks, CA: Sage (1998-06).

Driechova, Alena., Itay Fischhendler, and Mark Giordano. 2010. The Role of Uncertainties in the Design of International Water Treaties: An Historical Perspective. *Climate Change* 105: 387–408.

El Fadel, M., Y. El-Sayeg, K. El-Fadl, and D. Khorbotly. 2003. "The Nile River Basin: A Case Study in the Surface Water Conflict Resolution." *Journal of Natural Resources and Life Sciences Education* 32.

El-Fadl, El-Sayegh M., and D. Khorbotly. 2003. "The Nile River Basin: A Case Study in Surface Water Conflict Resolution." *Journal of Natural Resources and Life Sciences Education* 23:107–117.

El-Sayed, Mustapha, K., and R. Soheil Mansour. 2017. "Water Scarcity as a Non-traditional Threat to Security in the Middle East." *India Quarterly* 73(2):227–240.

ENA [Ethiopian News Agency]. 2020. "Sudan Refuses to endorse Arab League Resolution Over GERD Row." March 5.

FAO. The Nile Basin. Retrieved from http://www.fao.org/3/w4347e/w4347e0k.htm.

FDI Team. "Water-Shortage Crisis Escalating in the Tigris-Euphrates Bain." *Future Directions International Pty Ltd*. Last modified August 2002. http://www.futuredirections.org.

Fink, Edward L., and Deborah A. Cai. 2002. "Conflict Style Differences between Individualists and Collectivists." *Communication Monographs* 69(1):67–87.

Fischhendler, I. 2015. The Securitization of Water Discourse: Theoretical Foundations, Research Gaps and Objectives of the Special Issue. *International*

Environmental Agreements 15:245–255. https://doi.org/10.1007/s10784-015-9277-6.

Furst, Heiko. n.d. *The Hungarian-Slovakian Conflict over the Gabcikovo-Nagymaros Dams: An Analysis*. Retrieved from http://www.columbia.edu/cu/ece/research/intermarium/vol6no2/furst3.pdf. October 30, 2020.

Galtung, Johan. 1966. "East-West Interaction Patterns." *Journal of Peace Research* 3(2): 146–177.

Garrett, Hardin. 1968. The Tragedy of the Commons. *New Series* 162(3859) (December 13):1243–1248.

Gebre, Samuel. 2020. "Ethiopia to Press Ahead With Africa's Biggest Hydropower Dam." Retrieved from https://www.bloomberg.com/news/articles/2020-04-10/ethiopia-vows-to-press-ahead-with-hydropower-dam-despite-virus. April 10.

Gebreuel, Goitom. 2014. "Ethiopia's Grand Renaissance Dam: Ending Africa's Oldest Geopolitical Rivalry." *The Washington Quarterly* (Summer).

Gelfand, Michele J., Marianne Higgins, Lisa H. Nishii, Jana L. Raver, Dominguez Alexandria, Fumio Murakami, Susumu Yamaguchi, and Midori Toyama. 2002. "Culture and Egocentric Perceptions of Fairness in Conflict and Negotiation." *Journal of Applied Psychology* 87(5):833–845.

Giardano, Mark. 2008. "International Water Treaties." *Journal of Environmental Planning and Management* 51(6):873–875.

Gleick, Peter H. 2008. *Water Conflict Chronology*. Pacific Institute for Studies in Development, Environment, and Security Database on Water and Conflict. N.P.

Godana, B. 1985. *Africa's Shared Water Resources: Legal and Institutional Aspects of the Nile, Niger, and Senegal River Systems*. Geneva: Graduate Institute of International Studies.

Hall, Edward. T. 1976. *Beyond Culture: Theory of Low/High Context Communication*. Garden City, NY: Anchor Books/Doubleday.

Hamner, Jesse H., and Aaron T. Wolf. 1998a. *Trends in Transboundary Water Disputes and Dispute Resolution*. Oregon State University, USA.

Hamner, Jesse H., and Aaron T. Wolf. 1998b. "Patterns in International Water Resource Treaties: The Transboundary Freshwater Conflict Database." In *Colorado Journal of International Environmental Law and Policy, 1997 Yearbook*. http://www.transboundarywaters.orst.edu/publications/patterns/.

Harris, Leila M., and Samer Alatout. 2010. "Negotiating Hydro-Scales, Forging States: Comparison of the Upper Tigris/Euphrates and Jordan River Basins." *Political Geography* 29:148–156.

Harrison and Sons, St. Martin's Lane, London. "Treaty Series, No 16." Treaties between the United Kingdom and Ethiopia, and between the United Kingdom, Italy, and Ethiopia, Relative to the frontiers between the Soudan,

Ethiopia, and Eritrea. Last modified May 15, 1902. http://treaties.fco.gov.uk/docs/pdf/1902/ts0016.pdf.

Hassen, Anwar. 2014. "The Geopolitics of Water Negotiations Succeeding the GERD Project in The Nile River Basin." Retrieved from https://www.academia.edu/31728758/The_Geopolitics_of_Water_Negotiations_succeeding_the_GERD_Project_in_the_Nile_River_Basin.

Hefney, M., and S. E. Amer. 2005. Egypt and the Nile Basin. *Aquatic Science* 67:42–50.

Hendawi, Hamza. 2021. "Egypt and Sudan Sign Defence Pact and Blame Ethiopia for Stalled Dam Talks". *The National News*, March 2. https://www.thenationalnews.com/mena/egypt/egypt-and-sudan-sign-defence-pact-and-blame-ethiopia-for-stalled-dam-talks-1.1176240.

Hernandez, Ariel M. 2014. *Strategic Facilitation of Complex Decision-Making: How Process and Context Matter in Global Climate Change Negotiations.* Springer. New York, London: Cham Heideberg.

Hillel, D. 1994. *Rivers of Eden: The Struggle for Water and the Quest for Peace in the Middle East.* New York: Oxford University Press.

Hoeffler, Anke. 2014–03. "Can Intervention Secure the Peace?" *International Area Studies Review* 17(1):75–94.

Hofstede, Geert. 1981. *Culture's Consequences: International Differences in Work-Related Values.* Beverly Hills: Sage.

Howell, P. P., and J. A. Allan. 1994. *The Nile: Sharing a Scarce Resource. A Historical and Technical Review of Water Management and of Economic and Legal Issues.* Cambridge: Cambridge University Press.

Hoyt, Alia. 2020. "How the Nile Works: The Nile Today." Retrieved from https://adventure.howstuffworks.com/nile-river.htm. April 14.

Huang, Yi-Hui, and Olwen Bedford. 2009. "The Role of Cross-Cultural Factors in Integrative Conflict Resolution and Crisis Communication: The Hainan Incident." *American Behavioral Scientist* 53. November 30.

Hume, David. 2000. Collective Action. Encyclopedia Britannica.

Integrated Water Quality: Limnology Study for Lake Victoria. 2002. Environmental Management Part II Technical Report. N.P.: COWI Consulting Engineers.

International Water Law Project. 2021. "Addressing the Future of Water Law and Policy in the 21st Century." *International Documents.* https://www.internationalwaterlaw.org/documents/intldocs/.

International Law Water Project, The Helsinki Rules. Last modified May 26, 2020. https://www.internationalwaterlaw.org/documents/intldocs/.

International Law Water Project, Transboundary Water Management Organizations. https://www.internationalwaterlaw.org/institutions/transboundary_wmos.html.

IPoE. 2013. International Panel of Experts (IPoE) on Grand Ethiopian Renaissance Dam Project. Final Report. Addis Ababa. May 31.

Jackson, Sukhan, and Adrian C. Sleigh.2001. "The Political Economy and Socio-Economic Impact of China's Three Gorges Dam." *Asian Studies Review* 25(1):52–80.

Johnson, Gene. "Judge: Plan for Restoring Northwest Salmon Runs Not Enough." AP News. Last modified May 5, 2016. https://apnews.com/163 2aef434b549259d7bd7f29490be66.

Kadayifci-Orllana. 2009. *Ethno-Religious Conflicts: Exploring the Role of Religion in Conflict Resolution.* https://doi.org/10.4135/9780857024701.n14. January.

Kahsay, Tewodros Negash, Onno Kuik, Roy Brouwer, and Pieter Van Der Zaag. 2015. "Estimation of the Transboundary Economic Impacts of the Grand Ethiopia Renaissance Dam: A Computable General Equilibrium Analysis." *Water Resources and Economics* 10(April):14–30.

Kenya—Sondu Miriu Hydro Power Project. Washington, DC: World Bank, n.d. http://documents.worldbank.org/curated/en/579441468273008142/Kenya-Sondu-Miriu-Hydro-Power-Project.

Khagram, Sanjeev. 2004. *Dams and Development: Transnational Struggles for Water and Power.* Ithaca and London: Cornell University Press.

Khaneman, Daniel, and Amos Tversky. 1979. "Prospect Theory: An Analysis of Decision under Risk." *Econometrica* 47(2).

Kimenyi, Mwangi S., and J. M. Mbaku. 2015. The limits of the new "Nile Agreement." *Brookings, Africa in Focus.* April 28, 2015.

Klare, Michael E. 2001. *Resource Wars: The New Landscape of Global Conflict.* New York: Metropolitan Books.

Kliot, N. 1994. *Water Resources and Conflict in the Middle East.* New York: Routledge.

Kong, Dejun, T. 2015. "Narcissists' Negative Perception of Their Counterparts' Competence and Benevolence and Their Reduced Trust in a Negotiation." *Personality and Industrial Differences* 74:196–201.

Kraft, Michael E., and Scott R. Furlong. 2013. *Public Policy: Politics, Analysis, and Alternatives.* 4th ed. Los Angeles: Sage.

Krantzberg, Gail. 2009. "Renegotiating the Great Lakes Water Quality Agreement: The Process for a Sustainable Outcome." *Sustainability,* 1. https://doi.org/10.3390/su1020254.

Lazerwitz, David J. 1993. "The Flow of International Water Law: The International Law Commission's Law of the Non-Navigational Uses of International Watercourses." *Indiana Journal of Global Legal Studies* 1(1), Article 12. Available at https://www.repository.law.indiana.edu/ijgls/vol1/iss1/12.

Lederach, John Paul. 1995. *Preparing for Peace: Conflict Transformation Across Culture.* Syracuse: Syracuse University Press.

Levy, Barry S., and Sidel W. Victor. 2011. "Water Rights and Water Fights: Preventing and Resolving Before They Boil Over." *American Journal of Public Health* 101(5) (May):778–780.

Levy, Jack E. 1992. Prospect Theory and International Relations: Theoretical Applications and Analytical Problems. *Political Psychology* 43(2): 283–310.

Lopez, Edwin. 2018. "Timeline: How a New North American Trade Deal Happened." *Supply Chain Dive* (October 2). Retrieved from https://www.supplychaindive.com/news/NAFTA-timeline-how-USMCA-happened/538663/; November 5, 2020.

Loures, F., Rocha, and Alistair Rieu-Clarke. *The UN Watercourses Convention in Force: Strengthening International Law for Transboundary Water Management*. London and New York: Routledge.

Lowi, Miriam R. 1993. Bridging the Divide: Transboundary Resource Disputes and the Case of West Bank Water. *International Security* 18(1) (Summer): 113–138.

Mabrouk, Mirette. 2019. "Events at MEI." *The New Arab*, December 3. https://www.mei.edu/events.

Maclin, Elizabeth, Matt Sicchio, Shawn Cantrell, Lisa Ramirez, Brian Graber, Sara Johnson, and Karen Tuerk. eds. 1999. *Dam Removal Success Stories: Restoring Rivers through Selective Removal of Dams That Don't Make Sense*. N.P.: American Rivers, Friends of the Earth, & Trout Unlimited.

Madani, Kareh. 2010. "Game Theory and Water Resources." *Journal of Hydrology* 381:225–238.

Mafaranga, Hope. 2020. "Heavy Rains, Human Activity, and Rising Waters at Lake Victoria." EOS Science News by AGU. July 7.

Magdy, Samy. 2021. "In Stark Warning, Egypt Leader Says Nile Water 'Untouchable.'" AP News; apnews.com. March 30.

Mohamoda, D. Y. 2003. "Nile Basin Cooperation: A review of the literature." *Current African Issues* 26. Nordiska Afrikainstitute.

Marit, Brochman, Paul R. Hansel, and Jaroslav Tir. 2012. *International Treaty Effectiveness*. San Diego: Annual Meeting of the International Studies Association. http://www.paulhensel.org/Research/isa12.pdf.

Maru, Mehari. 2020. "Can Trump Resolve the Egypt-Ethiopia Nile Dam Dispute?" AlJazeera.com (OPINION). April 26.

Masr, Mada. 2015. "Egypt's Battle over the Renaissance Dam: A Timeline." Mada. https://www.madamasr.com/en/2015/03/23/news/u/egypts-battle-over-the-renaissance-dam-a-timeline/.

McCaffrey, Stephen C. 2003. "The Need for Flexibility in Freshwater Treaty Regimes." *Natural Resources Forum* 27(2) (May):156–162.

McCaffrey, Stephen C. 2013. "The Progressive Development of International Water Law." In *The UN Watercourses Convention in Force: Strengthening International Law for Transboundary Water Management*, edited by Flavia

Rocha Loures and Alistar Rieu-Clarke, 10–19. London and New York: Routledge, Taylor & Francis Group.

Mehmet, Kucukmehmetoglu and Jean-Michel Guldmannô. 2004. "International Water Resources Allocation and Conflicts: The Case of the Euphrates and Tigris." *Environment and Planning A* 36:783–780.

Mekonnen, D. Z. 2010. "The Nile Basin Cooperative Framework Agreement Negotiations and the Adoption of a 'Water Security' Paradigm: Flight into Obscurity or a Logical Cul-de-sac?" *The European Journal of International Law* 21(2).

Merem, E. C. et al. 2020. "Issues in Transboundary Water Use in the River Nile Basin Area of Africa." *World Environment* 10(2):27–44.

Michaelson, R. 2019. "Mohammed Morsi: Ousted President of Egypt Dies in Court." *The Guardian*, June 3.

Mitchell, S. M., and Zawahri, Nade A. 2011. "The Effectiveness of Treaty Design in Addressing Water Disputes." *Journal of Peace Research* 52(2): 187–200.

Mnookin, Robert H. 2003. When Not to Negotiate: A Negotiation Imperialist Reflects on Appropriate Limits. *U. Colo. L. Rev* 74: 1077 (2003).

Moon, Sarah. 2012. "Strife on the Nile: The Battle for Water Rights." *Harvard International Review* 34(2) (Fall):8.

Muckleston, K. W. 2003. *International Management in the Columbia River System*. New York: International Hydrological Programme, UNESCO, and PC-CP.

Mwiandi, Mary C. 2010. "The Nile Waters: A Factor in Socio-Economic Development of Western Kenya, 1959–2000." In *The River Nile in the Post-Colonial Age: Conflict and Cooperation among the Nile Basin Countries*, edited by Terje Tvedt, 93–124. Cairo: American University Press.

Nader, Mina. 2020. "Egypt, Ethiopia, Sudan at Loggerheads over Nile Dam Agreement." Retrieved from https://themedialine.org/top-stories/egypt. January 19.

Natural Resources Management and Environmental Department. 2016. *Irrigation Potential in Africa: A Basin Approach*. Food and Agriculture Organization of the United Nations. http://www.fao.org/nr/nr-home/en/.

NBI [Nile Basin Initiative]. 2012. The State of the Nile River Basin 2012. Retrieved from https://lnsbr.nipissingu.ca/wp-content/uploads/sites/10/2013/12/NileBasinInitiative_2012_StateoftheNileRiverBasin.pdf.

NBI (Nile Basin Initiative). 2021. Demography: Estimated and projected total population in the Nile Basin Countries. Nile Basin Water Resources Atlas. Retrieved from https://atlas.nilebasin.org/treatise/estimated-and-projected-total-population-in-nile-basin-countries/. September 22.

Ngowi, Honest P. 2010. "Unlocking Economic Growth and Development Potential: The Nile Basin Approach in Tanzania." In *The River Nile in the*

Post-Colonial Age: Conflicts and Cooperation among the Nile Basin Countries, edited by Terje Tvedt, 57–71. Cairo: American University Press.

Nkurunziza, Pascal. 2010. "Burundi and the Nile: Water Resource Management and National Development." In *The River Nile in the Post-Colonial Age: Conflicts and Cooperation among the Nile Basin Countries*, edited by Terje Tvedt, 13–30. Cairo: American University.

O'Connor, Rush. 2017. "Water Security: Preventing Future Conflicts." *Case Western Reserve Journal of International Law* 49.

OKACOM. 2020. The Permanent Okavango River Basin Water Commission. https://www.okacom.org/documents.

Okidi, O. 1994. History of the Nile and Lake Victoria Basins through Treaties. In P. P. Howell & J. A. Allan (Eds.), *The Nile Sharing a Scarce Resource*. London, UK: School of Oriental and African Studies.

Okidi, C. O. 1995. *Environmental Legislation in Africa: Some Recent Rrends*. IUCN (ID: MON- 054562).

Okoth, Simon. 2009. A 'Seat at the Table': Exploring the Relationship between Pluralist A 'Seat at the Table': Exploring the Relationship between Pluralist Structures and Involvement in Decision-Making—The Case of the Structures and Involvement in Decision-Making—The Case of the Nile Basin Initiative Nile Basin Initiative. PhD Dissertation, Virginia Commonwealth University.

Olaka, L. 2020. Lake Victoria Could Burst Its Banks More Often in the Future: What Can Be Done. *The Conversation*. www.phys.org/news/2020-06.

Olson, Mancur. 1965. *The Logic of Collective Action. Public Goods and the Theory of Groups*. Cambridge: Harvard University Press.

Onencan, Abby Muricho, and Bartell van de Walle. 2018. "Reasonable Utilization: Reconstructing the Nile Basin Water Allocation Dialog." *Water* 10(6):707.

Ostrom, Elinor. 1999. "A Behavioral Approach to the Rational Theory of Collective Action Presidential Address, American Political Science Association, 1997." *The American Political Science Review* 92(1) (March):1–22.

Overview of the Case: Gabcikovo-Nagymaros Project (Hungary/Slovakia). Retrieved from www.icj-cij.org/en/case/92.

Parker, Donna. 2000. *Cross-Cultural Considerations in Mediation*. ProQuest Dissertation Publishing. California State University, Dominguez Hills.

Peterson, John. 2009. "Policy Networks." In *European Integration Theory*, edited by A. Wiener and Thomas Diez, pp. 105–123. 2nd ed. Oxford, UK: Oxford University Press.

Phillips, Peter, F. 2011. "Sulha: Traditional Arab Dispute Resolution." Business Conflict Blog. Business Conflict Management.com, April 8.

Posner, Michael. I. 1973. *Cognition: An Introduction (Scott, Forestman Psychological Concept Series)*. Glenview, Illinois.

Postel, Sandra L., and Aaron T. Wolf. 2001. "Dehydrating Conflict." *Foreign Policy* 126(September/October):60–67.

Rahman, Kazi, S., Zahidul Islam, Umme, Navera, K., and Fulco Ludwig. 2019. "A Critical Review of the Ganges Water Sharing Arrangement." *Water Policy*, 21(2) (April 1).

Rathbun, Brian C. 2014. *Diplomacy's Value: Creating Security in 1920s Europe and the Contemporary Middle East.* Ithaca and London: Cornell University Press.

Reuters. 2019. "Trump Speaks with Egypt's Sisi, Back Talks on Disputed Ethiopia Dam." September 23.

Rieu-Clarke, Alistair, and Alexander Lopez. 2012. "Why Have States Joined the UN Watercourses Convention?" In *The UN Watercourses Convention in Force: Strengthening International Law for Transboundary Water Management*, edited by Flavia Rocha Loures and Alistair Rieu-Clarke, pp. 36–45. London and New York: Routledge.

Rieu-Clarke, Alistair, and Guy Pegram. 2013. Impacts on the International Architecture for Transboundary Waters. In *The UN Watercourses Convention in Force: Strengthening International Law for Transboundary Water Management*, edited by F. Rocha Loures and Alistair Rieu-Clarke, pp. 67–76. London and New York: Routledge.

Rieu-Clarke, Alistair, and Flavia R. Loures. 2013. An Institutional Structure to Support the Implementation Process. In *The UN Watercourses Convention Force*, edited by Flavia Rocha Loures & Alistair Rieu-Clarke, pp. 263–269. London and New York: Routledge.

Rieu-Clarke, A., and Flavia Rocha Loures. 2013. Possible Reasons Slowing Down the Ratification Process. In *The UN Watercourses Convention in Force: Strengthening International Law for Transboundary Water Management*, edited by F. Rocha Loures and Alistair Rieu-Clarke. London and New York: Routledge.

Rinehart, Lloyd M., and Thomas J. Page. 1992. "The Development and Test of a Model of Transaction Negotiation." *Journal of Marketing* 56(4):18. October.

River Nile Basin Cooperative Framework. 2010. Agreement on the Nile River Cooperative Framework (Accord-cadre Sur la Cooperation dans le Bassin du Fleuve Nil).

Roberts, M. 2007. *Developing the Craft of Mediation: Reflections on Theory and Practice.* London: Jessica Kingsley Publishers, American Journal of Clinical Hypnosis 50(4):355–356. https://doi.org/10.1080/00029157.2008.10404305.

Sabatier, Paul A., and Christopher M. Weible. eds. 2014. *Theories of the Policy Process.* Colorado: Westview Press.

Sadoff, C., and D. Grey. 2002. "Beyond the River: the Benefits of Cooperation on International Rivers." *Water Policy* 4:389–403.

Saha, Sagatom. 2019. "How Climate Change Could Exacerbate Conflict in the Middle East." Atlantic Council, May 14. www.atlanticcouncil.org/blogs.

Saled, Mohamed. 2020. "Ethiopia Bans Flights over Nile Dam." *Al-Monitor*, October 11.

Saleth, R., and Ariel Dinar. 1999. Evaluating water institutions and water sector performance." *The World Bank Technical Paper*. Washington D.C.

Salman, Salman M. A. 2013. "Misconceptions Regarding the Interpretation of the UN Watercourses Convention." In *The UN Watercourses Convention in Force: Strengthening International Law for Transboundary Water Management*, edited by Flavia R. Loures and Alistair Rieu-Clarke, 28–45. London and New York: Routledge.

Salman, Salman M. A. 2016. "The Grand Ethiopian Renaissance Dam: The Road to the Declaration of Principles and the Khartoum Document." *Water International* 41(4):512–527.

Sandu, Antonio. 2013. Communicative Action and Philosophical Practice. *Romanian Journal for Multidimensional Education / Revista Romaneasca pentru Educatie Multidimensionala* 6(1):39–66, 28. June 2014.

Schmeier, Susanne. 2015. "The Institutional Design of a River Basin Organizations—Empirical Findings from Around the World." *International Journal of River Basin Organization* 13(1)

Schmidt, S., D. Hawkins, and K. Guerra. 2017. "188,000 Evacuated as California's Massive Oroville Dam Threatens Catastrophic Floods." *The Washington Post*, February 13.

Sergio, Domingues, and Dejan Zlatkovic. 2015. "Renegotiating PPP Contracts: Reinforcing the 'P' in Partnerships." *Transport Reviews* 35(2) (March):204–225.

Spencer-Churchill, Lieutenant Winston. 1989. "The Fashoda Incident." *The North American Review* 167(505) (December):736–743.

St. John, Ronald B. 2019. Andean Water Wars: The Silala Case. Council on Hemispheric Affairs, August 5.

Strobl, Eric, and Robert O. Strobl. 2011. "The Distributional Impact of Large Dams: Evidence from Cropland Productivity in Africa." *Journal of Development Economics* 96:432–450.

Strzepek, Kenneth M., Gary W. Yohe, Richard S. J. Tol, and Mark W. Rosegrant. 2008. "The Value of the High Aswan Dam to the Egyptian Economy." *Ecological Economics* 66:117–126.

Sudan Tribune. 2017. "Egypt to establish military base in Eritrea." Retrieved from www.middleeastobserver.org/2017/04/18/egypt-to-establish-military-base-in-eritrea. February 15, 2021.

Suleiman, Ramzi. 2016. "Effects of Expectations, Type of Relationship, and Prior Injustice on Trust Honoring: A Strategic-Experimental Approach." In *Role of Trust in Conflict Resolution: The Israeli-Palestinian Case and Beyond*, edited by Ilai Alon and Daniel Bar-Tal, 23. Gewerbestrasse, Switzerland: Springer Nature.

Swain, Ashok. 2002a. "The Nile River Basin Initiative: Too Many Cooks, Too Little Broth." *SAIS Review*.

Swain, Ashok. 2002b. "Managing the Nile River: The Role of Sub-Basin Cooperation." In *Conflict Management of Water Resources*, edited by Manas Chatterji, Saul Arlosoroff, and gauri Guha. Aldershot: Ashgate.

Swain, A. 2004. *Managing Water Conflict: Asia, Africa and the Middle East*. New York: Routledge.

Sztompka, P. 2016. "Two Theoretical Approaches to Trust; Their Implications for the Resolution of Intergroup Conflict." In *The Role of Trust in Conflict Resolution: The Israeli-Palestinian Case and Beyond*, edited by I. Alon and D. Bar-Tal, 15–21. Springer International Publishing AG. https://doi.org/10.1007/978-3-319-43355-4_2.

Tadros, Amjad. 2020. "Ethiopia Filling Mega-Dam that Egypt Calls an "Existential" Threat." CBS News, July 17.

Talozi, S., A. Altz-Stamm, H. Hussein, and P. Reich. 2019. "What Constitutes An Equitable Water Share? A Reassessment of Equitable Apportionment in the Jordan–Israel Water Agreement 25 Years Later." *Water Policy* 21(5):911–933.

Taylor, A. J. P. 1950. "The Question of the Upper Nile 1894–5." *The English Historical Review* 65(254) (January):52–80.

Tekle, Tesfa-Alem. 2013. "Egypt to Establish Military Base in Eritrea." Sudan Tribune, April 18.

Tekle, T. 2017. Egypt to Establish Military Base in Eritrea. *Sudan Tribune*, April 18, 2013.

Tesfa, Belachew. 2013. "Benefit of Grand Ethiopian Renaissance Dam Project (GERDP) for Sudan and Egypt." Discussion Paper. *EIPSA Communicating Article: Energy, Water, Environment & Economic* 1(1). Available at http://eprints.hud.ac.uk/id/eprint/19305/. December.

Tesfaye, Aaron. 2012. "Environmental Security, Regime Building, and International Law in the Nile Basin." *Canadian Journal of African Studies* 46(2):271–287.

Tvedt, T. 2004. *The River Nile on the Age of the British: Political Ecology and the Quest for Economic Power*. New York: I.B. Tauris & Co., Ltd.

The World Bank. 2018. Ethiopia Economic Update: The Untapped Benefits of Services Reforms. Press Release, June 11. Retrieved from https://www.worldbank.org/en/news/press-release/2018/06/11/ethiopia-economic-update-the-untapped-benefits-of-services-reforms.

Ting-Tommy et al. 1991. Culture, Face Maintenance and Styles of Handling Interpersonal Conflict: A Study in Five Cultures. *The International Journal of Conflict Management* 2–4: 275–296.

Ting-Tomney, S., and J. G. Oetzel. 2001. *Managing Intercultural Conflict Effectively.* Thousand Oaks, CA: Sage.

Tir, Jaroslav, and Douglas M. Stinnett. 2011. The Institutional Design of Riparian Treaties: The Role of River Issues. *Journal of Conflict Resolution* 55(4):606–631.

Torbati, Yeganeh, and Hudson, John. 2021. "U.S. Policy Toward Egypt Sparks Conflict between Congressional Democrats and Biden." *Washington Post,* April 2.

Tvedt, T. 2004. *The River Nile on the Age of the British: Political Ecology and the Quest for Economic Power.* New York: I.B. Tauris & Co., Ltd.

UN News. 2020. "UN Officials Welcome Court's Guilty Verdict in Charles Taylor Trial." Retrieved from https://news.un.org/en/story/2012/04/409542-un-officials-welcome-courts-guilty-verdict-charles-taylor-trial. October 30.

UNDP. 2013. Human Development Report 2013. Retrieved from https://www.undp.org/publications/human-development-report-2013. April 13, 2021.

UNDP (United Nations Development Programme). 2020. Human Development Index (HDI) Ranking. From the 2020 Human Development Report. Retrieved from: http://hdr.undp.org/en/countries/profiles/ETH.

United Nations Environmental Programme (UNEP). 2013. Annual Report-2014 UNEP Annual Report 2013-LR(1).

United Nations Security Council. 2020. Highlights of the Security Council. https://www.un.org/securitycouncil/.

UNEP [United Nations Environmental Programme]. 2016. "Transboundary River Basins: Status and Trends." Vol. 3, River basins. January.

UNWC (UN Watercourses Convention). n.d. User's Guide Fact Sheet Series: Number 5 No Significant Harm Rule. Retrieved from https://www.unwatercoursesconvention.org/documents/UNWC-Fact-Sheet-5-No-Significant-Harm-Rule.pdf. November 7, 2020.

UNWC Online User's Guide. Part III Planned Measures. Retrieved from http://www.unwatercoursesconvention.org/the-convention/part-iii-planned-measures/.

Uprety, Kishor, and Salman, Salman M. A. 2011. "Legal Aspects of Sharing and Management of Transboundary Waters in South Asia: Preventing Conflicts and Promoting Cooperation." *Hydrological Sciences Journal.* Special Issue: Water Crisis: From Conflict to Cooperation 56(4).

U.S. State Department. 1994. "Text of Jordan-Israel Treaty of Peace. U.S. State Department, Nov. 94." *Supplement Middle East,* 5(44):6, 9. Signed October 26.

Villiers, Marque. 2000. *Water: The Fate of Our Most Precious Resource.* Boston and New York: Houghton Mifflin.

Vucic, Mihajlo. 2017. "Silala Basin Dispute—Implications for The Interpretation of the Concept of International Watercourse." *Annals FLB—Belgrade Law Review* LXV(4).

Walton, Douglas. 2008. *Informal Logic: A Pragmatic Approach.* 2nd ed. Excerpt. Cambridge University Press.

Wassara, Sampson S. 2013. "South Sudan in Volatilities of Sharing the Nile Resources." In *Forging Two Nations: Insights on Sudan and South Sudan,* edited by Elke Gravert, 234–247. Addis Ababa: Organization for Social Science Research in Eastern and South Africa.

Waterbury, J. 2002. *Nile Basin: National Determinants of Collective Action.* New Haven, CT: Yale University Press.

Weiner, A., and T. Diez. 2009. *European Integration Theory.* 2nd ed. Oxford & New York: Oxford University Press.

Weiss, D., and U. Wurzel. 1998. *The Economies and Politics of Transition to an Open Market Economy: Egypt.* Paris, France: OECD.

Wheeler, K. G., M. Basheer, Z. T. Mekonnen, S. O. Eltoum, A. Mersha, G. M. Abdo, E. A. Zagona, J. M. Hall, and Simon J. Dadson. 2016. *Cooperative Filing Approaches for the Grand Ethiopian Renaissance Dam.* Water International. N.P.

Widakuswara, Patsy. 2019. "Trump Meets with Egypt, Ethiopia, Sudan, FMs About Dam Feud." Voice of America. https://www.voanews.com/a/usa_trumpmeets-egypt-ethiopia-sudan-fms-about-dam-feud/6178950.html. November 6.

Wolf, Aaron. 1997. "International Water Conflict Resolution: Lessons from Comparative Analysis". *International Journal of Water Resources Development* 13(3):333–365.

Wolf, Aaron T. 1995. International Water Dispute Resolution. The Middle East Multilateral Working Group on Water Resources. *Water International* 20(3): 141–150.

Wolf, Aaron T. 2000. "Indigenous Approaches to Water Conflict Negotiations and Implications for International Waters." *International Negotiations* 5:357–373

Wolf, Aaron T. 2007. Shared Waters: Conflict and Cooperation. *Annual Review of Environment and Resources* 32:241–269.

Wolf, Aaron T., Annika Kramer, Alexander Carius, and Geoffrey D. Dabelko. 2006. *Water Can Be a Pathway to Peace, Not War.* Navigating Peace. N.P.

Wolf, Aaron T., Kerstin Stahl, and Marcia F. Macomber. 2003. "Conflict and Cooperation within International River Basins: The Importance of Institutional Capacity." *Water Resources Update* 125.

Wolf, Aaron T., Kramer. A, Carius. A, and Dabelko. J. D. eds. 2005. Chapter 5: Managing Water Conflict and Cooperation. In *State of the World 2005: Redefining Global Security by World Watch Institute.* Washington D.C.

World Bank. 2001. *Nile Basin Initiative – Shared Vision Program. Transboundary Environmental Analysis*. World Bank.

World Bank. 2020. Population, Total—Middle East & North Africa. The World Bank. Retrieved from https://data.worldbank.org/indicator/SP.POP.TOTL?locations=ZQ.

Working Paper No. ESA/P/WP.241. 2015. World Population Prospects: The 2015 Revision, Key Findings, and Advance Tables. N.P.: United Nations, Department of Economic and Social Affairs, Population Division.

Wouters, Patricia. 2002. The Legal Response to International Water Scarcity and Water Conflicts: The UN Watercourses Convention and Beyond, in Allocating and Managing Water for a Sustainable Future: Lessons from Around the World (Natural Research Law Center, University of Colorado School of Law).

Wouters, Patricia., and Moynihan, Ruby. 2013. "Water Security—Legal Frameworks and the UN Watercourses Convention." In *The UN Watercourses Convention in Force: Strengthening International Law for Transboundary Water Management*, eds. F. Rocha Loures and Alistair Rieu-Clarke, 336–351. London and New York: Routledge.

Zakhirova, Leila. 2013. The International Politics of Water Security in Central Asia. *Europe-Asia Studies* 65(10): 1994–2013.

Zaman, A. M., H. M. Malano, and B. Davidson. 2008. "An Integrated Water-Trading Allocation Model, Applied to a Water Market in Australia." *Agricultural Water Management* 96(1).

Zawahri, Neda A. 2008. "Designing River Commissions to Implement Treaties and Manage Water Disputes: The Story of the Joint Water Committee and Permanent Indus Commission." *Water International* 33(4):464–474.

Zawahri, Neda A. and Andrea K. Gerlak. 2009. "Navigating International River Disputes to Avert Conflict. *International Negotiation* 12:211–227.

Zawahri, Neda A., and Mitchell, Sara M. 2011. "Fragmented Governance of International Rivers: Negotiating Bilateral Versus Multilateral Treaties. *International Studies Quarterly* 55: 835–858.

Zawahri, Neda A., Dinar, Shlomi, and S. McLaughlin Mitchell. 2011. "Facilitating Treaty Formation to Govern International Rivers." *International Studies Quarterly* 55:803–807.

Index

A

Absolute Territorial Integrity, xvi
Abu Dhabi, xiii
Addis Ababa, xxii, xxiii, 4, 13, 16, 18, 20, 39, 46, 47, 51, 57, 63, 68–70, 74, 76, 78, 81, 90, 97, 104, 139, 142, 144, 153, 166, 187, 212, 214, 219, 221, 233–235
Afghanistan, xiii
Africa, xviii, xix, xxv, 5–7, 12, 13, 25, 32, 33, 35–38, 40, 46, 52, 63, 83, 88, 96, 107, 125, 146, 165, 167, 173, 182, 224, 234, 236
African Union, xxii, 3, 5, 48, 58, 69, 70, 82, 83, 88, 90, 123, 138, 154, 162, 224, 233, 235, 239
AHD. *See* Aswan High Dam
Ahmed Ali, Abiy, xxiii
Alexandria, xiv, 13
Algeria, xix
Amhara, 11
Anglo-German Agreement, 36
Arab League, xxii, 71, 74, 82, 84–86, 88, 90, 95, 101, 106, 123, 139, 142, 213, 233, 234, 236, 242
arbitration, xxvi, 65, 66, 71, 87, 110, 134, 160, 172, 173, 204, 224, 228, 237
Arid, xvi
Arizona, xvii
Aswan Dam, xx, 8, 10, 18, 95
Aswan High Dam, 9, 15, 18, 26
asymmetry, xvi, xx, xxi, 212
Asyut Barrage, 8
Ataturk Dam, xxiv
Awach. *See* Kenya

B

Bahr-el-Ghazal, 36
Bangladesh, xvi, 78, 200, 201
Bekele, Selishi, 5
1884 Berlin Conference, 37
bilateral agreement, xxvi, xxvii, 134, 135, 159–161, 163, 168, 170, 217, 219, 223, 225
Biological warfare, xvii

© The Editor(s) (if applicable) and The Author(s), under exclusive license to Springer Nature Switzerland AG 2021
S. H. Okoth, *The MENA Powers and the Nile Basin Initiative*,
https://doi.org/10.1007/978-3-030-83981-9

Blue Nile, xiv, xx, xxii, xxiv, 6, 7, 13, 32, 38, 41, 96, 98, 101, 119, 204, 212
Bonaparte, Napoleon, 33
Bottled drinking water, xvii
Bottom Billion, 18
Brazil, 23, 78, 167
Britain, 12, 21, 33, 38–40, 43, 68, 78, 82, 102, 107, 218
British, xxvi, 17, 21, 33, 35–40, 42, 43, 65, 71, 86, 98, 101, 102, 107–109, 142, 145, 195, 216
Brussels, 36, 37
Bureau of Reclamation, 9
Burundi, xix, xxvi, 21, 32, 144, 177, 186, 189, 192, 228

C

Cairo, xiv, xxii, xxiii, 9, 13, 16, 22, 24, 27, 33, 39, 47, 51, 60, 62, 68–71, 74–76, 79, 82, 86, 88–90, 95, 97, 100, 104, 106, 109, 122, 139, 143, 147, 153, 163, 182, 212, 214, 233, 235, 237, 242
Cairo University, xiv, 62
California, xvii
Cambodia, xvi, xxiv, 78, 84, 218
Canada, xvi, 61, 77, 78, 167, 180, 183, 184
Ceasefire solution, xxvii
CFA. *See* Cooperative Framework Agreement
China, xvi, xxiv, 23, 33, 82, 84, 185, 199, 200, 215, 218, 232
Churchill, 35–37
climate, xv, xxiii, xxiv, xxvii, 4, 46, 62, 64, 133, 159, 173, 178, 179, 190, 196, 197, 201, 219, 224, 237
Coercive Diplomacy, 103, 104

Collective Action Theory, xxv, 112, 118, 122, 190, 222
Collier, Paul, 18
colonial treaties, xxi, 6, 20–22, 31, 42, 51, 71, 76, 87, 95, 98, 119, 144, 197
Colorado River, xvi, 185, 198, 199, 215
conflict, xv–xviii, xx–xxvi, 3–5, 7, 14, 15, 24, 25, 27, 31, 41, 46–48, 51–53, 55, 56, 59, 71–76, 78, 81–85, 87, 89, 90, 95, 97–103, 105, 106, 108–110, 118–121, 123–126, 131, 133–140, 142–147, 149–155, 159–163, 169, 171, 173, 177, 180, 182, 187, 189, 190, 193, 195, 197, 199–205, 211, 213–215, 217–219, 221, 223–228, 231, 233, 235–237
conflict resolution, 4, 52, 56, 81, 98, 99, 109, 111, 135, 152, 161, 162, 180, 203, 218, 225, 228
Congo Free State, 36, 37
Cooperative Framework Agreement, xxvi, 14, 16, 17, 22, 42, 48, 51, 54, 55, 57–61, 63–67, 71, 77, 78, 80, 87–89, 96–99, 102, 103, 106, 108–110, 127, 141, 144, 162, 177–179, 181, 182, 184–188, 190, 193, 197, 213, 221, 222, 226–228, 232, 239
Coptic Christians, 34
cost-benefit, 23, 183
coup, 14, 213
Cross-Cultural Communication Theory, xxv, 118, 124
cybersecurity, 5
Cyril Ramaphosa, 83

D

Dahlak Island, 7

dam, xiv, xx–xxiv, 3–10, 12–26, 31, 32, 39, 41, 46, 47, 51–53, 55, 62, 63, 68, 69, 71, 74, 76, 78–83, 85–90, 95, 96, 99, 100, 103–106, 108–112, 119, 120, 127, 139, 141–143, 145, 146, 149, 153, 161, 163, 165, 166, 170, 172, 179, 180, 182, 187, 190, 193, 212–214, 225, 227, 231–234, 236, 237, 239–242
Damascus, xxiv
Danube River, 52, 169, 216
Darwin, Charles, xiv
data, xx, xxvi, 4, 21, 32, 55, 65–67, 69, 101, 103, 108, 121, 122, 126, 164, 166, 181, 196, 200, 218
Declaration of Principles, xxii, 3, 5, 25, 47, 48, 69–71, 73, 75–78, 80, 89, 96, 97, 100, 103, 106, 108, 109, 124, 139, 141, 144, 145, 154, 161–167, 223, 227, 241
Delta Barrage, 8
Derg, 11
Desalinize, xiv
diversion, xx, 24, 26, 96, 139, 199
Djibouti, 11
downstream, xv, xvi, xviii–xxii, 3, 6, 8, 13, 15, 16, 21, 23, 26, 31, 41, 47, 48, 55, 62, 68, 69, 84, 87, 89, 95, 96, 99, 100, 103, 109, 111, 119, 121, 123, 131, 132, 135, 163–165, 168, 171, 178–182, 185, 188, 193, 194, 200, 211, 212, 215, 232
Dubai, xiv
Dulles, John Foster, 9

E

Eastern Technical Regional Office, 52

economic growth, xv, xvi, xxiii, xxiv, xxvii, 9, 11, 18, 23, 44, 64, 66, 79, 133, 159, 178, 194, 224
EDU, 11
Egypt, xiv, xv, xvii, xix–xxvi, 3–6, 8–10, 12–14, 16–27, 31–34, 36–41, 43–47, 51–56, 58–60, 62, 63, 65, 67–72, 74–90, 95, 97, 99–112, 118–121, 124–127, 132, 134, 135, 138–140, 142–147, 149, 151, 153–155, 160–168, 170–172, 177, 178, 180–182, 184–190, 193, 195, 197, 204, 205, 211–214, 216–223, 225–228, 231–236, 239–242
el-Kanater, 8
Emperor Menelik II, 20, 38, 39, 98, 107
employment, 13, 23
energy security, 46, 52, 219
EPRP, 11
equitable, xviii, 17, 22, 42, 43, 46, 51, 55, 59, 61, 63, 64, 82, 89, 96, 99, 126, 132, 171, 180, 182, 185, 195, 198, 199, 223
Eritrea, xix, 7, 10, 11, 21, 32, 98, 120, 146, 214, 235, 236
Ethiopia, xiv, xv, xvii, xix–xxvi, 3–6, 8–14, 16–27, 31, 32, 37–41, 46, 47, 51, 53, 55–57, 59, 62, 63, 67, 69–72, 74–86, 88, 90, 95–112, 118–121, 124, 125, 127, 132–135, 138–140, 142–149, 151, 153–155, 160–167, 170, 171, 177, 179, 180, 182, 185–187, 189, 190, 193, 195, 197, 204, 205, 211–214, 217–221, 223, 225–228, 231–236, 239–242
Ethiopian Democratic Union, 11
Ethiopian People's Revolutionary Party, 11

Ethiopians, xiv, 6, 11, 18, 40, 63, 108, 139, 145
Euphrates, xvi, xxiv, 84, 132, 168, 172, 199, 215, 218, 232
Euphrates and Tigris, 84, 132, 199, 215, 232
Europe, xvi, 38, 133, 147
European Space Agency, 5, 82
evaporation, 32, 41, 197, 198
externality, 22

F
Farid, Farid, 33
Fashoda Incident, 35
Fattah al-Burhan, Abdel, xxiii
Fattah el-Sisi, Abdel, xxiii, 14, 148
filling policy, 23
floods, 6, 23, 33, 34, 71, 74, 164, 170, 180, 233
French, 33, 35–37
freshwater, xiii, xvi, 62, 64, 95, 179, 196, 237

G
Ganges, xvi, 77, 78, 172, 194, 198, 200, 201, 215, 216, 232
GAP, xxiv
Garstin study, 38
Garstin, William, 38, 101
Gaza Strip, xix
Germany, 68, 83, 219
Ghana, 23, 138
Gigawatt, 26
Giza, xiv
Globalization, xvii
Grand Ethiopian Renaissance Dam, xv, xx, xxv, 3, 6, 15, 212
Grand Millennium Dam. *See* Grand Ethiopian Renaissance Dam
Grand Renaissance Dam, xiv, xvii, xx, 18, 23, 180, 182, 185, 187
Greeks, 33, 35
Gulf, xiii, xiv, 85, 169, 237

H
Hacking, xvii
Haile Mariam, Mengistu, 10
Halayeb territory, 25, 71, 74, 233
Halayeb Triangle, xxiii, 213
Hapi, 33
HDI. *See* Human Development Index
hegemon
  hegemons, xvii, 97, 119, 120, 168, 198, 199, 215, 218, 232
Helsinki Rules, xxvi, 22, 63, 64, 89, 98, 112, 131, 132, 198, 223
history, xv, xxvii, 6, 15, 17, 31, 33, 56, 76, 86, 133, 137, 138, 140, 143, 145, 147, 155, 160, 171, 195, 197, 203, 217, 221, 225, 233, 235
Homer, 33
Hoover Dam, 25
Human Development Index, 12, 18
hydrology, 23, 59, 66, 68, 100, 133, 163, 196, 197, 201
Hydromet Regional Project, 103
hydropower, 18, 23, 26, 41, 180
hypothesis, xvi, 140, 143, 184

I
India, xvi, 23, 33, 52, 78, 84, 164, 172, 200, 201, 215, 218, 232
Indonesia, 23, 83
Indus River, 52, 77, 78, 84, 164, 172
industrialization, 10
Intergroup Contact Theory, xxv, 125
International Court of Justice, xvii, xxvi, 87, 110, 134, 136, 160, 168, 170, 224, 228
international law, xx, 76, 198

International Panel of Experts, 23, 25, 67, 69, 70, 89, 96, 97, 99, 103, 163
international relations, xvi, 72, 85, 120, 140, 234
Iraq, xvi, xxiv, 84, 132, 168, 172, 218
irrigation, xx, 10, 15, 21, 26, 38, 40, 41, 44, 68, 96, 101, 108, 119, 131, 139, 193
Isna (Esna) Barrage, 8
Israel, xix, 16, 19, 63, 83–86, 108, 164, 172, 199–201, 213, 223, 236, 237
Italy, 36, 38, 39

J
junta, 11

K
Kabul, xiii
Kabul River, xiii
Kenya, xiii, xviii, xix, xxvi, 21, 32, 43, 138, 144, 150, 160, 177, 186, 189, 192, 239
Khartoum, xxii, 22, 31, 47, 68–71, 74, 81, 100, 106, 139, 143, 213, 233, 240, 241
King Leopold II, 36
King Menelik II, 40, 102

L
Lake Nasser, 9, 24
Lake Tana, 39, 204
Lake Tsana, 20, 38, 98
Lake Victoria, 6, 31, 43, 44, 111
Lancang, xxiv
land, xiii, xv, 15, 16, 23, 79, 111, 122, 171
Laos, xvi, xxiv, 78, 84, 218
La Plata, 77, 78, 85, 167

Lebanon, xix, 149
Libya, xix, 13, 143
Libyans, 33
litigation, xxvi, 65, 102, 134–136, 170, 224, 225
LNB, xxvi, 192, 193
London, 36, 37
long-term, xxii, xxiv, xxvii, 4, 23, 46, 69, 72, 75, 83, 108, 109, 135, 161, 162, 164, 181, 193, 212, 216, 229, 233, 241
Lord Cromer, 38, 101
Luo, xviii

M
Mackinnon, Sir William, 36
Mamluks, 33, 35
mediation, xvii, xxvi, 3, 5, 47, 51, 59, 65, 66, 69, 71–75, 77–79, 81–83, 87, 88, 90, 96, 97, 100, 102, 104–106, 108, 109, 119, 124, 131, 134–150, 153–155, 160, 163, 165, 173, 202–204, 221, 225–228, 235
Mediterranean Sea, xix, 32
Megawatts, 25
Mekong, xvi, xxiv, 44, 52, 77, 78, 84, 85, 185, 194, 199, 215, 216, 218, 232
Memphis, 34
MENA, xviii, xix, xxii, xxv, 5, 13, 35, 47, 48, 62, 63, 82–85, 95, 101, 107, 108, 118, 132, 146, 159, 162, 231, 234, 236
Mengistu Haile Mariam, 143, 148
Mexico, xvi, 44, 52, 84, 167, 183–185, 198, 199, 218
Middle East, xviii, xix, xxi, xxv, 5, 237
Mnuchin, Steve, xxiii, 241
Morocco, xix
Morsi, Mohamed, xiv, 7, 13, 14, 24, 62, 104, 142, 148, 240

Moscow, 9, 17
Mubarak, Hosni, xiv, 6, 7, 13, 62, 142, 143, 147, 239, 240
Munadee el-Nil, 34
Muslim Brotherhood, 13
Mussolini, 38

N
Nasser, Gamal Abdel, 9, 13, 17, 18, 26, 68, 86, 95, 119, 147, 239
NBI. *See* Nile Basin Initiative
negotiated settlements, 90, 160
the Night of the Drop, 34
Nile, xiv, xvii–xxvi, 3, 5–10, 12–14, 16–18, 20–22, 24, 25, 31–48, 51–53, 55–64, 67, 71, 76, 78–80, 82, 84, 85, 87–90, 95–99, 101–105, 107–111, 118–121, 123, 126, 127, 132, 133, 135, 140, 142, 144, 145, 151, 155, 159, 162, 164–166, 171, 177–180, 182, 183, 185–195, 197, 199, 201, 203, 204, 211–214, 216, 218, 219, 222–225, 227–229, 231–234, 236, 237, 239–241
Nile Basin, xviii, xix, xxiv–xxvi, 3, 21, 22, 25, 31, 37–39, 42–45, 48, 51–53, 55, 57–62, 64, 67, 84, 85, 87, 88, 96, 97, 99, 101–103, 108–111, 118, 123, 126, 127, 132, 133, 135, 144, 159, 162, 165, 166, 177, 178, 182, 183, 185–190, 192–195, 201, 212, 216, 219, 222, 223, 225, 227, 229, 231, 232, 236, 237
Nile Basin Initiative, xviii, xxv, 21, 31, 42–45, 48, 51–53, 57, 58, 61, 84, 85, 87, 89, 96, 97, 99, 101, 103, 109, 110, 118, 123, 126, 144, 162, 165, 166, 183, 185, 186, 189, 193, 194, 212, 219, 227, 229, 231, 236, 237

Nile Equatorial Lakes Subsidiary Action Program Coordination Unit, 46, 52
Nile-SEC, 52
Nubian communities, 17

O
Ocean, xviii
Ogaden, 11
oil, xiv, xv, xix, 85, 87, 150
Okavango River, 52, 61
Oromo Liberation Front, 11
Oxford University, 5

P
Pakistan, 52, 78, 84, 164, 172, 218
papyrus, 33
Pareto-Improvement principle, xxv, 112
Paris, 37
Pasha, Mohammed, xx
Persians, 33
Pharaoh, 34, 35
pluralist, 67, 86, 87
Pompeo, Mike, xxiii, 80
Population increase, xxiii, xxvii
poverty, xviii, 6, 7, 10
power, xvi, xviii–xxii, 4, 6, 9–11, 16–18, 20, 21, 23, 25, 26, 38, 40, 44, 54, 67, 68, 71, 74, 79, 80, 84–86, 95, 96, 104, 107, 108, 119–122, 124, 140, 170, 173, 180, 182, 185, 189, 212–215, 219, 220, 232, 233
Pragmatic Statecraft, 103
Prospect Theory, xxv, 112, 118–120, 122, 153, 188
pyramids, xiv, 33

Q
Qatar, xix, xxii, 19, 83, 85, 86, 213

R

rain, xiv, 6, 24
Ras Doumeira, 11
Rathbun, Brian, 103
Reasoned Dialogue, 103, 105
Red Sea, xiv, 7, 87, 236, 237
regional power, xix, xxi, 25
reservoir, xx, xxiv, 3, 5, 17, 23, 25, 26, 41, 47, 68, 75, 78–81, 90, 95, 109, 111, 119, 140, 145, 151, 163, 164, 166, 180, 234, 241
resettlement, 15, 18
Retribution, xvii
rights, xiv–xviii, xx–xxii, xxiv, xxvi, 3, 4, 13, 15–17, 22, 31, 41–43, 48, 55, 59–61, 71, 75–77, 82–86, 88–90, 95, 99, 100, 102, 104, 107–111, 119, 123, 126, 131–133, 140, 142–145, 159, 160, 171, 172, 178–180, 185–187, 194, 197, 199, 200, 202, 211, 212, 215, 216, 218, 223–225, 231, 237, 239, 241
Rio Grande, 44, 52
river, xvi, xviii, xxiii, xxiv, 32, 34, 36, 37, 45, 51, 53, 55, 57, 60, 64, 66, 84, 85, 87, 103, 111, 122, 123, 131, 133, 134, 159, 161, 171, 188, 190, 191, 194, 198, 204, 212, 217–219, 228, 231
Romans, 33, 35
Rosaries, 24, 26
Russia, 9, 82
Rwanda, xix, xxvi, 21, 32, 44, 46, 144, 177, 186, 187, 189, 192, 239

S

Sadat, Anwar, 16, 62, 147
Sallah, Tijan M., xxi
Sameh Shoukry, 80, 82, 149
Saudi Arabia, xiv, xix, 83, 85, 236, 237
Scandinavia, xvi
Secretariat, 46, 52, 53, 54, 57, 67, 103, 166, 194, 219, 228, 229. *See also* Nile-SEC
Selassie, Haile, 10, 40, 86, 148
Sennar, 8, 16, 24, 26, 68
Shadoof, xx
Short-term strategy, xxvii
Sobat, 20, 38, 98
South Africa, 68, 218
Soviet Union. *See* Russia
Structural Adjustment Policies, 9
Sudan, xix, xxi–xxiii, xxvi, 3, 5, 7–9, 11, 12, 16, 17, 20–27, 31, 32, 35, 36, 39–41, 43–45, 47, 52–55, 60, 65, 67–71, 74, 76–78, 80–82, 86, 87, 90, 95, 98–102, 105, 106, 108, 111, 119–122, 124, 126, 127, 138–140, 142–144, 146, 150, 154, 161–163, 165–167, 177, 178, 186, 188–190, 193, 195, 197, 203, 213, 214, 216, 218, 223, 227, 231, 233–236, 239–242
Suez Canal, xxi, 17, 33, 236
Syria, xvi, xix, xxiv, 13, 63, 84, 132, 168, 172, 199, 218

T

Tahba Dam, xxiv
Tahrir Square, xiv, 13, 60, 142
Tanzania, xix, xxvi, 21, 32, 43, 44, 48, 138, 144, 177, 186, 189, 192, 239
Technical Advisory Committee, 66
Thailand, xvi, xxiv, 23, 78, 84, 218
Thebes, 34
Tigray, 11, 235, 236
Tigray People's Liberation Front, 11
Tigris, xvi, xxiv, 168, 172, 218

TPLF, 11
trade, xviii, 6, 10, 20, 23, 25, 38, 74, 84, 86, 110, 189, 213, 219, 220, 234
transboundary, xx, 46, 47, 52, 53, 61, 66, 96, 132, 159, 219, 220, 225, 232
Tripartite National Committee, 70, 78, 89, 97, 100, 103
Trump, Donald, xxiii, 77, 78, 80, 81, 90, 100, 106, 108, 150, 180, 221, 234, 237
Tunisia, xix, 13, 60, 83
turbines, 4, 26, 79
Turkey, xvi, xix, xxii, xxiv, 19, 83–86, 132, 168, 172, 199, 213, 215, 218, 232
Turks, 33
Twain, Mark, 3

U

Uganda, xix, xxvi, 6, 21, 32, 37, 43, 44, 46, 57, 144, 166, 177, 186, 189, 192, 194, 239
UNB, xxvi, 192
unilateral, xvii, 20, 31, 47
United Arab Emirates, xiii, xiv, 83, 85, 86, 237
United Nations, xxiii, 10, 12, 44, 53, 62, 71, 82, 88, 90, 117, 154, 168, 194, 199, 239
United States, xvi, xvii, xxii, xxiii, 3, 5, 9, 13, 44, 47, 61, 76, 77, 82, 84, 88, 90, 96, 100, 101, 105, 106, 120, 122, 124, 125, 139, 145, 150–154, 167, 183, 184, 198, 199, 205, 215, 232, 235, 236
United States-Mexico-Canada Agreement, 167, 184
UN Watercourses Convention, 65, 186, 201, 224
upstream, xiv–xvii, xix–xxi, xxiv, 3, 4, 6, 7, 13, 15, 16, 21, 22, 24, 31, 40–48, 51, 55, 56, 62, 68, 84, 87, 88, 90, 95, 96, 102, 103, 107, 109–111, 119, 123, 131, 132, 135, 139, 144, 164, 168, 179, 181, 184–189, 192, 193, 195, 197–200, 211, 213, 215, 216, 218, 222, 223, 227, 232, 233, 236
U.S.. *See* United States

V

Vietnam, xvi, xxiv, 78, 83, 84, 218

W

war, xiv–xvii, xix, xxiv, 7, 10–12, 16, 27, 31, 35, 75, 100, 104, 120–122, 142, 143, 211–213, 215, 217, 218, 226, 233–236
Washington Post, xxiii, 237
water, xiii–xxiv, xxvi, xxvii, 3–7, 9, 10, 12, 16–18, 21–26, 31, 33–35, 37–48, 51–55, 57–69, 71, 74–86, 88, 89, 95, 96, 98–103, 106–108, 110, 111, 117, 119, 122, 123, 126, 127, 131–136, 139, 140, 144, 145, 149, 151, 155, 159–166, 168–172, 174, 177–182, 184–187, 192–202, 204, 211–213, 215–227, 229, 231, 232, 234, 236, 237, 239, 241, 242
water management, xvi, 44, 85, 168, 192, 219, 222
water security, xiv, xxiv, xxvi, 7, 16, 22, 25, 46, 47, 52, 55, 60–64, 67, 71, 82, 84, 86, 89, 95, 98, 99, 106, 117, 141, 177, 178, 181, 184–187, 211, 219, 222, 226, 232, 242

Water-starved, xvii, xix
Water wars, xv, xvi
Wheeler et al., 23
Wheeler, Kevin, 5
White House, xxiii, 80, 165
White Nile, xiv, 6, 31, 95, 233
World Bank, xxi, 8, 44, 45, 47, 53, 62, 79–81, 96, 104, 241
World Commission on Dams, 14, 15

Y
Yarmouk River, 84

Z
Zayed University, xiii
Zenawi, Meles, 5, 6, 10, 11, 51, 89, 119, 142, 148, 239
Zifta Barrage, 8

Printed in the United States
by Baker & Taylor Publisher Services